E4-98.

D1002934

THE ARDEN SHAKESPEARE

GENERAL EDITOR: RICHARD PROUDFOOT

TITUS ANDRONICUS

THE ARDEN SHAKESPEARE

THE ARDEN EDITION OF THE
WORKS OF WILLIAM SHAKESPEARE

TITUS ANDRONICUS

Edited by
J. C. MAXWELL

ROUTLEDGE

LONDON and NEW YORK

The general editors of the Arden Shakespeare have been
W. J. Craig (1899–1906), R. H. Case (1909–44),
Una Ellis-Fermor (1946–58), Harold F. Brooks (1952–82),
Harold Jenkins (1958–82) and Brian Morris (1975–82)

Present general editor: Richard Proudfoot

This edition of *Titus Andronicus*, by J. C. Maxwell,
first published in 1953 by
Methuen & Co. Ltd
Third edition 1961
Reprinted twice

First published as a University Paperback in 1968
Reprinted twice
Reprinted 1985

Reprinted 1989
by Routledge
11 New Fetter Lane, London EC4P 4EE
29 West 35th Street, New York, NY 10001

ISBN 0 416 47280 X (hardbound edition)
ISBN 0 415 02706 3 (paperback edition)

Printed in Great Britain by
Richard Clay Ltd, Bungay, Suffolk

All rights reserved. No part of this book may be reprinted or reproduced or
utilized in any form or by any electronic, mechanical or other means, now
known or hereafter invented, including photocopying and recording, or in
any information storage or retrieval system, without permission in writing
from the publishers.

CONTENTS

PREFACE

DETAILS of editorial method are discussed below in the Introduction. Here I have only to make some general remarks and acknowledge obligations.

This edition is not based on the earlier *Arden* edition, though of course that is among those which I have consulted. The commentary is designed to meet the requirements of relatively elementary as well as of more advanced students. Hence there are glosses on classical allusions and common Elizabethan usages which the latter will not need, while some of the more elaborate notes may presuppose more knowledge than the former possess. But I hope that each note will be intelligible and helpful to those readers to whom it is primarily directed.

Where possible I have acknowledged specific debts in the notes. In addition, I have to thank the General Editor for giving generously of her time and thought, and also the following scholars who have helped me in various ways: Mr J. M. Nosworthy, Mr K. D. Paxton, Professor H. T. Price, and Dr Alice Walker. My debt to Professor Dover Wilson calls for special mention. His name probably occurs in the Introduction and commentary more often than that of any other scholar, and a good many times I quote his views in order to question them. But that is principally because his edition of the play is the only really substantial one that there is. I have taken advantage of its existence to cut down the number of parallel passages cited: in this direction I have seldom struck on anything significant that has escaped his notice. He has also helped me by answering privately a number of questions. Among the earlier editors, those from whom I have most often learnt what I should probably not have discovered without their aid are, I think, Capell, Dyce, and Delius.

J. C. MAXWELL

King's College, Newcastle upon Tyne
University of Durham

PREFACE TO 1961 EDITION

This reprint has given me the opportunity of correcting many errors and of indulging in second thoughts on many passages. I am indebted to reviewers of the earlier edition, especially the late Sir Walter Greg, *M.L.R.*, 49 (1954), 360–4; Dr Alice Walker, *R.E.S.*, n.s. 6 (1955), 80–2; and Professor Clifford Leech, *Durham University Journal*, n.s. 15 (1953–4), 77–8. Professor Leech has also given me, privately, further corrections and suggestions, as have Mr N. S. Brooke, Mr John Crow, Dr G. K. Hunter, Dr J. H. P. Pafford, and Professor F. P. Wilson. But my greatest debt is to Dr H. F. Brooks, who has not only provided a valuable Appendix for this edition, but has also gone through the original edition, and the draft of my new material, with the greatest care. The closeness of his scrutiny gives me some hope that little that is wholly indefensible has got through into the present edition.

Apart from the correction of positive errors, I have been able to correct and supplement acknowledgements to earlier editors, but, in the light of past experience, I am sure that I have not traced all explanations, and citations of parallels, to the scholars originally responsible for them. I have remedied a deficiency which my critical apparatus shared with those in all other editions by recording in brackets the places where Edward Ravenscroft's adaptation anticipated emendations by later editors.

I have unfortunately been able to make only a very few references to the monograph by Horst Oppel, *Titus Andronicus: Studien zur dramengeschichtlichen Stellung von Shakespeares früher Tragödie* (1961), which has just come into my hands, and which I shall be reviewing in a forthcoming number of *Modern Language Review*. [56 (1961), 629–30]

The three new notes, on misunderstood attempts at proof-correction of F (at i. i. 214, 259; iii. ii. 39), added in the 1963 edition, are based on the findings of Charlton Hinman, *The Printing and Proof-Reading of the First Folio of Shakespeare* (1963). [1963]

A few further additions and corrections have been made. [1968]

ABBREVIATIONS

The abbreviated titles of Shakespeare's works are those of Onions, *Shakespeare Glossary*. Line numbers as in W. J. Craig's Oxford Shakespeare.

Editions of *Titus*:

Baildon	H. B. Baildon, Arden Shakespeare, London, 1904.
Camb.	W. A. Wright, Cambridge Shakespeare (2nd ed.), London, 1892.
Chambers (1907)	E. K. Chambers, Red Letter Edition, London, 1907.
Delius	N. Delius, Shakespere's Werke (3rd ed.), Elberfeld, 1872.
Herford	C. H. Herford, Eversley Edition, London, 1899.
Hudson	H. N. Hudson, Era Shakespeare, London, n.d.
Lee	S. Lee, University Press Shakespeare, New York, 1908.
Ridley	M. R. Ridley, New Temple Shakespeare, London, 1936.
Rolfe	W. J. Rolfe, Friendly Edition, New York, 1890.
Stoll	E. E. Stoll, Tudor Shakespeare, New York, 1913.
Verity	A. W. Verity, Henry Irving Shakespeare, London, 1890.
Wilson	J. D. Wilson, New Shakespeare, Cambridge, 1948.
Witherspoon	A. M. Witherspoon, Yale Shakespeare, New Haven, 1926.

Other references:

Abbott	E. Abbott, *A Shakespearian Grammar* (3rd ed.), London, 1870.
Adams	J. Q. Adams (ed.), *Titus Andronicus, 1594*, New York, 1936.
Baldwin	T. W. Baldwin, *William Shakspere's Small Latine and Lesse Greeke*, Urbana, 1944.
Baldwin (1959)	T. W. Baldwin, *On the Literary Genetics of Shakespeare's Plays, 1592–4*, Urbana, 1959.
Chambers	E. K. Chambers, *William Shakespeare*, Oxford, 1930.
Franz	W. Franz, *Die Sprache Shakespeares*, Halle, 1939.
J.E.G.P.	*Journal of English and Germanic Philology*.
M.L.R.	*Modern Language Review*.
N.E.D.	*New English Dictionary*, Oxford, 1884–1928.
Noble	R. Noble, *Shakespeare's Biblical Knowledge*, London, 1935.
O.D.E.P.	*Oxford Dictionary of English Proverbs* (2nd ed.), Oxford, 1948.
On.	C. T. Onions, *A Shakespeare Glossary* (2nd ed.), Oxford, 1919 (last corrected impression, 1946).
Parrott	T. M. Parrott, 'Shakespeare's Revision of "T.A." ', *Modern Language Review*, 14 (1919), 16 ff.
P.M.L.A.	*Publications of the Modern Language Association of America*.
Ravenscroft	E. Ravenscroft, *Titus Andronicus, or the Rape of Lavinia*, London, 1687.
R.E.S.	*Review of English Studies*.

Schmidt   A. Schmidt, *Shakespeare-Lexicon* (3rd ed.), ed. G. Sarrazin, Berlin,
                 1902.

Sh. Jb.   *Shakespeare-Jahrbuch* (formerly *Jahrbuch der Deutschen Shakespeare-
                 Gesellschaft*).

Simpson   P. Simpson, *Shakespearian Punctuation*, Oxford, 1911.

S.P.   *Studies in Philology.*

Tilley   M. P. Tilley, *A Dictionary of the Proverbs in England in the Sixteenth
                 and Seventeenth Centuries*, Ann Arbor, 1950.

T.L.S.   *Times Literary Supplement.*

W. S. Walker   W. S. Walker, *A Critical Examination of the Text of Shakespeare*,
                 London, 1860.

Wyld   H. C. Wyld, *A History of Modern Colloquial English* (3rd ed.),
                 Oxford, 1936.

INTRODUCTION

There are three Quarto editions of the play before the First Folio.[1]

First Quarto (Q1). Title-page: THE / MOST LA- / mentable Romaine / Tragedie of Titus Andronicus: / As it was Plaide by the Right Ho- / nourable the Earle of *Darbie*, Earle of *Pembrooke*, / and Earle of *Sussex* their Seruants. / [Device] / LONDON, / Printed by Iohn Danter, and are / to be sold by *Edward White* & *Thomas Millington*, / at the little North doore of Paules at the / signe of the Gunne. / 1594.

Head-title: [Device with initials I.D.] / The most Lamen- / table Romaine Tragedie of / *Titus Andronicus*: As it was Plaide by / the Right Honourable the Earle / of *Darbie*, Earle of *Pembrooke*, / and Earle of *Sussex* their / Seruants.

Running-title: The most Lamentable[2] Tragedie[3] / of Titus[4] Andronicus.

Collation: A–K[4].

Only one copy is known. It was discovered in Sweden in December 1904, and collated in *Sh. Jb.*, 41 (1905), 211 ff. It is now in the Folger Shakespeare Library. Sporadic use of its readings was made by editors in the next thirty years, but it was not until after a facsimile had appeared, edited by J. Q. Adams (Folger Shakespeare Library Publications, 1936), that editions based on it throughout were published: those of G. L. Kittredge (1936), Neilson and Hill (1942), etc. Adams's edition gives full details of this Quarto. It is a poor piece of book-production, and very deficient in punctuation (the rule seems to have been: 'when in doubt, put a comma at the end of the line'[5]), but it provides what is to all appearance a very

1. A full bibliographical description of all the early editions is to be found in W. W. Greg, *A Bibliography of the English Printed Drama to the Restoration*, Vol. 1 (1939), No. 117.
2. Sometimes: lamentable.   3. Sometimes: *T*ragedie.   4. Once: *T*itus.
5. On this see A. C. Baugh, 'A Medieval Survival in Elizabethan Punctuation' (*Studies in the English Renaissance Drama in Memory of Karl Julius Holzknecht* (1959), pp. 1–15).

accurate text, and is the only source for a number of lines which appear in quite a different form in all later editions (see below on Q2). A number of features of the Q1 text, such as the wording of the stage-directions (see on I. i. 69) and the irregularity of the speech-prefixes (see on I. i. 299), make it fairly certain that the printer's copy consisted of the author's manuscript ('foul papers'), not always finally tidied up for the stage (see on I. i. 35*a*, II. iii. 294, III. i. 36, 281, IV. iii. 97–8, v. iii. 171).[1]

Second Quarto (Q2). Title-page: The most lamenta- / ble Romaine Tragedie of *Titus* / *Andronicus*. / As it hath sundry times beene playde by the / Right Honourable the Earle of Pembrooke, the / Earl of Darbie, the Earle of Sussex, and the / Lorde Chamberlaine theyr / Seruants. / [Ornament] / AT LONDON, / Printed by I. R. for Edward White / and are to bee solde at his shoppe, at the little / North doore of Paules, at the signe of / the Gun. 1600.

Head-title: [Ornament] / [leaf-sign] The most lamentable Romaine / Tragedie of *Titus Andronicus*: As it was plaid / by the Right Honorable the Earle of Darbie, Earle / of Pembrooke, and Earle of Sussex / theyr Seruants.

Running-title: *The most lamentable Tragedie / of Titus Andronicus.*
Collation: A–K⁴.

'I. R.' is James Roberts. Two copies of this edition are known. One is in the Edinburgh University Library, and the other, at one time in Bridgewater House, is now in the Huntington Library, California. The latter copy has the outer forme of sheet D and the outer forme of sheet I in a corrected state, thus differing from the Edinburgh copy in eight readings (Adams, p. 19). The Edinburgh copy has been unsatisfactorily reproduced in facsimile by Ashbee (1866) and Praetorius (1886). The Huntington copy was discovered in 1800, and readings from it transcribed (not very accurately, and by no means fully) by H. J. Todd are recorded in the 1803 Variorum. Malone's copy of Q3, collated by him with Q2, is in the Bodleian (Malone 37).

Apart from corruptions and minor corrections, Q2 differs from Q1 at a number of points. It omits the obscure and contradictory passage I. i. 35 (from *and*) to 35*c*, and it diverges from Q1 at the following places near the end of the play, evidently because the copy of Q1 from which it was set up was damaged: v. ii. 71, 106 (line 1 of sig. I4 in Q1); v. iii. 25 S.D., 60 (third last and second last lines of sig. K2); v. iii. 93–7, 129–33 (last five lines of sig. K3); v. iii. 164–9, 200 (last six lines of sig. K4. Here the last five lines had completely perished, with the result that at the place corresponding to the end of the verso in Q1, which in Q1 was blank except for '*Exeunt*' and '*Finis the Tragedie of Titus Andronicus*', Q2 added four new lines). A single injury to the foot of the page would account for all but the first of these losses. The divergence at the top of sig. I4 involves only one word in each of the two lines concerned, but since the two words are in precisely the same position on recto and verso, there must have been an injury here too.

This edition tidies up the text (and especially the punctuation) here and there, but (with the possible exception of II. iii. 231, *Piramus* for *Priamus*) contains nothing 'beyond the powers of an intelligent and ingenious compositor' (Adams, p. 20). The Cambridge editors in 1865 referred to Q2 as 'printed with remarkable accuracy'; most of the credit is due, already, to Q1.

Third Quarto (Q3). Title-page: [Ornament] / THE / MOST LAMEN- / TABLE TRAGEDIE / *of Titus Andronicus*. / *AS IT HATH SVNDRY* / *times been plaide by the Kings* / Maiesties Seruants. / [Device] / LONDON, / Printed for Eedward White, and are to be solde / at his shoppe, nere the little North dore of / Pauls, at the signe of the / Gun. 1611.

Head-title: [Ornament] / [paragraph sign] The most lamentable Romaine / Tragedie of *Titus Andronicus*: As it was plaid / by the right honorable the Earle of Darbie, Earle / of Pembrooke, and Earle of Sussex / their Seruants.

Running-title: *The most lamentable Tragedie* / *of Titus Andronicus.*
Collation: A–K⁴.

Fourteen copies of this edition are recorded. There is a facsimile by Ashbee (1867). Pope was the first editor to make use of Q3. When Steevens in 1766 brought out his very accurate reprint, he knew of no other copy than the one he used. Q3 supplies a handful of corrections and a great many more corruptions.[1] The chief interest of Q3 is that the First Folio text (except for III. ii) was set up from a copy of it to which some stage-directions had been added.

First Folio (F). The text of *Titus* in this was set up from a copy of Q3 to which a number of stage-directions, especially flourishes, a couple of lines (I. i. 398, and 'what booke?' after IV. i. 36), and a whole scene, III. ii (from manuscript) were added. The folio introduces even more errors, and even fewer corrections, than its imme-

---

1. Bolton (*P.M.L.A.*, 44 (1929), 769) notes '19 errors corrected, 16 new errors made, 56 minor variations introduced'. Not all the corrected 'errors' are real ones: apart from the most elementary misprints of Q2, I reckon only 5 genuine corrections in Q3. Moreover, the distinction between new 'errors' and 'variations' is arbitrary: they are all errors, even though the 56, as opposed to the 16, may not be *manifestly* false.

diate predecessor. The new stage-directions, as Greg (see review cited on p. viii) pointed out in correction of a remark in my 1953 edition, presumably go back to the original production.

The presence of one entirely new scene, evidently from manuscript, raises the question why no further use was, apparently, made of that manuscript. Wilson (p. 97) rightly holds that a scribe preparing copy for the Folio by adding III. ii, and stage-directions, from the prompt-book would not necessarily have bothered to read through the whole play. It must, after all, have been well known that, apart from the missing scene, the Quartos offered a good text. Wilson also points out shrewdly that I. i. 398 is at a point where 'stage-directions are thick on the page', so that an omission in the printed text would catch the scribe's eye. There is one folio reading which looks too good for conjecture (though it could easily have given rise to the Quarto reading) and which I believe to be correct: v. ii. 18 (see note). The halting metre, as well as the uncertain meaning, might well lead the scribe to consult the prompt-book there. It remains odd that he did so nowhere else (except perhaps at III. i. 36: see note): but this is merely an extreme case of what we find in *Richard II*, *Much Ado about Nothing*, and *The Merchant of Venice*, where, according to Greg, the collation of Quarto used as copy with manuscript was (respectively) 'rather perfunctory', 'rather casual', and 'not systematic'.[1]

The Longleat Manuscript. This consists of a drawing representing Tamora and her two sons on their knees pleading to Titus. Aaron stands over the sons with a drawn sword. Beneath the drawing are the words 'Enter Tamora pleadinge for her sonnes going to execution,' followed by a transcript of I. i. 104–20 and v. i. 125–44, the two extracts being linked 'by three lines partly derived from I. i. 121 and I. i. 126 and partly concocted by the scribe' (Wilson, p. 98). The last line is followed by '& *cetera*', and then the name 'Alarbus' is written in the margin (where speech-prefixes occur in the rest of the transcript), followed by lines across the page. The source seems to have been the First Folio rather than any Quarto, although the margin contains, in the same hand as the text, the words 'Henricus Peacham Anno mᵒ qᵒ g qᵗᵒ' which a later hand has interpreted as '1595'.[2] Who this Peacham was, and whether the date has any authority, we do not know. The main discussions of the MS. are as follows: E. K. Chambers, *The Library*, 4 Ser. 5 (1925), 326–30 (reprinted in *Shakespearean Gleanings* (1944)); Adams, pp. 31–40; Wilson, pp. 98–9 (and more fully in *Shakespeare*

---

1. *Editorial Problem in Shakespeare*, pp. 121, 123, 124.
2. This involves taking the 'g' as a '9'; see Adams, p. 33, for the difficulties.

Survey, 1 (1948), 17–22); J. Munro, *T.L.S.*, 10 June 1949, p. 385[1] (reply by Wilson, 24 June, p. 413). Wilson holds that the lines were added to the drawing 'by someone knowing very little about the play and at a loss to discover the dramatic moment depicted'. I find this rather difficult to follow. The transcription is made with fair accuracy from a good text, and the pains taken to join together the two passages of which it consists point to someone who had a purpose, however obscure to us. I do not see how a scribe at a loss to interpret the drawing would have been made any happier by constructing this cento, which he himself must have realized did not represent any single situation in the play. I cannot help thinking that drawing and text belong together. Perhaps the compiler's purpose was to string together (for private theatricals?) two striking and popular speeches from the play, and perhaps it is a private performance that the drawing represents, rather than, as Wilson suggests, 'the actual action and grouping of Shakespeare's fellows in Shakespeare's theatre at a particular moment of a play in which he had a hand'. But problems still remain: the name of Peacham and the date, and the incongruity between the representation of Aaron and his situation in either Act I or Act V. Our one comfort is that the MS. is of no textual importance.

There are two entries in the Stationers' Register that may refer to the play. On 6 February 1594, Danter, the printer of Q1, registered 'a booke intituled a Noble Roman Historye of Tytus Andronicus' together with 'the ballad thereof'. It has been suggested (Adams, p. 9) that this may refer to the Prose History preserved along with the ballad in the eighteenth-century chap-book discussed below under 'Sources'. The same may apply to 'a booke called Titus and Andronicus' transferred by Thomas Millington to Thomas Pavier on 19 April 1602. (For later transfers of ballad and, possibly, prose history, see Adams, p. 9.) The subject is obscure, but we may readily agree with Greg (*Bibliography*, p. xxv) that 'it would be quite in keeping with Danter's character to make one entrance serve for two separate publications.'

The present edition is based on Q1. Though not in principle 'conservative'—I have no initial prejudice against emendation—it departs less often from Q1 than Professor Dover Wilson's, the only other edition that follows Q1 closely.[2] Spelling and punctua-

---

1. See also Oppel, ch. viii, who persuasively develops Munro's views, and concludes (p. 115) that no single occasion is depicted but 'drei Hauptgestalten zu einem repräsentativen Gesamtbild vereinigt werden.'

2. This was written before the publication of Professor Alexander's one-volume Shakespeare (1951). I think Professor Alexander and I are about equally conservative in essentials, but I have retained more archaic forms.

tion are modernized, but certain features of the text will be novel
to anyone accustomed to the usual modernized texts of Shakespeare. In accordance with the principles of this series, I have retained all older forms that are more than variant spellings: hence
the reader will find 'murther', 'banket', and 'cur'sy'. Absolute consistency is not attainable: I have, for instance, printed 'mart'red'
at III. i. 81, while stopping short of 'tortering' at II. iii. 285. I have
also rejected what may be called pseudo-modernizations: forms
that were modernizations when they became part of the accepted
text but that have lingered on although they are now just as obsolete as the forms they supplanted: a good example is 'swounded'
(v. i. 119). The most important word in this class is 'and'. In Elizabethan English 'and' and 'and if' were both used as equivalents of
'if'. In the course of the seventeenth century it became customary
to write 'an' instead of 'and' in this sense, and 'an' became uni-
versal in the eighteenth-century editions. But now that the usage
is completely obsolete, it seems to me high time to return to the
original spelling, and I have done so throughout. Where there is
some doubt whether 'and if' means 'and+if' or simply 'if', I have
left it to the reader to decide if I have no strong views myself. On
another point of spelling I have adhered religiously to Q1. The
past tense of a verb such as 'scatter' appears in three different spellings (I ignore the presence or absence of apostrophe), 'scattered',
'scattred', and 'scatterd'. Whether the difference between the first
and the second reflects a real difference of pronunciation I do not
know; but I have retained the first form where it occurs in Q1,
even where the metrical norm would be one syllable rather than
two, in case the intention should be to slur and not to elide the
penultimate syllable. The editorial tendency has been to introduce
the third form, which is far the rarest in Shakespeare and in many
of his contemporaries.[1] Examples are I. i. 425, 427, and 432, where
I have restored '(dis)honoured' for the '(dis)honour'd' of (respectively) F4, F1, and Pope. This subject is fully discussed in *English
Institute Essays: 1947* (1948), pp. 147–51, by Professor H. T. Price,
but for whom I should probably not have been sufficiently alive to
this problem.

On lineation I have followed the current practice, for convenience of reference. In the early editions, when a speech begins in
the middle of a line of verse, there is no typographical indication
of the fact. Thus II. i. 45, which is printed here, as in other modern
editions,

1. H. T. Price, *op. cit.* in text, p. 151, notes that Jonson and Massinger, however,
prefer this form.

> *Dem.* Ay, boy, grow ye so brave?
> *Aar.*   Why, how now, lords!

appears in the early editions (ignoring minor variations)

> *Demetrius.* I boy, grow yee so braue?
> *Moore.*   Why how now Lords?

This is purely a change of convention, and it would have been pointless to record it in the critical apparatus. The same applies to the practice, particularly common in F1, of dividing the opening line of a speech. At I. i. 56, for instance, where Q1 has as in a modern edition (except that the speech-prefix *Saturninus* is centred in a line by itself)

> Friends that haue beene thus forward in my right.

F1 has

> *Saturnine.* Friends, that haue beene
> Thus forward in my Right,

I have ignored all such variations, except where there is doubt as to the metrical arrangement intended. The whole subject of lineation, with special reference to the peculiarities just discussed, is dealt with by R. B. McKerrow, *Prolegomena for the Oxford Shakespeare*, pp. 44–9.

One other detail may be mentioned here. Editors have in general been too timid about introducing hyphenated compounds. Writers and printers of Shakespeare's time were not in the least systematic in distinguishing between two adjectives, both qualifying the same noun, and two words, both adjectival in form, of which the first is in meaning an adverb modifying the second. Modern practice in the second case hyphenates the two words. W. S. Walker was particularly fond of introducing the hyphenated forms into the text of Shakespeare. He may have overdone it, but most of his proposals deserve serious consideration. This is not a question of emendation, it is a question of interpretation, and every case must be decided on its merits, with no presumption in favour of retaining the unhyphenated form.

As *Titus* is neither a play with a complicated staging nor one which will ever be widely read, I have thought it worth while, at the cost of a few oddities, to sweep away almost the whole paraphernalia of later editorial stage-directions and return to Q1, with only occasional supplements. I have, of course, retained the traditional act- and scene-divisions, and have normalized the speech-prefixes, which in Q1 show the variations characteristic of author's manuscript (see on I. i. 299).

In the critical apparatus I have tried to record, besides all textual variants,[1] any interesting spellings, especially of Q1. When not all the four early editions are mentioned, it is to be assumed that those omitted have the reading printed in the text. Thus '*morn*] *Moone* Q1–2' means that the reading 'morn' (in whatever spelling or spellings) is that of Q3 and F. Where a later editor has conjecturally restored the substantive text, I have sometimes added his name in brackets (e.g. v. iii. 146). When several of the early editions are cited as agreeing in a reading different from that in the text, I give the spelling of the earliest edition concerned. I have sometimes, in the lemma of a collation, given the modernized spelling or punctuation of my text without indicating when it first made its appearance, but only, I hope, when it is the obvious (or at least *an* obvious) representation in a modern text of the original reading.

The subject of punctuation presents peculiar difficulties in a modern-spelling text of an Elizabethan play. I have made no special attempt to represent unusual punctuations by a modern equivalent, and in any case this play presents (in Q1) few interesting oddities. In the apparatus I have recorded the original punctuation only where it would, according to modern conventions, be definitely misleading. I have ignored minor vagaries of the later Quartos and of the Folio where Q1 is either correct or at least not misleading. I cannot leave this subject without expressing my indebtedness to the Cambridge edition (2nd ed. 1892). Its critical apparatus is wonderfully complete and accurate (though it contains too much that is of no intrinsic interest), and I have relied on it without verification for many minor points,[2] though not, I hope, for any on which the true reading in the text may depend. I have often omitted the word 'conj.' when I have seen no reason to doubt that the author of a proposal who is not himself an editor would have been prepared to print it in the text. This may be questionable procedure, but it seems preferable to citing without 'conj.' only editors who have actually printed the reading in question.

2. DATE AND AUTHORSHIP

The date and authorship of *Titus Andronicus* seem at first sight to offer no problems at all. Shakespeare's authorship is vouched for,

---

1. I omit obvious misprints found in only one edition, where the correction is too evident to be classed as an emendation.

2. One detail had better be mentioned here: in my apparatus, 'Rowe, 2nd ed.' refers to the second edition, dated 1709 but probably published 1710, which McKerrow distinguished from the first edition in *T.L.S.*, 8 March 1934, p. 168; 'Rowe, 3rd ed.' refers to the 1714 edition, the Cambridge edition's 'Rowe, 2nd ed.'.

not only by the inclusion of the play in the First Folio, but also by the mention of it as his by Francis Meres in *Palladis Tamia* (1598).[1] As to date: Henslowe in his diary[2] notes a production as 'ne' of 'Titus & Ondronicous'[3] by Sussex's men on 24 January 1594. Shortly afterwards, on 6 February 1594, as noted above, 'a booke intituled a Noble Roman History of Tytus Andronicus' was entered to John Danter in the Stationers' Register, and an edition printed by Danter appeared in the same year.

Yet few have been convinced by the whole of this simple and consistent story. The first recorded denial of Shakespeare's authorship comes from Edward Ravenscroft in 1687, in the *Address* to his adaptation of the play. He claims to 'have been told by some anciently conversant with the Stage, that it was not Originally his, but brought by a private Author to be Acted, and he only gave some Master-touches to one or two of the Principal Parts or Characters; this I am apt to believe, because 'tis the most incorrect and indigested piece in all his Works; It seems rather a heap of Rubbish then a Structure.'[4] There is no evidence that Ravenscroft had any good authority, and (though it seems unlikely that he simply invented the whole story) his chief motive may well have been to justify his own rewriting of the play. Langbaine was not slow to point out that Ravenscroft had accepted Shakespeare's authorship in the prologue to his adaptation when it was produced.[5] All that the story shows is that the inferiority of *Titus* to Shakespeare's other tragedies made such a story plausible long before wholesale disintegration of the Shakespeare canon became popular. Thus Theobald, in rejecting Shakespeare's authorship, claims to be in the company of 'the better judges',[6] and the main eighteenth-century scholars, Johnson, Farmer, Steevens, and Malone, took the same

1. Chambers, ii. 194.   2. Ed. W. W. Greg, i. 16.

3. The form 'Titus and Andronicus' persists in a very odd fashion. It is found in the Stationers' Register for 1602, 1624, 1626, and 1630 (Chambers, i. 313–14; Adams, p. 9), where the reference is to the prose history and/or the ballad. It also occurs in several seventeenth-century references to the play, where it is hard to imagine a direct connection either with Henslowe's diary or with the Stationers' Register: the catalogue attached to T. Goff's *Careless Shepherdess* (1656), in which the play is not attributed to Shakespeare (*Shakspere Allusion Book*, ed. J. Munro, ii. 58); and the list in Henry Oxinden's commonplace book (started in 1647) of plays in his possession (*Library*, 4 Ser. 15 (1934–5), 448). J. M. Robertson, *Introduction to the Study of the Shakespeare Canon*, p. 69, pointed out that Titus and Andronicus figure as separate characters in the same story in E. Hellowes's translation of *The Familiar Epistles of Antonie Guevara* (1584). The story is the one more familiar as that of *Androcles* and the lion. Robertson tentatively suggested that this might have been made into a play, and its title might have lingered in people's memories.

4. Chambers, ii. 255.   5. *Ibid.*   6. Quoted in 1821 Variorum, xxi. 379.

view, though Malone thought the play was probably included in the Folio because Shakespeare 'wrote a few lines in it, or gave some assistance to the author, in revising it, or in some other way aided him in bringing it forward on the stage'.[1] Capell, Tyrwhitt (who first called attention in print to Meres's reference[2]), and Ritson[3] favoured the attribution to Shakespeare. There is no need to trace the later history of the play in scholarly opinion—though the spirited defence of Shakespeare's authorship by Charles Knight (*Studies of Shakspere*, 1849) is still worth reading—but the early establishment of an orthodox opinion hostile to the Folio attribution is notable.[4]

Apart from a natural reluctance on artistic grounds to attribute the play to Shakespeare, what are the difficulties about the 1594 date? The first is an allusion in the anonymous play, *A Knack to Know a Knave*, to an incident not known to occur anywhere but in *Titus*: Osric greets King Oswald as being as welcome

> As Titus was unto the Roman Senators
> When he had made a conquest on the Goths.
> (Sig. F 2v; Hazlitt's *Dodsley*, VI. 572)

A Knack is recorded by Henslowe as 'ne' when performed on 10 June 1592 by Strange's men at the Rose, and it was registered on 7 January 1594. This is not conclusive—it might be an allusion to Shakespeare's source, not as yet identified with certainty[5]—and I discuss below an attempt to undermine it.[6] Verbal echoes of *Titus*

1. Quoted in 1821 Variorum, XXI. 258.

2. *Observations and Conjectures upon some Passages of Shakespeare*, Oxford, 1766.

3. *Remarks on the Last Edition of Shakespeare*, London, 1783, p. 158.

4. Chambers, I. 316, understates the position when he says that 'Shakespeare's original authorship has been very generally doubted from the days of Malone onwards.'

5. See below, p. xxvii. The prose story contains no ceremonial reception of Titus by the senators.

6. Mr P. E. Bennett (*Notes and Queries*, 200 (1955), 422–4, 462–3) has argued that *A Knack to Know a Knave* is a Bad Quarto, that 'Goths' is a reporter's substitution, under the influence of *Titus*, for 'Jews', and that the 'Titus' in question is the Flavian Emperor. The contamination, he thinks, took place about the end of 1593, when some of Strange's men were rehearsing *Titus*, which he believes really was 'new' on 24 January 1594. (He interprets the Q1 title-page as referring to this production by 'a mixed company of actors, mostly Sussex's, as Henslowe notes, but also with a few of Derby's [Strange's] and Pembroke's'.) I think the other evidence against such a late date remains strong, but I agree that caution is advisable in using the lines from *A Knack*. The passage is inept as a reference to the Titus of our play (but then, much of *A Knack* is inept, and it can scarcely all be the reporter's fault). Mr Bennett certainly goes much too far in holding that, with the substitution of 'Jews' for 'Goths', we have a perfectly normal reference to the emperor Titus. To say of the senators that they

in writings earlier than 1594 are more elusive,[1] but I believe there is one in *The Troublesome Reign of King John*, published in 1591. At the end of that play, John is melodramatically repenting of his crimes, and says:

> How, what, when, and where, have I bestow'd a day
> That tended not to some notorious ill?
> > (Pt II. viii. 85–6 in the text ed. by
> > F. J. Furnivall and J. Munro, *The
> > Shakespeare Classics*, 1913)

This can hardly be independent of Aaron's speech, v. i. 125–7:

> Even now I curse the day, and yet, I think,
> Few come within the compass of my curse,
> Wherein I did not some notorious ill.

Which passage is the debtor? I do not think a confident answer can be given, but the author of *The Troublesome Reign* is a shameless borrower,[2] and these lines seem to me much more at home in Aaron's speech than in John's: 'some notorious ill' is happier as a boast than in a penitential context. I think there is also a connection between the following passages, though there is nothing that strongly suggests the priority of one rather than the other:

> No funeral rite, nor man in mourning weed,
> No mournful bell shall ring her burial;
> But throw her forth to beasts and birds to prey.
> > (v. iii. 196–8)

> Lo, lords, the wither'd flower,
> Who, in his life, shin'd like the morning's blush,
> Cast out o' door, denied his burial rite,
> A prey for birds and beasts to gorge upon.
> > (*Troublesome Reign*, Pt II. i. 33–6)

A date about 1590 or a little earlier would be consistent with the immaturity of the play as a specimen of Shakespeare's art, and

---

> in requitall of his service done
> Did offer him the imperiale Diademe

would be a most confused way of referring to the fact that, as Mr Bennett himself puts it, 'Titus Vespasianus was welcomed back from Jerusalem by the senators and by them made co-emperor with his father, virtually on the spot.' It is certainly not so much more apt than a reference to the Titus of our play as to entitle us to accept Mr Bennett's restoration with confidence, though I should myself be prepared to refrain from making any use at all of *A Knack* in view of the uncertain nature of its text. If its author did write 'Goths', his mind may have been in a state of glorious confusion about the two Tituses.

1. See also note on II. iii. 39.
2. See P. Alexander, *Shakespeare's Life and Art*, p. 85.

would also be easier to reconcile with the famous allusion by Ben Jonson which must now be quoted. In the *Induction* to *Bartholomew Fair* (1614) he writes: 'Hee that will sweare, *Ieronimo*,[1] or *Andronicus* are the best playes, yet, shall passe vnexcepted at, heere, as a man whose Iudgement shews it is constant, and hath stood still, these fiue and twentie, or thirtie yeeres.' No doubt Jonson need not have meant his arithmetic to be taken too literally, and he was certainly likely, if anything, to exaggerate the antiquatedness of the plays mentioned, but as far as it goes his remark favours an early date: it would not be so easy if *Titus* had been a bare twenty years old in 1614. Jonson may, indeed, not have known its date with any accuracy, but there is no need to multiply hypotheses of this kind.

One of the other arguments for a date earlier than 1594 is, I believe, a mare's nest. It is the suggestion that Henslowe's 'Tittus and Vespacia', produced as 'ne' by Strange's men on 11 April 1592, is either identical with *Titus* or an earlier form of it. In spite of all the ink that has been spilt on the subject, I can see no reason to reject the obvious explanation that *Titus and Vespasian* (which is presumably what Henslowe meant) was a play about the two Flavian emperors, probably dealing with the destruction of Jerusalem (so Adams, p. 10; a possible objection (Chambers, I. 319) is that Strange's men had another play called 'Jerusalem' running concurrently with 'Titus & Vespacia' in 1592, but this, as Chambers himself allows (*Elizabethan Stage*, III. 341), is very likely about the First Crusade, not about Titus' destruction of Jerusalem). It is true that the German *Tragœdia von Tito Andronico*, indirectly derived from *Titus*, substitutes the name 'Vespasian' for 'Lucius', but as Chambers (I. 319) says, a natural process of association would readily suggest that name in a play whose hero was called Titus.

These considerations, none of them conclusive, raise the question: how much weight, and what exact meaning, is to be attached to Henslowe's 'ne'? Chambers (I. 320) writes: 'Henslowe's "ne", whatever its precise significance, is certainly a mark attached to a play "the first tyme yt wasse playde". Generally it seems to have been a new play in the full sense. It is probable that it was sometimes a revised play, and possible that it was sometimes an old play, given by a particular company for the first time. But there is no clear case of this last type, and there are several clear cases in which such a performance was not marked "ne".' His more detailed account in *The Elizabethan Stage*, II. 144–6, does not entirely bear this out. For 'Jeronimo', which is universally agreed to be identical with Kyd's *Spanish Tragedy*, is given as 'ne' when pro-

---

1. I.e., Kyd's *Spanish Tragedy*.

duced by the Admiral's men on 7 January 1597. It is possible that the play had been revised since its original appearance in the 1580's, but this is not certain, and the most natural interpretation is that the play had not previously been produced by this particular company. Since the title-page of *Titus*, Q1, mentions the 'servants' of the Earls of Derby and Pembroke before those of the Earl of Sussex, it seems reasonable to suppose that it was only to the last-named company that *Titus* was new in 1594. When and where the other two companies played it,[1] we must be content not to know. The Earl of Derby, who succeeded to the title on 25 September 1593, had previously been Lord Strange, and performances of *Titus* in which the Chamberlain's company, including many of Strange's men, was associated with the Admiral's men are recorded by Henslowe on 5 and 12 June 1594.[2] Strange's men may easily have produced the play earlier, though not (assuming that 'Titus and Vespacia' is irrelevant) in the London season of 1592 which Henslowe records in full. Those who believe in a late date for *Titus* may be conceded the point that it is odd that such a popular play should not have been put on in 1592, if it were already in existence and in the company's repertoire. The career of Pembroke's men is a more obscure one, but they seem to have come to grief in the latter part of 1593, and do not emerge again as an important company. On the title-page of Q2, the name of Pembroke precedes that of Derby. If the transposition has any authority, a difficulty arises for an early dating of *Titus*, since Pembroke's men are not recorded as active before 1592.[3] (In my 1953 edition, I suggested that 1594 might be the date of the first London production of the play,

1. I know of no evidence in support of the following statement by Hardin Craig, *An Interpretation of Shakespeare* (New York, 1948), p. 38: 'This [the title-page of Q1] has caused more confusion than it warrants. It does not necessarily mean that all these companies had acted this particular play, but only that they had all acted a play on the same subject. The Elizabethans did not discriminate among versions, but among subjects.' He compares the non-entry of Shakespeare's *King John* for the Folio and Danter's prose history of *Titus*. On the latter, see Greg's remark, quoted above, p. xv. As for the former, *The Troublesome Reign of King John*, though not strictly a 'bad Quarto', may have been a rehash of Shakespeare's play, as is argued by E. A. J. Honigmann (Arden ed., 1954), so that its publication would make it unnecessary to register the latter for the Folio.

2. Chambers, II. 319.

3. A plausible theory according to which Pembroke's Men came into existence in May 1591 has been put forward by J. Dover Wilson, *New Shakespeare* edition of *2H6* (1952), p. xii. Mr A. S. Cairncross has kindly shown me a number of echoes of *Titus* in the Bad Quarto of *2H6* (see Arden, 1957, pp. 183–4) and the Bad Octavo of *3H6*. These were Pembroke plays, as we learn from the title-page of the latter (*The True Tragedy*). The former (*First Part of the Contention*) was entered in the Stationers' Register on 12 March 1594. Their contamination by *Titus* may have taken place during provincial performances.

Strange's and Pembroke's men having played it on tour. I agree with Greg (review cited on p. viii) that this is unlikely.)

The evidence, it can be seen, forms a tangled web, and I have not tried to conceal what is fragmentary and conflicting about the external evidence for the date and early stage-history of the play. But there does not seem to be anything that flatly contradicts a date of about 1589–90. The internal evidence that has been adduced for a later date is more formidable, and carries us back to the question of authorship, which I have left aside for some time.

A larger number of significant parallels with *Titus* have been found in *Venus and Adonis* and *The Rape of Lucrece*, especially the latter, than in any other works of Shakespeare. It has been argued that this is evidence in favour of a date for *Titus* fairly close to that of the poems, and this (on the assumption that the latter were published soon after they were written) would be 1593–4. I do not see that this carries much weight. *Titus* is, apart from the poems, the work of Shakespeare in which the Ovidian mode is most clearly discernible. Moreover, it is linked in subject with *Lucrece*, so that Shakespeare's mind might easily revert to the play when he was writing the poem. Still, it must be allowed to the late-daters that it is an odd coincidence that the parallels with *Lucrece* are consistent with the obvious interpretation of Henslowe's 'ne'.

The other items of internal evidence which are adduced in support of a late date for *Titus* are bound up with the contention that Shakespeare is not entirely responsible for the play and must now be dealt with in relation to that contention. In the palmy days of disintegration of the Shakespeare canon, almost all practising dramatists of 1585–95 were called in to take a hand in *Titus*, but at present the only serious candidate for a share in the play is George Peele. There is general agreement, too, that there is much better evidence of his presence in Act I than in the rest of the play. A number of scholars, most recently Dover Wilson, have pointed to striking resemblances between Act I and the plays and poems of Peele, and probably more suggestive than any individual verbal parallels is the tendency to mechanical repetition of words and phrases (Wilson, pp. xxviii–xxix; cf. my note on I. i. 294). To this may be added an argument from syntax. At I. i. 5–6 we have:

> I am his first-born son that was the last
> That ware the imperial diadem of Rome.

The construction 'his . . . that' is not uncommon in sixteenth- and seventeenth-century English, but it is unusually frequent in this Act, occurring six or seven times in 500 lines, i.e. six or seven times as often as in the rest of the play (four times in 2,000 lines). In

Peele's non-dramatic poetry the construction is also about six times as common as in *Venus and Adonis* and *The Rape of Lucrece*, and the absolute frequency is not very different. This is not conclusive, but it is at any rate quite independent of the other arguments that have been brought forward for Peele's hand in Act I of *Titus*.[1]

So much for the outline of the case for Peele's hand in Act I of *Titus*. It has been further claimed that the parallels favour a particular date, 1593. There are specially close resemblances between *Titus* and Peele's poem, *The Honour of the Garter*, which must belong to May and June 1593, and Wilson (p. xlv) argues that 'despite Peele's habit of repeating his clichés year after year, the parallels with *Titus Andronicus* make it tolerably certain that play and poem were being written at the same time.' It seems to me more reasonable to say that in view of Peele's habit it is far from certain. There is one parallel that calls for special attention, since it involves a word found only in *Titus* and in *The Honour of the Garter*. *Titus*, I. i. 182, runs:

> This palliament of white and spotless hue,

the 'palliament' being thought of as the white robe of the candidate for office. In *The Honour of the Garter* (lines 91–2), Edward III is

> A goodly king in robes most richly dight,
> The upper like a Roman palliament.

Later in the poem come the lines (313–16):

> O sacred loyalty! in purest hearts
> Thou build'st thy bower! thy weeds of spotless white,
> Like those that stood for Rome's great offices
> Make thee renown'd, glorious in innocency.

Opposite conclusions have been drawn from the comparison of these passages. Wilson (who believes that Peele wrote both) argues that the *Titus* passage is the earliest, since the reference to a 'palliament' (apparently a quasi-classical coinage based on one or both of the words 'pallium' and 'paludamentum') is out of place in the poem, as indeed Peele himself admits, for he goes on:

> Indeed a chaperon, for such it was—

'that is to say,' Wilson writes, 'it was not a "pallium" or cloak at all but a hood!' This seems a good argument for the priority of the play, though telling, if anything, against common authorship. Wilson does not make clear what he takes to be the connection between the *Titus* line and lines 313–16 of the poem: the implica-

1. For a detailed account, with statistics for some other dramatists, see my paper in *J.E.G.P.*, 49 (1950), 557–61.

tion seems to be that here again Peele recalled his own *Titus* line. The same three passages have been used by H. T. Price[1] to prove that the *Titus* line is (*a*) posterior to the poem, (*b*) not by Peele. Pointing out justly that Peele does not identify his 'palliament' with the candidate's white robe as earlier scholars (joined, since Price wrote, by Wilson, p. xlvi) had asserted, he claims that Shakespeare confused the two Peele passages so as to produce his white palliament. This ignores the greater appropriateness of the reference in *Titus*, and proves nothing. There is no means of telling in advance whether the original coiner of the word 'palliament' referred it to a white garment or a coloured one such as the Garter robes, and neither application of the word need be a confused version of the other. The comparison of these passages, then, neither proves nor disproves common authorship, but I think (with Wilson against Price) that the *Titus* passage is probably the earlier.[2]

The case for Peele's hand in *Titus* is primarily a stylistic one. The case (from internal evidence) against it rests on considerations of structure. That the structure of the play is like Shakespeare and unlike Peele is not a conclusive argument against all theories which attribute some share in the play to Peele, but it is an argument against the most popular type of theory, according to which Peele is the original author of the play, and Shakespeare a reviser and adapter. The most recent, and most elaborate, version of this theory is that of Wilson, who postulates (*a*) a short play by Peele written for a travelling company in 1593; (*b*) an expansion of (*a*) for London production, carried out towards the end of 1593, in which Peele was assisted by Shakespeare, 'partly [because] Shakespeare was known to be working just then upon the kindred theme of Lucrece, but mainly [because] the Earl of Sussex's men were in a hurry' (p. xxxvii). Any such theory comes up against the objection that the firmness of construction evident in *Titus* is quite unlike anything in any of Peele's plays. It is true that most of these are preserved in bad texts, but it is impossible to believe that they were ever well constructed. In an important article, 'Plot Structure in Peele's Plays as a Test of Authorship' (*P.M.L.A.*, 51 (1936), 689–701), A. M. Sampley has, on these grounds, argued strongly against Peele's responsibility for a number of plays with which he has been associated, including *Titus*. There is only one other dramatist besides Shakespeare writing at the time who might conceivably have plotted *Titus*, and that is Kyd; J. M. Robertson showed a sounder

1. *Papers of the Michigan Academy of Science, Arts, and Letters*, 21 (1935), 506–7; *J.E.G.P.*, 42 (1943), 61.

2. See the elaborate discussion in Baldwin (1959), pp. 404 ff., briefly referred to on p. xxxviii below.

instinct than Wilson in invoking him as the original plotter of the play, though in fact there is nothing in the writing to suggest that he had any hand in it. The detailed consideration of the structure of the play (which I rate more highly than Wilson does) must be left to the final section of this Introduction. Meanwhile, it is enough to point out that the apparent discontinuity in style between Act I and the rest of the play is not paralleled by any discontinuity in construction, and that the structure of the whole play suggests Shakespeare rather than Peele.

It may seem tempting to assert roundly that the whole play is by Shakespeare and no one else. This has been ably argued by H. T. Price,[1] and may be the right solution after all. My only defence is that I can never quite believe it *while* reading Act I.[2] At the same time the alternative to which I find myself driven is not a very plausible one, since it involves holding that as early as 1589–90 Peele, already a well-established dramatist, acted as a very subordinate collaborator with a writer a number of years his junior in both age and experience.[3]

3. SOURCE

No source for *Titus* survives in a form which we know to have been available to Shakespeare. But a single copy (in the Folger Library) of a mid-eighteenth-century chap-book giving a version not based on Shakespeare may be in essentials pre-Shakespearian:[4] see G. Bullough, *Narrative and Dramatic Sources of Shakespeare*, VI (1966), and R. M. Sargent.[5] Its title-page claims that it is 'Newly Translated from the Italian Copy printed at Rome', and it may indeed be of Italian origin. The ballad, 'The Lamentable and Tragicall History of Titus Andronicus', which is printed with

1. *J.E.G.P.*, 42 (1943), 55–81.

2. Actually if there is a clean break between the two authors, I should be inclined to put it after II. i. 25.

3. An elaborate attempt at dating the play has recently been made by T. W. Baldwin, *The Literary Genetics of Shakspere's Poems & Sonnets* (Urbana, 1950), pp. 4–9. (Baldwin had earlier argued that the play was later than *Venus and Adonis*: see note on II. iv. 36–7.) He compares the handling of the image of the sun taking leave of the morning in the following passages: *3H6*, II. i. 21–2, *Titus*, II. i. 5–9, Spenser, *Faerie Queene*, I. v. 2, Peele, *Descensus Astraeae*, 4, and concludes that the order of the first three is Spenser (1590), *3H6*, *Titus*, and also that Peele (1591) precedes *Titus*. I ought to add that the passage in *Titus* (cf. the previous note) is one which I incline to attribute to Peele. (See now Baldwin (1959), ch. 22–6.)

4. This chap-book was known to Farmer and to Halliwell-Phillipps (Chambers, I. 321).

5. *S.P.*, 46 (1949), 167–83; see also Baldwin (1959), pp. 427–30.

the prose story, and is also included in Percy's *Reliques* as 'Titus Andronicus's Complaint', is entirely dependent on the prose story, though some of the stanzas have been rearranged to bring the order of events into closer conformity with the play.[1] All the differences between the prose story and the play are compatible with the hypothesis that the former is substantially identical with the source of the latter.

The vague late-Roman setting of the play is localized 'in the Time of Theodosius' (late fourth century A.D.) in the story. Italy has been plundered by the Goths. Titus Andronicus, a Roman senator, raises the siege of Rome, and becomes engaged in a ten-year struggle with the Goths, at the end of which he kills the Gothic king in a battle, and captures the queen Attava. The dead king's two sons Alaricus and Abonus continue the struggle, and eventually the Roman emperor decides on a political marriage with Attava and enters into it against the advice of Titus. After becoming empress, Attava secures the key positions for Goths and vows revenge on Titus, whose banishment she procures, but at this the people rise in revolt and the decision has to be reversed. Attava hates Titus all the more for this. At this point in the story comes the account of the empress's intrigue with a (nameless) Moor. She does not succeed in concealing her blackamoor child, but persuades the emperor that it was 'conceived by the Force of Imagination',[2] whereupon the Moor is exiled, but the empress later secures his return. It is only now that Lavinia comes on the scene. She becomes betrothed to the emperor's only son by a former wife. As the marriage would frustrate Attava's plans to secure the empire for her own sons, she decides to make away with the prince. She, the Moor, and her two sons murder him, and throw him into a pit. Lavinia persuades her brothers to go in search of him. They fall into the pit, are discovered and accused of murder, and are condemned, partly because of the false witness of the Moor. As in the play, the Moor (but at the instigation of the empress, not on his own initiative) persuades Titus to let him cut off his hand by a false offer of clemency to his sons if he does so, but they are executed notwithstanding and their headless bodies sent to Titus. The next disaster is the rape and mutilation of Lavinia by Attava's sons. She eventually discloses her story as in the play, and Titus vows revenge. He feigns madness, and shoots arrows to heaven. The citizens become alarmed at the arbitrary behaviour of the empress. Titus and some friends ambush and kill the empress's sons, and the

1. Sargent, p. 171.

2. This motif occurs in R. Head and F. Kirkman, *The English Rogue*, Part III, ch. 2.

grim banquet takes place. Titus orders his friends to kill the emperor and empress. At this stage the Moor discloses his share in the
wicked deeds and is tortured to death. Titus finally, 'to prevent the
Torments he expected, when these things came to be known, at
his Daughter's Request, . . . killed her; and so, rejoicing he had
revenged himself on his enemies to the full, fell on his sword and
died.' There is nothing about what happens in Rome after his
death.

One part of the political background is clearer in the story than
in the play—the purpose of the marriage of the emperor with the
Gothic queen. It may be conjectured that Shakespeare, having
decided to send Titus' son Lucius (a character not in the prose
story) to join the Goths, had to represent Tamora as having cut
herself from her compatriots. That being so, there could be no
political end to be secured by the emperor's marriage with her.

The main differences may be summed up as follows:

(1) There is no problem of succession in the prose story. Titus
is never a candidate for the throne, and he has no occasion to make
the fatal decision he makes in the play.

(2) The sacrifice of Alarbus is an addition.[1]

(3) Lavinia is betrothed to the emperor's son, not his brother,
and the murder of her betrothed is not part of the same plot as her
rape: nor is either brought into close connection with the intrigue
between the empress and the Moor. Here the play shows effective
concentration.

(4) The Moor 'never emerges as an independent character; he
remains, until his concluding confession, the instrument of the
Queen'.[2] His attitude towards his son, and his defiance at the end,
are also peculiar to the play.

(5) The survival of one of Titus' sons, and his flight to the Goths,
are absent: 'the triumph of civic justice through the instrumental-
ity of Lucius is wholly the creation of Shakespeare.'[3] Shakespeare
himself (IV. iv. 67–8) makes the comparison with the story of Coriolanus.

(6) The emperor is a weakling rather than the villain he is in
the play.

(7) 'The play deliberately obscures the clear-cut nature of the
foreign-native conflict for power . . . the vendetta between the

1. This has been thought to be indebted to Seneca's *Troades* (Kittredge, cited
by R. A. Law, *S.P.* 40 (1943), 145). In *Titus* itself Alarbus has been thought to be
an addition to the original version, but see note on I. i. 69. Alarbus and Mutius are
both absent from the seventeenth-century Dutch and German versions which are
in some way derived from *Titus*.

2. Sargent, p. 176.   3. *Ibid.*, p. 178.

Queen and Andronicus assumes more nearly the status of an inter-family feud.'[1]

(8) 'The play concludes (as the story does not) with the authority of the Roman state once more centred in a strong, just emperor.'[2]

Perhaps the most interesting consequences of the assumption that we have in the chap-book what is substantially Shakespeare's source are that it confirms the impression that Aaron is peculiarly Shakespearian, that it gives to Shakespeare the typical concern both in the first and in the fifth act with civil order and the forces which threaten to overthrow it, and that it makes the notion that Titus' misfortunes follow in large part from a misguided decision of his own, a Shakespearian innovation.

In view of the discovery of what may be, in essentials, Shakespeare's immediate source, speculation on more remote origins becomes of doubtful value. Of the names which are new in the play,[3] Bassianus may have been suggested by the emperor Antoninus Bassianus Caracalla (d. A.D. 217), whose character, however, is more reminiscent of Saturninus'. A Latin university play about him survives.[4] Saturninus is the name of a legate in Germany who raised a revolt in A.D. 88, and also of a third-century emperor.[5] Tamora may recall Tomyris, queen of the Massagetae, mentioned in *1H6*, II. iii. 6, who revenged her son's death on the Persian king Cyrus. The name of Mutius may be connected with Mutius Scaevola, who burned off his right hand as a proof of fortitude. He belongs to the time of Tarquin, and the name might have been suggested by the story of Lucrece, which Shakespeare clearly had in mind while writing the play. No parallels have been suggested for the name Alarbus, though it is not far from the Alaricus of the prose story.

Of the names that appear also in the prose story, only that of Andronicus calls for comment. It has been thought to point to a Byzantine origin for the whole story. The emperor Andronicus Comnenus (1183–5) was noted for his cruelty. He was eventually mutilated (his right hand being cut off) and killed by the mob. The pronunciation 'Andrónicus', instead of 'Andronícus', may be an example of the tendency to treat the Greek tonic accent as a

1. Sargent, pp. 182–3.   2. *Ibid.*, p. 183.

3. Most of this paragraph is based on W. Keller, *Sh. Jb.*, 74 (1938), 137–62; see also R. A. Law, *S.P.*, 40 (1943), 145–53, where, amongst other things, it is suggested that the play is indebted to Plutarch's Life of Scipio Africanus, which contains a large number of the play's Roman names.

4. See *Cambridge Bibliography of English Literature*, I. 661.

5. Miss F. A. Yates (see note on IV. iii. 4) suggests that the name connotes 'the evil opposite of the golden age of Saturn', and cites IV. iii. 56.

stress accent: see P. Simpson on 'The Elizabethan Pronunciation of Accented Greek Words', *M.L.R.*, 45 (1950), 509–10, and Baldwin, II. 391.

The resemblances to the story of Tereus and Philomela in Ovid, which is referred to several times in the play, are already in the chap-book version, except that the outraged female does not in the chap-book take an active part in the revenge, as she does in *Titus* and in Ovid: cf. H. Baker quoted below. Keller (pp. 139, 157) unconvincingly suggests that Shakespeare also used the version in Chaucer's *Legend of Good Women*. He may have read Gower's version in the *Confessio Amantis*: see note on v. ii. 59; but Nørgaard's parallels for 'rapine' = 'rage' weaken the argument.

The most interesting analogue is the novella by Bandello (III. 21), which tells of the rape and murder by a revengeful Moorish slave of the wife of his master, and of the murder of their sons. The Moor promises his master to spare the sons if he will cut off his nose, and he breaks his promise like the Moor in the prose story and Aaron in the play. The story was translated into French by Belleforest (*Histoires Tragiques*, vol. 2, Paris, 1570) and there is an English ballad version (*Roxburghe Ballads*, vol. 2, Hertford, 1874, pp. 49–55). The parallel was first pointed out by E. Koeppel, *Englische Studien*, 16 (1891), 365–71, and though it is no longer necessary to suppose it a main source if the chap-book version was accessible to Shakespeare, it gives us a Moor with a more Aaron-like character and power of initiative, especially in the delight he takes in his villainy. This is not prominent in the chap-book, though when the Moor cut off Titus' hand he 'inwardly laugh'd at the Villainy'.[1]

The relative importance for the play of Ovid's story of Tereus and Philomel and Seneca's of Thyestes has been much discussed, and the wider question of Ovid and Seneca as influences is raised in the last section of this Introduction. Where Shakespeare's version corresponds to the chap-book, it would be rash to read any particular significance into the fact that it also agrees with Ovid against Seneca, or *vice versa*, but a few remarks may be made. It is the Ovidian story alone that is referred to in the play itself,[2] and it is in some ways the closer analogue. The banquet is related to the other events as in Ovid: 'revenge for a rape followed by the cutting out of the victim's tongue. The further mutilation of the victim—amputation of her hands—is, according to the text (II. iv. 40), a device intended directly to prevent her from using Philomel's

---

1. Sargent, p. 178; Bullough (cited on p. xxvii), p. 41.

2. Such a reference, however, is itself a Senecan parallel: Atreus appeals to the story of Philomel and Progne in *Thyestes*, 275–6.

method of revealing the crime.'[1] Titus and Lavinia prepare the banquet together as in Ovid: in *Thyestes*, Atreus works alone. 'For a deflowered and peculiarly mutilated woman to assist in contriving a peculiar gruesome revenge—this is what connects *Titus Andronicus* with Ovid and probably with Ovid alone.'[2] There are, on the other hand, points in which *Titus* is closer to *Thyestes*.[3] The summoning of Revenge from below (iv. iii. 38; v. ii. 3) recalls Seneca's apparitions from the underworld; two sons have been served up at the banquet in both Seneca and *Titus*, and one has been guilty of ambition, whereas in Ovid there is one—innocent—victim; the mother is not the slayer either in Seneca or in *Titus*, as she is in Ovid. In Seneca as in *Titus*, there are elaborate preparations for the killing, the killer is also the cook (this is at most implied in Ovid), the feast is public, and the head is not shown (this last may reflect a difference between drama and narrative: but heads were not uncommon on the Elizabethan stage, and, indeed, figure in iii. i of *Titus*). On balance, the resemblances to Ovid seem to me decidedly the more important, though most of them are already present in the prose story. There seems no strong evidence for any direct consultation of *Thyestes*, except perhaps in iv. iii (see note on line 64), and conceivably in the treatment of the figures supposed to have risen from the underworld.[4]

4. THE PLAY

The evaluation of *Titus Andronicus* has been intimately bound up with the question of its authorship. I have already indicated my conviction that the play is through and through Shakespearian in its planning, though there are strong indications that another hand, that of Peele, was responsible for the writing of Act i. But its inferiority to all Shakespeare's other tragedies remains to be discussed. It would help if a date about 1589, rather than the 1592–3 of many recent scholars, were to be accepted; but the whole *genre* to which the play belongs is one which it requires a special effort of imagination to appreciate, and a label such as 'tragedy of blood' is not really very helpful.

To my mind the most useful recent discussions[5] are in the follow-

1. H. Baker, *Induction to Tragedy*, p. 121.   2. *Ibid.*, p. 122.
3. All these are taken from A. Brandl, *Göttingische Gelehrte Anzeiger*, 1891, 723–4.
4. I have noted also a not very striking verbal parallel in v. iii. 72.
5. Two earlier accounts may be mentioned: the Introduction to the first Arden edition, which is diffuse and wayward but has some perceptive comments; and the Introduction to the Praetorius facsimile of Q2 by Arthur Symons (1885). I mention the latter because it has recently been praised by Wilson (p. xvii), but I cannot share his high opinion of it.

ing three books: M. C. Bradbrook, *Themes and Conventions of Elizabethan Tragedy* (1935), E. M. W. Tillyard, *Shakespeare's History Plays*
(1944), and, most fully, Howard Baker, *Induction to Tragedy* (1939).
Tillyard (pp. 137–8) writes:

> This play has exactly the same qualities as the *Comedy of Errors*:
> it is academic, ambitious and masterfully planned. Miss Brad-
> brook[1] sees the academicism very plainly:
>
>> *Titus Andronicus* is a Senecal exercise; the horrors are all class-
>> ical and quite unfelt, so that the violent tragedy is contra-
>> dicted by the decorous imagery. The tone is cool and cultured
>> in its effect.
>
> Actually there is just as much Ovid in the play as there is Seneca.
> The rape and mutilation of Lavinia comes from Ovid's story of
> Procne and Philomela, though the culminating scene of Tamora
> eating her son's[2] flesh in a pasty comes from Seneca's most
> popular play, the *Thyestes*.

In view of the chap-book version, 'comes from' may be too un-
qualified, but Shakespeare certainly did everything in his power
to remind his audience of the classical analogue (esp. iv. i. 41 ff.),
and it is Ovid that is uppermost in his mind. The relevance of this
to the gruesome elements in the play is well brought out by Baker
(p. 124), who calls attention to the difficulties of transferring such
a story, familiar in narrative form, to the stage.[3] He points out that
almost any 'metrical tragedy' of the *Mirror for Magistrates* type
(whose importance in the rise of Elizabethan drama he makes
clear) likewise contains more gruesome details than does a play of
Seneca. Whether the problems are as successfully solved as Miss
Bradbrook suggests by the 'cool tone' she mentions is perhaps open
to doubt, but it is interesting that the detachment of treatment was
noted by Coleridge in those poems which provide so many parallels
to *Titus*. Of *Venus and Adonis* Coleridge says: '[Shakespeare] works
exactly as if of another planet.'[4]

The considerations I have mentioned seem to me to tell very
strongly against Dover Wilson's suggestion that many of the most
gruesome passages in *Titus* are written with a burlesque intention.

---

1. Pp. 98–9; Miss Bradbrook has now given a fuller account of the play in
Shakespeare and Elizabethan Poetry (1951), pp. 104–10.

2. A slip for 'sons''; a few lines below Tillyard again writes 'son' for 'sons'.

3. The problems involved were already familiar to Aristotle: 'The epic
affords more opening [than Tragedy] for the improbable, the chief factor in the
marvellous, because in it the agents are not visibly before one. The scene of the
pursuit of Hector would be ridiculous on the stage . . . but in the poem the
absurdity is overlooked' (*Poetics*, tr. Bywater, rev. Fyfe, ch. 24).

4. *Shakespearean Criticism*, ed. T. M. Raysor (Everyman), i. 193.

Our usual critical vocabulary is perhaps not entirely adequate for discussing these questions, and it would be rash to say that a uniform attitude of deadly seriousness is presupposed. Certainly Aaron seems to owe much to Marlowe's Barabas, and *The Jew of Malta* is a play whose nature is notoriously difficult to define. When T. S. Eliot in 1918[1] described it as a farce, he was for long regarded as putting forward a paradox;[2] but professional scholarship has now caught up, and P. H. Kocher in a valuable analysis describes the play as 'more a malicious comedy than anything else'.[3] Yet no account that denied that it was also a melodrama would be adequate. More recently still, Miss Agnes Latham has ably argued for a strong burlesque element in the horrors of Nashe's *Unfortunate Traveller*.[4] All this goes to show the capacity of an Elizabethan audience for a mixed response—and Wilson's description[5] of Aaron as 'a humorous villain', comparable to 'humorous heroes and humorous lovers' such as the Bastard in *King John* and Berowne, may gladly be accepted—yet I cannot feel that in its broad outlines *Titus* is anything but a tragedy in intention. It is, of course, precisely the 'broad outlines' that Wilson denies to Shakespeare: his view is more plausible in the context of his own theory of Shakespeare revising a Peele play.

It is, then, to those outlines that we must now turn. From Ravenscroft in 1687 ('rather a heap of Rubbish then a Structure') to Wilson in 1947 ('like some broken-down cart, laden with bleeding corpses from an Elizabethan scaffold, and driven by an executioner from Bedlam dressed in cap and bells') the structure of the play has been severely criticized. But judged by the standards of its own day, not those of Shakespeare's maturity, it is a well-planned play. Most of the modifications made in the chap-book version (if that indeed represents the source) are purposeful, and such new difficulties as the dramatist involves himself in, like the relations of the Goths to Tamora on the one hand and to Lucius on the other, are easily accounted for by inexperience, combined with an ambition to treat political themes seriously.[6]

All this does not make *Titus* a good play, but it does make it a play that we can believe Shakespeare to have written seriously.

---

1. *The Sacred Wood* (4th ed., 1934), p. 92.

2. See, e.g., H. S. Bennett's edition (1931), p. 17. Wilson too, in his comparison of Barabas and Aaron (pp. lxii–lxiii), assumes without question that Barabas is to be taken entirely seriously. Marlowe, I believe, has done exactly what Wilson here says he can *not* do, viz. 'create a vivacious villain'.

3. *Christopher Marlowe* (1946), p. 279.

4. *English Studies, 1948* (ed. F. P. Wilson), pp. 85–100.

5. P. lxiv: cf. Tillyard, p. 138.   6. See especially Tillyard, pp. 139–40.

I should like to look, as an example, at one of Wilson's objections, which is not, I think, so much wrong as over-stated. He remarks (p. x) that Tamora 'takes a leading part in Act I, and is referred to in the rest of the play as an able schemer. But it is Aaron . . . who . . . afterwards contrives all the outrages against the family of the Andronici, not only without consulting Tamora, but professed- ly out of sheer devilry.' There is admittedly lack of skill and un- certainty of purpose here, but surely not of a kind surprising in an inexperienced dramatist, whose imagination has been caught by the potentialities of a character which occupies only a subordinate position in his source. The liaison between Aaron and Tamora, too, forms a much more satisfactory sub-plot than Wilson admits, and oddly points forward, as do so many things in this play, to *King Lear* and the intrigue between Edmund and the wicked sisters. What *Titus* here lacks is spiritual depth and imaginative signifi- cance, not (or at least not so much) constructional competence.

But it is clearly not enough to show that some criticisms of the play have been too strongly put. Its positive claims to be in any sense a tragedy depend on whether Titus himself has any of the qualities of a tragic hero. I think he has, but that he is much less interesting in himself than as foreshadowing several of Shake- speare's mature tragedies. The best discussion of this topic, and indeed of the play as a whole, is that of H. T. Price,[1] who sees hints especially of Othello and Lear. I should like to look at those in turn, after glancing at the more obvious but perhaps more super- ficial parallel with Hamlet. In both *Hamlet* and *Titus* we have a combination of feigned madness with some degree of real mental unbalance. In both plays, Shakespeare has clearly learnt from Kyd, and I doubt whether a development to *Hamlet* through *Titus* can be convincingly claimed. In the main, the two plays would seem to belong to different lines of development from Kyd. At any rate, the figure of Titus surely owes something to Kyd's Hieronymo in *The Spanish Tragedy*, just as Hamlet probably does to Kyd's own *Hamlet*. Even in *Titus* there is something more than the alternate presentation of real madness and of cunning revenge under the guise of madness which we find in *The Spanish Tragedy*, but, of course, nothing approaching the subtlety of Hamlet's 'antic dis- position'.

1. *J.E.G.P.*, 42 (1943), esp. pp. 70–80; it is to this essay that I would refer those interested in comparing the structure of *Titus* with that of Shakespeare's other tragedies. Professor Price has returned to the subject in *Construction in Shakespeare* (Ann Arbor, 1951), of which pp. 37–41 are devoted to *Titus*. Some similarities have, I hope, emerged from the discussion of the play and the chap-book in the section on *Source* in this Introduction.

The comparison with Othello is more illuminating. Titus, writes Price,[1] 'has something of the simplicity of Othello; although he can estimate a man's capacity in the field, he is hopeless in the hands of a dishonest schemer at home'. Further resemblances can be detected.[2] His idealism leads him to kill his daughter as a tribute to the ideal of purity, as he has earlier killed his son in the name of honour. He is, like Othello, essentially an isolated figure, though Shakespeare has not yet devised an adequate presentation of this: the feigned madness is the best he can do at the culminating point. The resemblance between Aaron and Iago is obvious, and Chiron and Demetrius are somewhat analogous to Roderigo as at once crude villains and dupes.

The resemblance to Lear is even more striking. The errors and crimes into which Titus' anger and inflexibility betray him in Act I have the same function in the play as those of Lear. The sense that errors and crimes alike spring from the same personality strikes me as already particularly Shakespearian. The man who slays his virtuous son in a bad quarrel (I. i. 342) is the same man who, when called upon to arbitrate on the rival claims for the empire, makes the fatal decision of accepting the invidious role, and then comes down on the side of the principle of primogeniture without reference to the merits of the case. Where he diverges from Lear is that he 'never arrives at healing self-knowledge'.[3] Price, from whom I take this phrase, acutely remarks that Marcus represents the moderation which Titus rejects, and that 'roughly speaking, Lear is a Titus who becomes a Marcus, but a revenge-play necessarily precluded this type of development.'[4] Later in the play, too, suggestions of *King Lear* are frequent: notably the sub-plot turning on the lust of a principal female character for a flamboyant villain, and the calling in of foreign aid to re-establish internal order.[5] Some affinities between *Titus* and *Lear* were noted by P. Allen, *Shakespeare, Jonson and Wilkins as Borrowers* (1928), pp. 13–18. The gulf between the plays is about as great as there could be between any two works by the same author, but at any rate one already sees Shakespeare in *Titus* planning on the grand scale, and achieving a result that, however little it may appeal to us, is beyond the powers of any other dramatist writing at the time.

To assign to *Titus* a definite place in Shakespeare's development is difficult, especially in view of the conflicting theories about its dating (absolute and relative); but I should like to conclude with

1. *J.E.G.P.*, 42 (1943), 74.
2. I am here indebted to some notes given me by Mr E. A. J. Honigmann.
3. Price, p. 73.   4. *Ibid.*
5. The former motif, but not the latter, is in the chap-book.

a few remarks, made on the assumption of early date and serious (i.e. non-burlesque) intention.

It is, I think, the one play of Shakespeare which could have left an intelligent contemporary in some doubt whether the author's truest bent was for the stage, and this in spite of its superiority in sheer competence over most contemporary drama. It is true that the drama of the time had, as a whole, close connections with non-dramatic poetry,[1] but even when allowances have been made for that, we may still feel with Miss Bradbrook that *Titus* is 'more like a pageant than a play'.[2] What is not yet present is any sustained power of building up to a climax: as W. H. Clemen puts it, 'instead of preparing us for *one* great event, for *one* climax, and leading us through all the stages of development up to this peak, Shakespeare overwhelms us from the first act on with "climaxes", with a multiplicity of fearful events and high-sounding words.'[3] Professor Clemen, in the discussion from which this extract is taken, is specially concerned with Shakespeare's failure to make the imagery of the play subserve a genuinely dramatic purpose, and I have nothing to add to his account. But in concentrating on Shakespeare's failure to do what he does with increasing mastery in his mature plays, there is a danger of overlooking how far he has already got. He has a sense of the play as a whole, and a sense of the individual episode. It is principally in bringing the two into relation that he is still deficient. So too on the side of language: the individual phrase or line, and the rhetorical outline of a speech, are often successful; what is lacking is commonly the sense of appropriateness of speech to situation and character, and above all the power to convey a real impression of dramatic interchange:[4] 'the characters are not yet talking with *each other*, but are delivering pompous orations to the audience.'[5]

Yet the very fact that we can point to so many things that are wrong with *Titus* is itself evidence of dramatic life: no one dwells on defects, and suggests improvements, in the irremediably dull and worthless. And even if the things in *Titus* which look forward to the later tragedies derive most of their interest from what be-

1. Two books already mentioned are relevant here: H. Baker, *Induction to Tragedy*, and M. C. Bradbrook, *Shakespeare and Elizabethan Poetry*.

2. *Op. cit.*, p. 110.

3. *The Development of Shakespeare's Imagery* (1951), p. 25.

4. But the scenes involving Aaron, Chiron, and Demetrius seem to me to represent a tolerable level of achievement in this respect.

5. Clemen, *op. cit.*, p. 29; so in his *Die Tragödie vor Shakespeare* (1955) he discusses the process 'wie sich aus dem starren und beziehungslosen Nebeneinanderstehen und Aneinandervorbeireden der Redepartner ein beziehungsreiches Zueinanderreden entwickelt' (p. 12).

comes of them in those tragedies, they have some impressiveness in their inchoate state. *Romeo and Juliet* is on almost every count a vastly superior play to *Titus*, but it could be maintained that *Titus* is strictly speaking more *promising*. The author of *Romeo and Juliet* could conceivably have gone in that play as far as he was destined to go in tragedy—and indeed Shakespeare's tragic development does not exactly proceed through *Romeo and Juliet*—but the author of *Titus* was obviously going *somewhere*: though it was not yet certain whether he would steer clear of violent episodic melodrama on the one hand and exaggeratedly Ovidian narrative in dialogue on the other.

5. RECENT WORK ON TITUS

Since my 1953 edition was published, a number of important scholarly and critical contributions to the study of *Titus* have appeared.

On the bibliographical side, there are Sir Walter Greg's last words on the play in *The Shakespeare First Folio* (1955). I discuss some of his views in the later part of the note on III. i. 36. Fredson Bowers, *Studies in Bibliography*, 9 (1957), 3–20, has argued that the Folio *Titus*, like *Romeo and Juliet*, was set up not, as has generally been believed, by one of the two principal compositors (B), but, except for the first page, by a less skilled workman whom he has renamed E. In *The Printing and Proof-Reading of the First Folio of Shakespeare* (1963), Charlton Hinman agrees. For the press-variants Bowers mentions (p. 12, n. 13), see Hinman, I. 286–90, and, for the only three of importance, p. viii above.

Two important new editions have appeared: that of C. J. Sisson, supplemented by his *New Readings in Shakespeare* (1956), in which I have found some welcome confirmation, some arguments that have convinced me, and some others which leave me still of my original opinion; and the posthumously published *London Shakespeare* of John Munro (1958).

The book which discusses *Titus* at greatest length is T. W. Baldwin's *On the Literary Genetics of Shakspere's Plays 1592–1594* (1959). I have given my views on this book as a whole in *Notes and Queries*, 205 (1960), 354–5. Baldwin believes, largely on grounds of its structure and 'casting-pattern', that *Titus* 'was first written for the Admiral's men around 1588 or 1589' (p. 234), not by Shakespeare (p. 445), and that the existing version represents a 1594 revision by Peele and Shakespeare (p. 420), but that 'the *Old Titus* ran in much the same fashion as the *Titus* of 1594.' He re-examines the Peele links, notably the 'palliament' (pp. xxv–xxvi above). The fact that 'pallium' was the recognized term for the Garter mantle gives some weight to his contention that the poem precedes the passage in the play (p. 412), and his whole discussion (ch. XXII) strengthens the case for Peele's hand in *Titus*. He emphasizes that at II. iii. 129–30 (see note) it is easier to see Nashe as the source than as the debtor (pp. 416–18). A claim for the priority of *Venus and Adonis* to II. iii. 17–20 (see note on l. 17) is less persuasive to me (pp. 418–20). Baldwin also examines the Dutch and German versions, which I ignored in my earlier edition because I could see no reason to dissent from E. K. Chambers's view (*William Shakespeare*, I. 319) that 'the facts are quite consistent with the natural hypothesis of divergence from a common source in an adaptation of [the surviving] *Titus Andronicus* for continental travel.' Baldwin's claims for a debt to the *Old Titus* are not far-reaching, but modest as they are, they have not persuaded me that Chambers was wrong. The hypothesis of revision has its attractions—it does some justice to Henslowe's 'ne', and accounts for certain 1593–4 links (p. xxiv above)—but I find it hard to believe in a completely non-Shakespearian *Old Titus* which yet resembled the existing play in structure as closely as Baldwin holds that it did.

Shakespeare Survey, vol. 10 (1957), contained three excellent articles relevant to *Titus*. Terence Spencer's brilliant 'Shakespeare and the Elizabethan Romans' brings out the way in which *Titus* must have been less un-Roman to the Elizabethans than it is to us: 'One could almost say without paradox that, in many respects, *Titus Andronicus* is a more typical Roman play, a more characteristic piece of Roman history, than the three great plays of Shakespeare which are generally grouped under that name' (p. 32). He also emphasizes the oddly eclectic treatment of Roman institutions of all periods: 'The author seems anxious, not to get it all right, but to get it all in' (*ibid.*). R. F. Hill, in 'The Composition of *Titus Andronicus*', is studiedly agnostic on the authorship question. He still leans towards crediting it all to Shakespeare as his first play, but his analysis of the use of certain rhetorical devices shows marked divergence between *Titus* and any of the other ten early plays chosen for comparison. I think he has established beyond all reasonable doubt that 'to contend for sole Shakespearian authorship of *Titus* and composition in 1593–4 is nonsense' (p. 68). His acute analysis (p. 63) of the play's structural weaknesses is a corrective to more indulgent accounts, including that on pp. xxxiv–xxxv above, though I would still hold (and Hill does not deny) that it is beyond the ascertained power of any contemporary dramatist except Kyd (Marlowe's whole approach to drama being radically different). Finally, E. M. Waith in 'The Metamorphosis of Violence in *Titus Andronicus*' follows out some of the implications of Shakespeare's Ovidianism, concluding (p. 48) that 'in taking over certain Ovidian forms Shakespeare takes over part of an Ovidian conception which cannot be fully realized by the techniques of drama' (cf. p. xxxiii above). He also notes how the play answers to the Renaissance demand for 'admiration' as one main effect of a tragedy.

In a paper in *Essays in Criticism*, vol. 10 (1960), 275–89, 'Wilderness of Tigers: Structure and Symbol in *Titus Andronicus*', Mr Alan Sommers discusses the conflict between Rome and 'the barbarism of primitive, original nature' (p. 276) embodied in Tamora and Aaron.

Shakespeare Survey, 14 (1961), includes two articles bearing on *Titus*. Gustav Ungerer prints and discusses an account of a performance on New Year's Day, 1596, for Sir John Harington at Burley-on-the-Hill; the critical comment is worth quoting: 'la monstre a plus valeu q̄ le suiect.' Nicholas Brooke, writing on 'Marlowe as Provocative Agent in Shakespeare's Early Plays', deals with *Titus* on pp. 35–7.

TITUS ANDRONICUS

DRAMATIS PERSONÆ[1]

SATURNINUS, *son to the late Emperor of Rome and afterwards Emperor.*
BASSIANUS, *brother to Saturninus.*
TITUS ANDRONICUS, *a noble Roman, general against the Goths.*
MARCUS ANDRONICUS, *tribune of the People, and brother to Titus.*
LUCIUS,
QUINTUS,
MARTIUS, } *sons to Titus Andronicus.*
MUTIUS,
Young LUCIUS, *a boy, son to Lucius.*
PUBLIUS, *son to Marcus Andronicus.*
SEMPRONIUS,
CAIUS, } *kinsmen to Titus.*
VALENTINE,
ÆMILIUS, *a noble Roman.*
ALARBUS,
DEMETRIUS, } *sons to Tamora.*
CHIRON,
AARON, *a Moor, beloved by Tamora.*
Messenger, and Clown.
Goths and Romans.
TAMORA, *Queen of the Goths.*
LAVINIA, *daughter to Titus Andronicus.*
A Nurse, and a black Child.
Kinsmen of Titus, Senators, Tribunes, Officers, Soldiers, and Attendants.

SCENE : *Rome, and the Country near it.*

[1] First given imperfectly by Rowe.

TITUS ANDRONICUS

ACT I

SCENE I

Enter the Tribunes and Senators aloft; and then enter SATURNINUS *and his followers at one door, and* BASSIANUS *and his followers at the other, with drums and trumpets.*

Sat. Noble patricians, patrons of my right,
 Defend the justice of my cause with arms;

ACT I

Scene 1

Act I Scene 1] *Actus Primus. Scæna Prima. F; not in Qq.*   *Enter*] *Flourish. Enter F.*   *at the other*] *not in Qq.*   *drums*] *Drum Q3,F.*   *trumpets*] *Colours F.*

Scene 1] Except for scene-division, and a few F and editorial supplements, I have throughout gone right back to Q stage-directions. Such additional information as 'Rome' or 'the Capitol' is evident from the text when it is of any importance.

Enter . . . aloft] This does not mean that we see them coming on, but that they are 'discovered' by drawing back the curtains of the upper stage: G. F. Reynolds, *The Staging of Elizabethan Plays*, p. 48, quotes for this use of *Enter* from *George a Greene*, sc. xi: 'Enter a Shoemaker sitting upon the stage at worke.' The staging of the play is throughout very simple and any standard account, e.g. the brief one by C. J. Sisson in *Companion to Shakespeare Studies*, ed. Granville-Barker and Harrison, will give the necessary information.

at one door . . . at the other] The specification of 'at one door' in Q1

makes it clear that the contrasting 'at the other', supplied by F, is required. On this form of expression in stage-directions cf. W. Archer and W. J. Lawrence in *Shakespeare's England*, II. 304–5: 'Though there were in fact three doors opening upon the stage, two of them were so much more prominent and more frequently used, that playwrights often expressed themselves as though they alone existed. They would, indeed, be the only doors visible when the curtains of the Rear Stage were closed'—as they would be in this scene.

Flourish (F)] trumpet-call. F has a number of additional directions of this kind, originating in the prompt-book with which the copy of Q3 used by the printer has been very roughly collated.

1. Sat.] This (unabbreviated) and the speech prefixes at ll. 9, 18, 46, 47, and 56, and also at v. i. 121–4, are centred in Qq. At I. i. 64, 157, II. iii.

And, countrymen, my loving followers,
Plead my successive title with your swords:
I am his first-born son that was the last   5
That ware the imperial diadem of Rome;
Then let my father's honours live in me,
Nor wrong mine age with this indignity.
Bass. Romans, friends, followers, favourers of my right,
    If ever Bassianus, Cæsar's son,   10
    Were gracious in the eyes of royal Rome,
    Keep then this passage to the Capitol,
    And suffer not dishonour to approach
    The imperial seat, to virtue consecrate,
    To justice, continence, and nobility;   15
    But let desert in pure election shine,
    And, Romans, fight for freedom in your choice.
Marc. [*holding the crown*] Princes, that strive by factions and
        by friends
    Ambitiously for rule and empery,
    Know that the people of Rome, for whom we stand   20

5. am his] was the *F*.   6. ware] wore *F*.   14. virtue consecrate,] *Rowe* (*2nd ed.*); vertue, consecrate *Qq;* Vertue: consecrate *F*.   18. *Marc.* [*holding the crown*]] *Bolton; Marcus Andronicus with the Crowne Qq* (*centred*); *Enter Marcus Andronicus aloft with the Crowne F* (*centred*).

192, II. iv. 11, a centred entry serves instead of a speech-heading. For I. i. 358, 360, see critical apparatus.

4. *successive title*] title to the succession. Cf. *2H6*, III. i. 49: 'successive heir'.

5. *his . . . that*] of him who. Q1 gives a comma after *son*. This is in keeping with the practice of Shakespeare's time (cf. Simpson, p. 42), but I omit the comma, here and in ll. 39–40, 122, to make the construction clearer to the modern reader. For the possible bearing of the frequency of this construction on the authorship of Act I, see Introduction, pp. xxiv–xxv.

8. *mine age*] the fact that I am the elder. Delius's view that *age* virtually means 'youth', and that Shakespeare means he is too young to enforce recognition of his rights, is less plausible.

10–13. *If . . . And*] Wilson, pp. xxvii–

xxviii, notes the identity of structure with ll. 428–31.

11. *gracious*] acceptable: so ll. 170, 381 (graciously), 429, II. i. 32.

15. *continence*] self-restraint, with special reference to the use of power.

16. *pure election*] in contrast to Saturninus' claim from primogeniture.

18. Marc. [holding the crown]] Bolton's interpretation of the Q1 direction (*Modern Language Notes*, 45 (1930), 139–40) is undoubtedly correct. Marcus has been on stage with the other Tribunes from the beginning of the scene. Q1 centres the speech-heading of the two speeches that precede this and of the three that follow.

19. *empery*] status of emperor, as in ll. 22, 201, and *empire* in l. 183.

20–1. *people . . . party*] The very vaguely conceived Rome of this play is divided into patricians and plebeians

A special party, have by common voice,
In election for the Roman empery,
Chosen Andronicus, surnamed Pius
For many good and great deserts to Rome.
A nobler man, a braver warrior,   25
Lives not this day within the city walls:
He by the senate is accited home
From weary wars against the barbarous Goths,
That with his sons, a terror to our foes,
Hath yok'd a nation strong, train'd up in arms.   30
Ten years are spent since first he undertook
This cause of Rome, and chastised with arms
Our enemies' pride: five times he hath return'd
Bleeding to Rome, bearing his valiant sons
In coffins from the field, and at this day   35
To the monument of the Andronici   35a

23. Pius] *Pious F.*   35–35*c.* and ... Goths] *not in Q2–3,F.*   35*a.* the Andronici]
Chambers; *that* Andronicy *Q1.*

('people'), the latter being represented
by tribunes as in republican Rome
(and, as a nominal survival, under the
empire). The *factions* of l. 18 are both
patrician.

23. *Pius.*] Q1's colon after this word,
if it is not a sheer blunder, may be
analogous to the use of the colon to
introduce reported speech, cf. Simpson, pp. 77–8. The next line, as it were,
quotes the grounds for the assignment
of the 'surname'. Q2 (more normally)
prints a comma (and a colon at the end
of l. 24 where Q1 has a comma).

27. *accited*] summoned.

30. *yok'd*] brought under the yoke:
the symbol of conquest by Rome, cf.
l. 69.

32. *chastised*] Seven times in Shakespeare with this stress, against two
with 'chastíse' (On.).

35–35*c. and . . . Goths*] These lines,
omitted in Q2, conflict with the rest of
the scene. But it is doubtful whether
they belong to an earlier version. The
general account of Titus' return in
ll. 36 ff. reads very oddly after the more
specific account in these lines of what

he has done on his return. L. 36 sounds
like a fresh start, made after the preceding lines had already been, in intention, deleted. The whole speech
may never have been reduced to a
satisfactory state by the author.

35. *at this day*] W. W. Greg, *M.L.R.*,
48 (1953), 439–40 (so also Baldwin
(1959), p. 431) conj. 'as this day',
noting that if this means 'as he has
already done', it supports the view of
Dover Wilson and others that the sacrifice of Alarbus (ll. 96–119) is a later
insertion in the scene as originally conceived; but that if it means 'as he proposes to do' (so Baldwin), it supports
the integrity of the scene. H. F. Brooks
suggests that 'at this day' could mean
'on the day corresponding to this'—
i.e. always on the very day of return;
then 'at last' (l. 36) could mean 'for the
final time'.

35*a. the Andronici*] The MS. presumably had 'y^e', which could easily
be misread as 'y^t' by a compositor
who did not realize (note his spelling of it) that *Andronici* was plural.
The correction by Chambers ap-

Done sacrifice of expiation,   35*b*
And slain the noblest prisoner of the Goths.   35*c*
And now at last, laden with honour's spoils,
Returns the good Andronicus to Rome,
Renowned Titus, flourishing in arms.
Let us entreat, by honour of his name
Whom worthily you would have now succeed,   40
And in the Capitol and senate's right,
Whom you pretend to honour and adore,
That you withdraw you and abate your strength,
Dismiss your followers, and, as suitors should,
Plead your deserts in peace and humbleness.   45

Sat. How fair the tribune speaks to calm my thoughts!
Bass. Marcus Andronicus, so I do affy
In thy uprightness and integrity,
And so I love and honour thee and thine,
Thy noble brother Titus and his sons,   50
And her to whom my thoughts are humbled all,
Gracious Lavinia, Rome's rich ornament,
That I will here dismiss my loving friends,
And to my fortune's and the people's favour
Commit my cause in balance to be weigh'd.   55
                    [*Exeunt the followers of Bassianus.*

40. succeed] succeeded *Capell.*   41. Capitol] Capitall *Q1–2.*   54. fortune's]
Delius; fortunes *Qq;* Fortunes *F.*   55. *Exeunt . . . Bassianus*] *Capell; Exit Soldiers*
Qq,F.

pears in his 'Red Letter' edition, 1907.

39–40. *by honour . . . succeed*] The
ground of Marcus' appeal to the factions seems to be the respect each of
them feels for its own candidate. This
is a little odd, but not sufficiently so to
make acceptable Capell's ingenious
emendation, according to which *his
. . . whom* would refer to the late
emperor.

40. *Whom . . . succeed*] Stoll, with no
support from *N.E.D.*, gives the original text the sense of Capell's emendation by treating 'succeed' as a past
participle. H. F. Brooks suggests that
the meaning is: they want whoever is
chosen to succeed 'worthily', and this
requires that the election should be

carried on peacefully and without
intimidation.

41. *Capitol . . . right*] the right of the
Capitol and the senate. The omission
of inflection after the first of two co-
ordinate possessive nouns is common
(Abbott §397; Franz §684d, quoting
Mac., v. vii. 16: 'my wife and children's ghosts'), as indeed it is in colloquial modern English. The whole
phrase seems to mean 'with due respect
for the rightful claims of the Capitol
and the senate': cf. On. *right* sb.[1], 2.

42. *pretend*] claim.

47. *affy*] trust.

54. *fortune's*] Delius's interpretation
of the ambiguous *fortunes* seems preferable to treating it as plural.

Sat. Friends, that have been thus forward in my right,
      I thank you all and here dismiss you all,
      And to the love and favour of my country
      Commit myself, my person, and the cause.
                    [*Exeunt the followers of Saturninus.*
      Rome, be as just and gracious unto me   60
      As I am confident and kind to thee.
      Open the gates and let me in.
Bass. Tribunes, and me, a poor competitor.
                    [*They go up into the Senate-house.*

Enter a Captain.

Cap. Romans, make way, the good Andronicus,
       Patron of virtue, Rome's best champion,   65
       Successful in the battles that he fights,
       With honour and with fortune is return'd
       From where he circumscribed with his sword,
       And brought to yoke, the enemies of Rome.

*Sound drums and trumpets, and then enter two of Titus' sons, and
then two Men bearing a coffin covered with black; then two other sons;
then* TITUS ANDRONICUS; *and then* TAMORA, *the Queen of Goths,
and her sons,* ALARBUS, CHIRON, *and* DEMETRIUS, *with* AARON

59. Exeunt . . . Saturninus.] *Capell; not in* Qq,F.   63. They] *Flourish. They* F.
65. Patron] Pattern *Anon. conj. (in Camb.).*   68. where] whence *F.*   69. and
then two] After them, two *F.*   then Titus] After them, Titus *F.*   her ... Alarbus]
Rowe; her two . . . Qq,F.

61. *confident and kind*] a trusting and
loving son: *kind* = possessed of natural
affection.

65. *Patron*] Up to the sixteenth century, this spelling represented both the
meanings now differentiated as patron
and pattern (see *N.E.D.*, 'pattern'), as
still in French 'patron'. By Shakespeare's time the two had become
fairly distinct, but there are a few instances from Spenser which suggest
the earlier undifferentiated stage. In
F.Q., Argument to I. i, 'the Patron of
true Holinesse' and *Letter to Raleigh* 'of
the xii. other vertues, I make xii. other
knights the patrones', the appropriate
gloss might be 'representative', which

looks towards both the modern words.
Lodowick Bryskett in his account of
Spenser's plan stresses the 'patron'
aspect; 'assigning to every vertue, a
Knight to be the patron and defender
of the same' (*Discourse of Civill Life*,
1606, p. 27). In the present passage,
'representative' gives good sense. Another survival of the original identity
of the two words is recorded in *English
Dialect Dictionary*, 'patron *sb.*[1]', where
the form 'pattern' is quoted as current
in Ireland for 'a fair in honour of a
patron saint'.

68. *circumscribed*] brought within
bounds.

69. S.D.] There is no entrance for

the Moor, and others as many as can be; then set down the coffin,
and TITUS *speaks.*

Tit. Hail, Rome, victorious in thy mourning weeds!   70
Lo, as the bark that hath discharg'd his fraught
Returns with precious lading to the bay
From whence at first she weigh'd her anchorage,
Cometh Andronicus, bound with laurel boughs,
To re-salute his country with his tears,   75
Tears of true joy for his return to Rome.
Thou great defender of this Capitol,
Stand gracious to the rites that we intend.
Romans, of five and twenty valiant sons,
Half of the number that King Priam had,   80
Behold the poor remains, alive and dead.
These that survive, let Rome reward with love;

69. S.D. *then set*] *They set F.*   71. his] *F4.*   76. Rome.] *Rowe (Ravenscroft);*
Rome, *Qq,F.*   78. rites] rights *Q1–2.*

Alarbus (Rowe added one), though he
has an exit at l. 129. Since he has not a
speaking part, and since Q1 was set up
from author's 'foul papers' and not
from prompt-copy, the omission need
not indicate revision. J. Munro (*T.L.S.*,
10 June 1949, p. 388) holds that
Alarbus was never on the stage at all,
and that the mention of him at l. 129
S.D. is an erroneous addition by 'some-
body' unspecified. The book-keeper
could have made a jotting on the MS.
(cf. v. i, initial S.D.), but there is no
reason to think he would have done so
without justification.

others . . . be] A typical S.D. from
author's MS. At *2H6,* IV. ii. 33, F has,
less modestly, 'Enter Cade . . . with
infinite numbers.'

the coffin] The singular is surprising, as A. Koszul, *English Studies,* 31
(1950), 182, points out, since ll. 84, 89,
94 call for a number of corpses. But
this is probably how the author envisaged the staging and we cannot
safely emend. At l. 149, but not elsewhere, F emends to 'coffins'.

71. *his*] The alteration to *her* is, in the

light of l. 73, an obvious one, but the
irregularity may well go back to
author's MS. In the 1609 text of *Sonnet*
102, ll. 8 and 10, we have the same
sequence of 'his . . . her'. Other examples of similar mixtures are: Bacon,
Advancement of Learning, II. xxii. 1 (ed.
Aldis Wright, p. 203): 'so as it may
yield of herself'; Nashe, *Lenten Stuffe*
(ed. McKerrow, III. 157, ll. 25–7):
'vesselles . . . it hath given shelter to at
once in her harbour'.

73. *anchorage*] 'set of anchors' (On.);
but it seems to be scarcely more than a
rhetorical variation for 'anchors'.

77. *Thou . . . defender*] Jupiter
Capitolinus.

78. *rites*] The spelling of Q1–2 is not
uncommon, cf. l. 143, v. iii. 196, *Ham.*
(Q2), v. ii. 413.

80. *Half . . . had*] Priam's fifty sons
are so well known that a specific source
need not be sought. The total of Titus'
sons actually adds up to twenty-six,
cf. III. i. 10. This may (C. Crawford,
cited by Baildon) be because Mutius
was an afterthought: see Oppel, pp.
22–3.

These that I bring unto their latest home,
With burial amongst their ancestors.   84
Here Goths have given me leave to sheathe my sword.
Titus, unkind, and careless of thine own,
Why suffer'st thou thy sons, unburied yet,
To hover on the dreadful shore of Styx?
Make way to lay them by their brethren.

[They open the tomb.

There greet in silence, as the dead are wont,   90
And sleep in peace, slain in your country's wars.
O sacred receptacle of my joys,
Sweet cell of virtue and nobility,
How many sons hast thou of mine in store,

---

89. brethren] bretheren *Q3,F (so ll. 123, 160, 357)*.   90. the] *not in Q2.*
94. hast thou of mine] of mine hast thou *Q3,F.*

---

83. *Latest home*] Ultimately from Ecclesiastes, xii. 5, 'long home'. The quotation is from Coverdale's version (retained in A.V.): see *N.E.D. home* sb. 6. *O.D.E.P.*, p. 381, cites Brunne (1303): 'And thy traueyle shalt thou sone ende, / For to thy long home sone shalt thou wende'; Lyly's *Euphues and his England* (1580): 'Shal... a trauailer that hath sustained harm... disswade al Gentlemen to rest at their own home till they come to their long home?' Tilley, H533, has quotations with 'longest' (a. 1594) and 'last' (1611). *Locrine* (*Sh. Apocrypha*, ed. Tucker Brooke), v. iv. 237, has 'latest home'.

87–8. *Why ... Styx?*] Lee quotes Virgil, *Aen.*, vi. 325–9: 'haec omnis, quam cernis, inops inhumataque turba est ... volitantque haec litora circum.' The closeness of *hover* to *volitant* suggests an actual echo.

89. *brethren*] Q1 varies between the spellings *brethren* and *bretheren* (and similarly between *empress* and *emperess*). Since it never uses the longer form except where a trisyllabic scansion is appropriate, it is tempting to follow Wilson and Alexander in varying the spelling throughout according to scansion; but on balance it seems best to use the present-day spelling consistently. I have, however, recorded in the apparatus all occurrences of the longer form in Q1. In the history plays the name 'Henry' is constantly varying between a disyllabic and a trisyllabic pronunciation without any variation of spelling. This fact makes it extremely unlikely that the variations in *Titus* 'may point to difference of authorship' (Wilson on l. 240). On the allied question of divergent spellings of proper names as a clue to divergent authorship, cf. P. Alexander, *Shakespeare's* Henry VI *and* Richard III (Cambridge, 1929), pp. 178–84, whose conclusions are entirely negative.

92. *receptacle*] Stressed 'réceptácle' as in *Rom.*, IV. iii. 40, and as late as Wordsworth (*Prel.*, x. 170, and two other passages: the only ones in which he uses the word). Wilson glosses 'sepulchre, vault', which is too specific, though the word can be used, as here and in the *Rom.* passage, with reference to a sepulchre. The word is now more prosaic and more exclusively used of a *small* container.

94. *in store*] 'laid up as in a storehouse' (On.). Schmidt compares *Mac.*, II. iv. 34, 'The sacred storehouse of his predecessors'.

That thou wilt never render to me more!   95
Luc. Give us the proudest prisoner of the Goths,
    That we may hew his limbs, and on a pile
    Ad manes fratrum sacrifice his flesh
    Before this earthy prison of their bones,
    That so the shadows be not unappeas'd,   100
    Nor we disturb'd with prodigies on earth.
Tit. I give him you, the noblest that survives,
    The eldest son of this distressed queen.
Tam. Stay, Roman brethren! Gracious conqueror,
    Victorious Titus, rue the tears I shed,   105
    A mother's tears in passion for her son:
    And if thy sons were ever dear to thee,
    O, think my son to be as dear to me.
    Sufficeth not that we are brought to Rome,
    To beautify thy triumphs, and return   110
    Captive to thee and to thy Roman yoke;
    But must my sons be slaughtered in the streets
    For valiant doings in their country's cause?
    O, if to fight for king and commonweal
    Were piety in thine, it is in these.   115
    Andronicus, stain not thy tomb with blood:
    Wilt thou draw near the nature of the gods?

---

98. *manes*] *F3; manus Qq,F.*   flesh] *Stoll;* flesh: *Qq,F.*   99. earthy] earthly *F.*
103. this] his *Q3.*   108. son] sonnes *F.*   110. triumphs, and return] triumphs
and return, *Theobald.*   112. slaughtered] slaughtred *F.*

98. Ad manes fratrum] to the shades of (our) brethren.

101. *prodigies*] ominous events.

106. *passion*] grief; this word has a wide range of meanings in Shakespeare's English; for others, cf. II. i. 36, III. i. 217.

110.] Most editions (including my 1953 one) accept Theobald's repunctuation. But 'triumphs and return' is an awkward hendiadys for 'triumphal return', and there is really nothing wrong with saying that she and her sons 'return captive with thee' when the meaning is that he returns with them as his captives. There may also be a suggestion of the sense given by Schmidt 1 d as 'fall to, become the

share of': *Ham.*, I. i. 91–2, 'which had return'd / To the inheritance of Fortinbras'. Kittredge and Alexander retain the original punctuation.

112. *slaughtered*] I have throughout followed the Q spelling for words of this kind, except where rhythm tells strongly against it. Here the extra slurred syllable is quite unobjectionable.

116. *thy tomb*] thy family tomb.

117–18. *Wilt . . . merciful*] No specific source need be sought for this commonplace. Steevens quoted Cicero, *pro Ligario*, XII. 38. Mr G. K. Hunter refers me to *England's Parnassus* (ed. C. Crawford, nos. 1157, 1158).

Draw near them then in being merciful;
Sweet mercy is nobility's true badge:
Thrice-noble Titus, spare my first-born son.   120
Tit. Patient yourself, madam, and pardon me.
These are their brethren whom your Goths beheld
Alive and dead, and for their brethren slain
Religiously they ask a sacrifice:
To this your son is mark'd, and die he must,   125
T' appease their groaning shadows that are gone.
Luc. Away with him, and make a fire straight,
And with our swords, upon a pile of wood,
Let's hew his limbs till they be clean consum'd.
          [*Exit Titus' sons, with Alarbus.*
Tam. O cruel, irreligious piety!   130
Chi. Was never Scythia half so barbarous!
Dem. Oppose not Scythia to ambitious Rome.
Alarbus goes to rest, and we survive
To tremble under Titus' threat'ning look.
Then, madam, stand resolv'd, but hope withal   135
The self-same gods that arm'd the Queen of Troy
With opportunity of sharp revenge
Upon the Thracian tyrant in his tent
May favour Tamora, the Queen of Goths,
(When Goths were Goths, and Tamora was queen)   140
To quit the bloody wrongs upon her foes.

---

122. their] the *F.*   your] you *Q2–3,F.*   129. *Titus'*] *not in F.*   131. never
. . . barbarous!] neuer . . . barbarous. *Q1*; euer . . . barbarous? *Q2–3,F.*
132. not] me *F.*   134. look] lookes *F.*   138. his] her *Theobald.*   141. the]
her *Rowe;* these *Capell conj.*

121. *Patient yourself*] calm down;
so in *Arden of Feversham* (*Sh. Apocrypha*,
ed. Tucker Brooke), v. i. 86 (Steevens).

127. *fire*] Disyllabic, as often with
similar words: the best-known example is *R2*, i. iii. 294: 'O, who can
hold a fire in his hand'.

129. S.D. Exit . . . Alarbus] See on
l.69 S.D.

132. *Oppose*] compare: a Latinism,
for which *N.E.D.* has no exact parallel;
but its 5 is fairly close.

136–8. *Queen . . . tent*] Hecuba, who
killed the sons of Polymnestor in
revenge for the murder of her son
Polydorus. If the author knew the version in the *Hecuba* of Euripides, the
emendation *her* for *his* is probable. But
Steevens remarked that he 'might have
been misled by the passage in Ovid:
"vadit ad *artificem*" (*Met.*, XIII. 551),
and therefore took it for granted that
she found him in *his* tent.'

141. *the*] Capell's conjecture may
well be right.

Enter the sons of Andronicus again.

Luc. See, lord and father, how we have perform'd
        Our Roman rites: Alarbus' limbs are lopp'd,
        And entrails feed the sacrificing fire,
        Whose smoke like incense doth perfume the sky.   145
        Remaineth nought but to inter our brethren,
        And with loud 'larums welcome them to Rome.
Tit. Let it be so; and let Andronicus
        Make this his latest farewell to their souls.
                    [*Sound trumpets, and lay the coffin in the tomb.*
        In peace and honour rest you here, my sons;   150
        Rome's readiest champions, repose you here in rest,
        Secure from worldly chances and mishaps.
        Here lurks no treason, here no envy swells,
        Here grow no damned drugs, here are no storms,
        No noise, but silence and eternal sleep.   155
        In peace and honour rest you here, my sons.

Enter LAVINIA.

Lav. In peace and honour live Lord Titus long;
        My noble lord and father live in fame.

---

143. *rites*] *F2*; right(e)s *Qq,F*.   149. *Sound*] *Flourish. Then Sound F.*   *Coffin*]
Coffins F.   151. Rome's] Roomes *Q1* (*so ll. 164, 186, 193*).   154. drugs]
drugges *Q1–2*; grudgges *Q3*; grudges *F*.   157. *Lav.*] *not in Q1*.   158. father]
Father, *F*.

143. *rites*] See on l. 78.

143–4. *Alarbus' ... entrails*] The possessive can, I think, carry over the intervening phrase in a way that is not possible in modern English, though I can find no close parallel for this usage.

147. *'larums*] trumpet calls (lit. 'calls to arms'). Or (On.) the sense may be more general: 'tumultuous noises'.

151. *Rome*] For the Q1 spelling, representing the pronunciation, see Wyld, p. 239, and cf. *John*, III. i. 180: 'That I have room with Rome to curse awhile'. This, and the more normal spelling, alternate in what seems quite a random fashion in *Titus*.

154. *drugs*] plants which produce

poisons: 'poisons' is the commonest Shakespearean sense. For the absence of poisonous plants as an item in the praise of a country, Prof. R. A. B. Mynors refers me to the praise of Italy in Virgil, *Georg.*, II. 152: 'nec miseros fallunt aconita legentes'. Seneca, *Troades*, 145 ff., has been quoted as a source for this whole speech—not, I think, very convincingly.

156. S.D.] Wilson places Lavinia's entry after l. 155, in order to indicate that she has heard the last line of Titus' speech.

158. *live*] Probably third person ('let him live') rather than ordinary imperative. The absence of punctuation after *father* in Qq is not conclusive in

Lo, at this tomb my tributary tears
I render for my brethren's obsequies;   160
And at thy feet I kneel, with tears of joy
Shed on this earth for thy return to Rome.
O, bless me here with thy victorious hand,
Whose fortunes Rome's best citizens applaud.
Tit. Kind Rome, that hast thus lovingly reserv'd   165
The cordial of mine age to glad my heart.
Lavinia, live; outlive thy father's days,
And fame's eternal date, for virtue's praise.

Enter MARCUS ANDRONICUS *and Tribunes; re-enter*
SATURNINUS, BASSIANUS, *and others.*

Marc. Long live Lord Titus, my beloved brother,
Gracious triumpher in the eyes of Rome.   170
Tit. Thanks, gentle tribune, noble brother Marcus.
Marc. And welcome, nephews, from successful wars,
You that survive, and you that sleep in fame.
Fair lords, your fortunes are alike in all
That in your country's service drew your swords;   175
But safer triumph is this funeral pomp
That hath aspir'd to Solon's happiness
And triumphs over chance in honour's bed.
Titus Andronicus, the people of Rome,
Whose friend in justice thou hast ever been,   180
Send thee by me, their tribune and their trust,
This palliament of white and spotless hue,
And name thee in election for the empire,

---

162. this] the *Q2–3,F.*   164. fortunes] Fortune *F.*   168. *Enter ... others.*]
Dyce (substantially); not in Qq,F.   174. alike] all alike *F.*

favour of this, since they do not
habitually place commas after nouns
in the vocative (cf. Simpson, pp. 21–2),
but it is natural to take ll. 157 and 158
as parallel in construction.

166. *cordial*] comfort; cf. *R3*, II. i.
41–2: 'a pleasing cordial ... Is this thy
vow.'

168. S.D. Enter . . . others] As
Wilson says, F's S.D. at l. 233
shows that this entry is on the upper
stage.

177. *aspir'd*] risen, implying (in contrast to modern English) that the end
has been attained. But the modern
sense was also common in Shakespeare's time.

Solon's happiness] A reference to the
saying (first in Herodotus, I. 32) 'call
no man happy until he is dead.'

181. *trust*] trusted one.

182. *palliament*] See Introduction,
pp. xxv–xxvi.

183. *in election*] i.e. as a candidate.

With these our late-deceased emperor's sons:
Be *candidatus* then, and put it on,   185
And help to set a head on headless Rome.

Tit. A better head her glorious body fits
Than his that shakes for age and feebleness.
What should I don this robe, and trouble you?
Be chosen with proclamations to-day,   190
To-morrow yield up rule, resign my life,
And set abroad new business for you all?
Rome, I have been thy soldier forty years,
And led my country's strength successfully,
And buried one and twenty valiant sons,   195
Knighted in field, slain manfully in arms,
In right and service of their noble country.
Give me a staff of honour for mine age,
But not a sceptre to control the world:
Upright he held it, lords, that held it last.   200

Marc. Titus, thou shalt obtain and ask the empery.

Sat. Proud and ambitious tribune, canst thou tell?

Tit. Patience, Prince Saturninus.

Sat.   Romans, do me right:
Patricians, draw your swords, and sheathe them not
Till Saturninus be Rome's emperor.   205
Andronicus, would thou were shipp'd to hell,
Rather than rob me of the people's hearts!

Luc. Proud Saturnine, interrupter of the good
That noble-minded Titus means to thee!

---

184. late-deceased] *Theobald;* late deceased *Qq,F.*   189. What] What!
Theobald.   you?] *Q1 (F3);* you, *Q2–3,F.*   192. abroad] abroach *F3.*   all?]
Pope; all. *Qq,F.*   206. were] wert *Q3,F.*

185. candidatus] lit. 'clad in a white
robe'.

189. *What*] why; but Theobald may
be right.

190. *proclamations*] Five syllables.

192. *set abroad*] Not recorded elsewhere. F3's emendation, which was
accepted by Dyce, is tempting, and
restores a very common expression,
meaning 'set on foot'.

197. *In . . . of*] in support of the just
claims of, and in service to.

201. *obtain and ask*] obtain if only you
ask; perhaps (Baildon) to indicate 'the
certainty of Titus' election'. Tilley,
A343, quotes 'ask and have' as a proverb from Stewart's *Chronicle of Scotland*
(1535).

202. *canst thou tell?*] For this 'defi-
ant or evasive phrase' (On.) cf. *Err.,*
III. i. 52, *1H4,* II. i. 43. The meaning of the latter passage, as here,
seems to be: 'that's what *you* think,
is it?'

Tit. Content thee, prince; I will restore to thee   210
　　The people's hearts, and wean them from themselves.
Bass. Andronicus, I do not flatter thee,
　　But honour thee, and will do till I die:
　　My faction if thou strengthen with thy friends,
　　I will most thankful be; and thanks to men   215
　　Of noble minds is honourable meed.
Tit. People of Rome, and people's tribunes here,
　　I ask your voices and your suffrages:
　　Will ye bestow them friendly on Andronicus?
Tribunes. To gratify the good Andronicus,   220
　　And gratulate his safe return to Rome,
　　The people will accept whom he admits.
Tit. Tribunes, I thank you; and this suit I make,
　　That you create our emperor's eldest son,
　　Lord Saturnine; whose virtues will, I hope,   225
　　Reflect on Rome as Titan's rays on earth,
　　And ripen justice in this commonweal:
　　Then, if you will elect by my advice,
　　Crown him, and say 'Long live our emperor!'
Marc. With voices and applause of every sort,   230
　　Patricians and plebeians, we create
　　Lord Saturninus Rome's great emperor,
　　And say 'Long live our emperor Saturnine!'
Sat. Titus Andronicus, for thy favours done
　　To us in our election this day,   235

214. friends] *Q1 (F3) ;* friend *Q2-3,F.*   217. people's] Noble *F.*   219. ye] you
Q2-3,F.   Andronicus?] *Andronicus. Q1.*   223. suit] sute *Qq (F3) ;* sure *F.*
224. our] your *Q2-3,F.*   226. Titan's] Tytans *Q2-3,F;* Tytus *Q1.*   233.] *After
this line F has: A long Flourish till they come downe.*

214. *friends*] The 's' is very heavily
inked in Q1, and may have been mistaken for a semicolon by Q2, which
reads 'friend,'. The corrected state of
F has 'Friend?' for the uncorrected
'Friend,': a misunderstood attempt at
proof-correction.

217. *people's*] F's 'noble' is taken up
rom the previous line.

219. *Will . . . Andronicus?*] The Q1
punctuation (comma at the end of
l. 218 and full stop after *Andronicus*)
could perhaps be defended as some-

thing more tentative than a direct
question: 'I ask them, if you feel
inclined to give them'.

226. *Reflect*] shine.

Titan] the god of the sun; see W.
Kranz, *Philologus*, 105 (1961), 290-5.

230. *of every sort*] from all classes of
the community, patrician and ple-
beian alike (Delius).

231-3.] The first few letters of these
lines are torn away in the surviving
copy of Q1, but the text is obviously as
in later editions.

I give thee thanks in part of thy deserts,
And will with deeds requite thy gentleness:
And for an onset, Titus, to advance
Thy name and honourable family,
Lavinia will I make my empress,   240
Rome's royal mistress, mistress of my heart,
And in the sacred Pantheon her espouse.
Tell me, Andronicus, doth this motion please thee?

Tit. It doth, my worthy lord, and in this match
I hold me highly honoured of your grace: 245
And here in sight of Rome, to Saturnine,
King and commander of our commonweal,
The wide world's emperor, do I consecrate
My sword, my chariot, and my prisoners;
Presents well worthy Rome's imperious lord: 250
Receive them then, the tribute that I owe,
Mine honour's ensigns humbled at thy feet.

Sat. Thanks, noble Titus, father of my life.
How proud I am of thee and of thy gifts
Rome shall record, and when I do forget   255
The least of these unspeakable deserts,
Romans, forget your fealty to me.

Tit. Now, madam, are you prisoner to an emperor;
To him that for your honour and your state
Will use you nobly and your followers.   260

Sat. A goodly lady, trust me, of the hue

---

242. Pantheon] Panthæon *F2;* Pathan *Qq,F.*   250. imperious] imperiall *Q3,F.*
252. thy] my *F.*   258. you] your *F.*   259. for your] for you *F.*   261. me,]
Rowe; me *Qq,F.*   261–2.] [*Aside*] *Capell.*

---

236. *in part of*] as part of the reward
for. For this curious expression, cf. a
1601 quotation in J. E. Neale, *Eliza-
beth I and her Parliaments, 1584–1601*
(1957), p. 427, 'in part of the charges
bestowed for their defence'; Dryden,
All for Love, Act III (ed. Scott-Saints-
bury, v. 392), 'Take this in part of re-
compense'; Ford, *Broken Heart,* I. ii. 59.

238. *onset*] beginning; cf. *Gent.,* III.
ii. 94: 'give the onset to thy good
advice'.

240. *empress*] See on l. 89.

242. *Pantheon*] The errors 'Pathan'
here and 'Tytus' in l. 226 suggest the
writing of 'n' by a stroke above the
preceding vowel. The Pantheon was a
temple dedicated to all the gods in the
reign of Augustus.

243. *motion*] proposal.

250. *imperious*] imperial.

259. *for*] because of. Only the (mis-)
corrected state of F has 'you'; the
uncorrected has, rightly, 'your'.

261. *trust me*] No punctuation before or after this phrase in Qq,F. I take

That I would choose, were I to choose anew.
Clear up, fair queen, that cloudy countenance:
Though chance of war hath wrought this change of
    cheer,
Thou com'st not to be made a scorn in Rome: 265
Princely shall be thy usage every way.
Rest on my word, and let not discontent
Daunt all your hopes: madam, he comforts you
Can make you greater than the Queen of Goths.
Lavinia, you are not displeas'd with this?   270

Lav. Not I, my lord, sith true nobility
Warrants these words in princely courtesy.

Sat. Thanks, sweet Lavinia. Romans, let us go:
Ransomless here we set our prisoners free:
Proclaim our honours, lords, with trump and drum. 275

Bass. Lord Titus, by your leave, this maid is mine.

Tit. How, sir! Are you in earnest then, my lord?

Bass. Ay, noble Titus; and resolv'd withal
To do myself this reason and this right.

Marc. Suum cuique is our Roman justice: 280
This prince in justice seizeth but his own.

Luc. And that he will, and shall, if Lucius live.

Tit. Traitors, avaunt! Where is the emperor's guard?
Treason, my lord! Lavinia is surpris'd.

Sat. Surpris'd! by whom?

Bass.   By him that justly may   285
Bear his betroth'd from all the world away.
       [*Exeunt Marcus and Bassianus, with Lavinia.*

Mut. Brothers, help to convey her hence away,

---

264. chance] change *Q1*.   266–7. way. . . . discontent] waie . . . discontent.
Q1; way. . . . discontent, *Q2*.   269. you] your *F*.   270. this?] this. *Qq*.
280. cuique] *F2;* cuiqum *Q1–2;* cuiquam *Q3,F*.   286. Exeunt . . . Lavinia.] *Malone
(substantially); not in Qq,F*.

it as a parenthesis and hence put only
a comma after it, and not a semi-colon
or an exclamation mark, as some
editors have done.

  264. *chance of war*] The commonplace
that 'the chance of war is uncertain' is
quoted by Tilley, C223, from a va-
riety of sources beginning with Robinson's translation of the *Utopia* (1551).
  cheer] countenance.
  268–9. *he . . . Can*] the man who comforts you is one who can.
  271. *sith*] since.
  272. *Warrants*] justifies.
  280. Suum cuique] to each his own
(Tilley, M209).

And with my sword I'll keep this door safe.
> [*Exeunt Lucius, Quintus, and Martius.*

Tit. Follow, my lord, and I'll soon bring her back.

Mut. My lord, you pass not here.

Tit.   What, villain boy,   290
> Barr'st me my way in Rome?   [*He kills him.*
> > *During the fray, exeunt Saturninus, Tamora,*
> > *Demetrius, Chiron and Aaron.*

Mut.   Help, Lucius, help!

Re-enter LUCIUS.

Luc. My lord, you are unjust, and, more than so,
> In wrongful quarrel you have slain your son.

Tit. Nor thou, nor he, are any sons of mine;
> My sons would never so dishonour me.   295
> Traitor, restore Lavinia to the emperor.

Luc. Dead, if you will; but not to be his wife,
> That is another's lawful-promis'd love.   *Exit.*

Enter aloft the EMPEROR *with* TAMORA *and her two sons*
and AARON *the Moor.*

Sat. No, Titus, no; the emperor needs her not,
> Nor her, nor thee, nor any of thy stock: 300

---

288. *Exeunt . . . Martius.*] *Malone; not in Qq,F.*   290–1. What . . . Rome?] *divided by Pope; one line Qq,F.*   291. *He kills him.*] *not in Q1–2.*   *During . . . Aaron.*] *Camb. (substantially); not in Qq,F.*   292. *Re-enter* LUCIUS.] *Capell; not in Qq,F.* 298. lawful-promis'd] *W. S. Walker;* lawfull promist *Qq,F.*   *Exit.*] *Capell; not in Qq,F.*   299. *Sat.*] *Emperour. Qq;* Empe. *F.*

288. *door*] Disyllabic, cf. l. 127.

290–1. *My . . . help!*] For convenience of lineation I retain the traditional arrangement. But I find it hard to believe that 'What . . . Rome?' is not intended as a single line, as in Qq,F.

294. *Nor thou, nor he*] Wilson notes the repetition in ll. 300, 344, and 425. It carries with it a repetition of 'dishonour' (ll. 303, 345, 425) and ll. 303 and 344 are linked by the word 'confederates'. I share Wilson's reluctance to attribute these mechanical recurrences to Shakespeare at any point of his career.

298. *That is*] Almost equivalent to 'since she is'.

299. Sat.] Q1's '*Emperour*' is the first example of irregular speech-prefixes in this play. Cf. '*King*' in II. iii. 260, 262, 276, 281, 292, 299, IV. iv. 69, 79, 94, 104 (but not 113), and throughout V. iii, except for '*Emperour*' at l. 64. Oddly enough, at I. i. 459, 478, 482, Q3 introduces an irregularity ('*King*' for '*Saturnine*') where Q1 was normal. Such irregularities are characteristic of texts set up from author's 'foul papers' as R. B. McKerrow pointed out (*R.E.S.*, 11 (1935), 459–65).

I'll trust by leisure him that mocks me once;
Thee never, nor thy traitorous haughty sons,
Confederates all thus to dishonour me.
Was none in Rome to make a stale
But Saturnine? Full well, Andronicus,   305
Agree these deeds with that proud brag of thine
That said'st I begg'd the empire at thy hands.

Tit. O monstrous! what reproachful words are these?

Sat. But go thy ways; go, give that changing piece
To him that flourish'd for her with his sword.   310
A valiant son-in-law thou shalt enjoy;
One fit to bandy with thy lawless sons,
To ruffle in the commonwealth of Rome.

Tit. These words are razors to my wounded heart.

Sat. And therefore, lovely Tamora, Queen of Goths,   315
That like the stately Phœbe 'mongst her nymphs
Dost overshine the gallan'st dames of Rome,

---

304. Was none] Was there none els *F2*.   316. Phœbe] *F2; Thebe Qq,F.*
317. gallan'st] gallanst *Q1;* gallant'st *Q2–3,F.*

---

301. *by leisure*] not in a hurry.

304. *stale*] laughing-stock. There is no obvious supplement to make this a complete line. The parallel passage in *3H6*, III. iii. 260: 'Had he none else to make a stale but me?' perhaps gives some support to the conjecture of F2 (which, however, wrongly adds *of* at the end of the line, not omitted till Boswell, 1821).

306–7. *that . . . hands*] Titus had made no such boast, but Saturnine's jealousy of his influence over the people is an important factor in the play.

309. *changing piece*] Wilson quotes Peele, *Tale of Troy*, l. 288, for this phrase, applied to Cressida. The word 'piece' is a treacherous one in Elizabethan English. It can, as here, be a somewhat derogatory term for a woman, but it often = 'masterpiece', as in *H8*, v. v. 27 (which On. does not distinguish from the present passage), and *Lr.*, IV. vi. 138: 'O ruin'd piece of nature!' Though 'changing-piece' is

not recorded as a compound I am not sure that it is not one here and in the *Tale of Troy*, in the sense of 'a piece of small change', passing from hand to hand.

310. *flourish'd . . . sword*] brandished his sword in order to win her. The sense 'swaggered' is probably also present: cf. *Caes.*, III. ii. 193, with *New Shakespeare* Glossary.

312. *bandy*] brawl.

313. *ruffle*] swagger; 'very common, *c.* 1540–1650' (*N.E.D.*).

316–17. *Phœbe . . . Rome*] Cf. Virgil, *Aen.*, I. 498–501. The word 'overshine' suggests, as Ritson noted, that the author used Phaer's translation (1558; I quote from the 1607 edition): 'Most like vnto *Diana* bright when she to hunt goth out. . . . / Whom thousands of the lady Nimphes await to do her will, / She on her armes her quiuer beares, and all them ouershines.'

317. *gallan'st*] The spelling is phonetic, to avoid the almost unpronounceable combination *ntst*: *gallant*

If thou be pleas'd with this my sudden choice,
Behold, I choose thee, Tamora, for my bride,
And will create thee Empress of Rome.   320
Speak, Queen of Goths, dost thou applaud my choice?
And here I swear by all the Roman gods,
Sith priest and holy water are so near,
And tapers burn so bright, and everything
In readiness for Hymenæus stand,   325
I will not re-salute the streets of Rome,
Or climb my palace, till from forth this place
I lead espous'd my bride along with me.
Tam. And here in sight of heaven to Rome I swear,
If Saturnine advance the Queen of Goths,   330
She will a handmaid be to his desires,
A loving nurse, a mother to his youth.
Sat. Ascend, fair queen, Pantheon. Lords, accompany
Your noble emperor, and his lovely bride,
Sent by the heavens for Prince Saturnine,   335
Whose wisdom hath her fortune conquered.
There shall we consummate our spousal rites.
                                 [*Exeunt all but Titus.*
Tit. I am not bid to wait upon this bride.
Titus, when wert thou wont to walk alone,
Dishonoured thus, and challenged of wrongs?   340

Re-enter MARCUS, LUCIUS, QUINTUS, *and* MARTIUS.

---

320. Empress] Emperesse *Q1,3*.   333. queen, Pantheon.] *Pope;* Queene:
Panthean *Qq,F;* queen, the Pantheon. *W. S. Walker.*   337. *Exeunt . . . Titus*]
Exeunt. Manet Titus Andronicus Theobald; Exeunt Omnes Qq,F.   340. *Re-enter . . .*
MARTIUS] *Capell; Enter Marcus and Titus sonnes Qq,F.*

is 'loosely used as a gen. epithet of
praise' (On.).

325. *Hymenæus*] god of marriage:
'Hymen' elsewhere in Shakespeare.

stand] Plural because 'everything' is
plural in sense.

332. *a mother . . . youth*] Stresses the
disparity of age between Tamora and
Saturninus.

333. *Pantheon*] The correction of text
and punctuation must be right as far
as it goes, but since in l. 242 'Pantheon'

is stressed on the first syllable, and
since the corruption in Qq,F would in
any case lead to the omission of 'the',
Walker's further emendation is very
plausible.

336. *Whose wisdom*] The antecedent
is presumably 'bride'—she has shown
her wisdom in accepting Saturninus'
advances—though Delius takes it to be
'heavens'.

338. *bid*] invited.

340. *challenged*] accused.

Marc. O Titus, see, O see what thou hast done,
    In a bad quarrel slain a virtuous son.
Tit. No, foolish tribune, no; no son of mine,
    Nor thou, nor these, confederates in the deed
    That hath dishonoured all our family: 345
    Unworthy brother, and unworthy sons!
Luc. But let us give him burial, as becomes;
    Give Mutius burial with our brethren.
Tit. Traitors, away! he rests not in this tomb:
    This monument five hundreth years hath stood,   350
    Which I have sumptuously re-edified:
    Here none but soldiers and Rome's servitors
    Repose in fame; none basely slain in brawls.
    Bury him where you can, he comes not here.
Marc. My lord, this is impiety in you.   355
    My nephew Mutius' deeds do plead for him;
    He must be buried with his brethren.
Mart. And shall, or him we will accompany.
Tit. 'And shall'! What villain was it spake that word?
Mart. He that would vouch it in any place but here.   360
Tit. What, would you bury him in my despite?
Marc. No, noble Titus, but entreat of thee
    To pardon Mutius and to bury him.

---

348. Mutius] *Mucius Q1–2 (but Mutius at ll. 356, 362).*   358. *Mart.*] *Bolton;*
Titus two sonnes speakes Qq,F (centred); Quint. Mart. Capell.   360. *Mart.*] *Capell;*
Titus sonne speakes Qq,F (centred).

347. *as becomes*] as is fitting; a tag
used by Peele both in *Device of the
Pageant*, l. 35 (Wilson) and *Edw. I*, ix.
22.

348. *brethren*] See on l. 89.

350. *hundreth*] This form occurs in
the preface to the Authorized Version
of the Bible. In this line it was not
modernized until F3.

354. *Bury . . . here*] Q1 has no punctuation after *can*. Probably a tele-
scoped way of saying at once 'bury
him where you can' and 'wherever you
bury him he comes not here.' Cf. *Rom.*,
III. v. 190: 'Graze where you will, you
shall not house with me.'

358. Mart.] Bolton's correction
assumes that 'two sonnes' is an error

for '2. [i.e. second] sonne'. As he points
out, Titus' reply suggests that this line
belongs to only one speaker. The
assignment of names to the second
and third sons must be conjectural,
but Bolton compares II. iii. 251,
257, where Martius shows somewhat
more spirit than does his companion,
as the second son does in the present passage. Bolton's discussion is in
Modern Language Notes, 45 (1930),
140–1.

shall] For the peremptory implications, cf. *Cor.*, III. i. 87 ff. (G. K.
Hunter).

360. *vouch it*] Rowe's *vouch't* no doubt
represents the way the line was pronounced. 'Vouch' = maintain.

Tit. Marcus, even thou hast stroke upon my crest,
　　And with these boys mine honour thou hast
　　　　wounded:　　　　　　　　　　　　　　　365
　　My foes I do repute you every one;
　　So trouble me no more, but get you gone.
Quint. He is not with himself; let us withdraw.
Mart. Not I, till Mutius' bones be buried.

　　　　　　　　[*The brother and the sons kneel.*

Marc. Brother, for in that name doth nature plead,—　370
Mart. Father, and in that name doth nature speak,—
Tit. Speak thou no more, if all the rest will speed.
Marc. Renowmed Titus, more than half my soul,—
Luc. Dear father, soul and substance of us all,—
Marc. Suffer thy brother Marcus to inter　　　　　375
　　His noble nephew here in virtue's nest,
　　That died in honour and Lavinia's cause.
　　Thou art a Roman; be not barbarous:
　　The Greeks upon advice did bury Ajax
　　That slew himself; and wise Laertes' son　　　380

---

368. *Quint.*] *Capell; 3. Sonne. Qq; 1 Sonne. F; Luc. Rowe; Mart. Malone.*　with]
not in F.　　369, 371. *Mart.*] *Capell; 2. Sonne. Qq,F; Quint. Rowe.*　　373. Re-
nowmed] Renowned *Q3,F.*　　379. Ajax] *Ayax Q1.*　　380. wise] *not in F.*

---

364. *stroke*] This variant of the past
participle (properly a past indicative
form) should not be modernized to
'struck'. It occurs again at II. i. 93.

368. *not with*] beside.

372. *if . . . speed*] Perhaps 'if everything else is to go well', but the future
tense is awkward and the whole expression vague. Wilson's 'if the rest of
you wish to live' is unconvincing.

373. *Renowmed*] A normal Elizabethan spelling.

377. *in . . . cause*] See on l. 41.

379. *advice*] deliberation, as in
modern 'advisedly'.

380–1. *wise . . . funerals*] 'Laertes'
son' is Ulysses, who persuaded Aga-
memnon to give honourable burial to
Ajax when he had killed himself in
recovering from a fit of insanity in
which he had slaughtered sheep
which he mistook for the Greek
generals. He was angry with the latter

because the arms of Achilles had been
assigned to Ulysses instead of to him.
The ultimate source of the story is the
Ajax of Sophocles, and it has been
thought that it was not accessible elsewhere. But all that is required for this
reference could be got from Lambinus'
note on Horace, *Sat.*, II. iii. 187, which
reads: 'Vlysses clamore, & iurgio ex-
audito adueniens mitigatus iam, ac
placatus in Aiacem mortuum, Aga-
memnonem quoque flexit, atque
exorauit, vt Aiacem sineret sepeliri.'
For the wide currency of Lambinus'
commentary in sixteenth-century English grammar schools, see Baldwin, I.
422, II. 524: it is true that Baldwin
thinks the *Satires* were less familiar to
Shakespeare than the rest of Horace.
Except for Euripides, the Greek tra-
gedians were not very widely read in
Shakespeare's time even by tolerable
Greek scholars, and it is preferable to

Did graciously plead for his funerals.
Let not young Mutius then, that was thy joy,
Be barr'd his entrance here.

Tit.   Rise, Marcus, rise;
The dismall'st day is this that e'er I saw,
To be dishonoured by my sons in Rome!   385
Well, bury him, and bury me the next.

                                [They put him in the tomb.

Luc. There lie thy bones, sweet Mutius, with thy friends,
Till we with trophies do adorn thy tomb.

All. [*Kneeling.*] No man shed tears for noble Mutius;
He lives in fame that died in virtue's cause.   390

Marc. My lord, to step out of these dreary dumps,
How comes it that the subtle Queen of Goths
Is of a sudden thus advanc'd in Rome?

Tit. I know not, Marcus, but I know it is:
Whether by device or no, the heavens can tell.   395
Is she not then beholding to the man
That brought her for this high good turn so far?
Yes, and will nobly him remunerate.

---

389. *All.* [*Kneeling.*]] *they all kneele and say, Qq,F (centred).*   390.] *Exit all but Marcus and Titus. Qq; Exit. F; not in Rowe.*   391. dreary] dririe (dreary *Pope*) *Qq;* sudden *F.*   398.] *not in Qq; Malone (conj.) attr. to Marcus.*

avoid assuming that the author of this scene knew Sophocles, even if that author should be Peele rather than Shakespeare. The most ardent champion of the view that Shakespeare had a good first-hand knowledge of Greek tragedy was J. Churton Collins, *Studies in Shakespeare* (1904), but his evidence has carried conviction to few. 'Graciously' probably means 'acceptably' rather than kindly: for 'gracious' = 'acceptable', cf. ll. 170, 429. 'Funerals' is plural also in *Caes.*, v. iii. 105.

388. *trophies*] memorials. Not, On. notes, used by Shakespeare in the definite sense of 'spoil taken from the enemy'. Cf. *Ham.*, IV. v. 214: 'No trophy, sword, or hatchment o'er his bones'.

390.] For the deletion of the exit given in Qq,F, see ll. 474–6, which

belong to one of the sons. It is curious that the misattribution there should agree with a mistaken exit here.

391. *dumps*] melancholy, a common cliché in the third quarter of the sixteenth century, especially in alliterative phrases of this kind.

395. *Whether*] Presumably monosyllabic: often spelt *where* in Elizabethan texts, e.g. *Caes.*, I. i. 65.

device] scheming.

396. *beholding*] beholden; commoner than the latter in Elizabethan English.

398. *Yes . . . remunerate*] This line is probably genuine (see Introduction, p. xiii): it must have been added at the same time as the 'Flourish' added to the following S.D. It may belong to Marcus, but it is equally possible that Titus answered his own rhetorical question.

Enter the EMPEROR, TAMORA *and her two sons with the
Moor, at one door. Enter at the other door* BASSIANUS *and*
LAVINIA, *with others.*

Sat. So, Bassianus, you have play'd your prize:
    God give you joy, sir, of your gallant bride.   400
Bass. And you of yours, my lord: I say no more,
    Nor wish no less; and so I take my leave.
Sat. Traitor, if Rome have law or we have power,
    Thou and thy faction shall repent this rape.
Bass. Rape call you it, my lord, to seize my own,   405
    My true-betrothed love, and now my wife?
    But let the laws of Rome determine all;
    Meanwhile am I possess'd of that is mine.
Sat. 'Tis good, sir: you are very short with us;
    But, if we live, we'll be as sharp with you.   410
Bass. My lord, what I have done, as best I may,
    Answer I must, and shall do with my life.
    Only thus much I give your grace to know:
    By all the duties that I owe to Rome,
    This noble gentleman, Lord Titus here,   415
    Is in opinion and in honour wrong'd,
    That, in the rescue of Lavinia,
    With his own hand did slay his youngest son,
    In zeal to you, and highly mov'd to wrath
    To be controll'd in that he frankly gave: 420
    Receive him then to favour, Saturnine,
    That hath express'd himself in all his deeds
    A father and a friend to thee and Rome.

---

398. S.D. *Enter*] *Flourish. Enter* F.   399. Bassianus] *Bascianus Q1–2.*   406
true-betrothed] *Theobald;* true betrothed *Qq,F.*   408. am I] I am *Q3,F.*

398. S.D. (app. crit.) Flourish] See
on S.D. before l. 1.

399. *play'd your prize*] won your bout.
According to A. Forbes Sieveking in
Shakespeare's England, II. 390, this was
'the technical term for qualifying for
the patent as a member of the fencing
fraternity'.

400. *gallant*] See on l. 137.

408. *that*] that which (very common
in Elizabethan English, cf. l. 420).

409–10. *short . . . sharp*] Cf. Tilley,
A168, 'All that is sharp is short' (F. P.
Wilson).

416. *opinion*] reputation: cf. *1H4*, v.
iv. 48: 'Thou hast redeem'd thy lost
opinion.'

420. *controll'd*] thwarted.

frankly] generously, unreservedly.

422. *express'd*] shown: cf. *Ham.*, I. iii.
70–1: 'Costly thy habit . . . But not
express'd in fancy'.

Tit. Prince Bassianus, leave to plead my deeds:
　'Tis thou, and those, that have dishonoured me.　425
　Rome and the righteous heavens be my judge
　How I have lov'd and honoured Saturnine.
Tam. My worthy lord, if ever Tamora
　Were gracious in those princely eyes of thine,
　Then hear me speak indifferently for all;　430
　And at my suit, sweet, pardon what is past.
Sat. What, madam, be dishonoured openly,
　And basely put it up without revenge?
Tam. Not so, my lord; the gods of Rome forfend
　I should be author to dishonour you!　435
　But on mine honour dare I undertake
　For good Lord Titus' innocence in all,
　Whose fury not dissembled speaks his griefs:
　Then, at my suit, look graciously on him;
　Lose not so noble a friend on vain suppose,　440
　Nor with sour looks afflict his gentle heart.
　[*Aside to Sat.*] My lord, be rul'd by me, be won at
　　last;
　Dissemble all your griefs and discontents:
　You are but newly planted in your throne;
　Lest then the people, and patricians too,　445
　Upon a just survey take Titus' part,
　And so supplant you for ingratitude,
　Which Rome reputes to be a heinous sin,
　Yield at entreats, and then let me alone:

---

442. [*Aside to Sat.*]] *Rowe; not in Qq,F.*　447. you] vs *Q3,F.*　448. sin,] *Rowe;*
sinne. *Qq,F.*

428–31. *if ever . . . And*] See on ll.
10–13.
　430. *indifferently*] impartially.
　433. *put it up*] submit to it (metaphor
from sheathing a weapon).
　434. *forfend*] forbid.
　435. *be author . . . you*] countenance
any action that would dishonour you.
N.E.D. author 1d. cites Hobbes:
'Author, is he which owneth an action,
or giveth a warrant for it.'
　436. *undertake*] vouch.

438. *Whose . . . griefs*] i.e. the fact
that he is not able to dissemble his rage
proves the genuineness of his grie-
vances.
　440. *suppose*] supposition; for a col-
lection of nouns of this type see Abbott
§451.
　442. *My lord*] A new paragraph in
Qq indicates the aside.
　449. *at entreats*] to entreaty.
　let me alone] Very common for 'leave
it to me', often, as here, with a sinister

I'll find a day to massacre them all,   450
And race their faction and their family,
The cruel father, and his traitorous sons,
To whom I sued for my dear son's life;
And make them know what 'tis to let a queen
Kneel in the streets and beg for grace in vain.   455
[*Aloud.*] Come, come, sweet emperor; come, Andronicus;
Take up this good old man, and cheer the heart
That dies in tempest of thy angry frown.

Sat. Rise, Titus, rise; my empress hath prevail'd.

Tit. I thank your majesty, and her, my lord.   460
These words, these looks, infuse new life in me.

Tam. Titus, I am incorporate in Rome,
A Roman now adopted happily,
And must advise the emperor for his good.
This day all quarrels die, Andronicus;   465
And let it be mine honour, good my lord,
That I have reconcil'd your friends and you.

---

456. [*Aloud.*]] *Hanmer; not in Qq,F.*   459. *Sat.*] *King. Q3,F (so ll. 478, 482).*
467. reconcil'd] reconciled *Q1-2.*

implication. In this sense already in Chaucer, *Troilus*, II. 1401, III. 413 (where see Robinson's note).

451. *race*] I retain the Qq,F spelling since here and elsewhere the sense seems to be 'root out'. There is no etymological connection with *race* = root (Latin *radix*) or *enrace* = implant (used by Spenser), but there is semantic influence. *N.E.D.* gives two verbs, *race*[3] as variant of *rase* and *race*[4] as aphetic form of *arace*, but the dividing-line is clearly hard to draw, as it admits in a note on *race*[3], 3b.

457. *Take up*] Surely (cf. *R3*, I. ii. 184-5: 'Take up the sword again, or take up me. / *Anne.* Arise, dissembler') 'raise to his feet', i.e. 'bid him rise', as Saturninus proceeds to do, rather than (Wilson) 'make friends with': where 'take up' = 'reconcile', as in IV. iii. 91, the object is the quarrel, not the enemy. The kneeling and rising in this scene are somewhat complicated, as

Professor Ellis-Fermor points out to me. There are never any S.D.s to say when the characters rise, and here there is none for Titus' kneeling either. He and Marcus must have risen at l. 391. I suppose he kneels again as soon as the Emperor enters. It would seem dramatically more effective for him to be in the same posture right from l. 415, when he is first mentioned, up to l. 459.

462. *incorporate*] On Latinate past participles of this kind, often adopted into English in this form earlier than as ordinary verbs, see H. Bradley in *Shakespeare's England*, II. 561-3, and Abbott §342. They seemed natural because of the existence of many common native English verbs in which the past participle had come to be identical with the stem, e.g. *cast, cut, hit, put.*

465. *die*] i.e. let them die, cf. *lie* in l. 387.

For you, Prince Bassianus, I have pass'd
My word and promise to the emperor
That you will be more mild and tractable.   470
And fear not, lords, and you, Lavinia;
By my advice, all humbled on your knees,
You shall ask pardon of his majesty.

Luc. We do, and vow to heaven and to his highness,
That what we did was mildly as we might,   475
Tend'ring our sister's honour and our own.

Marc. That on mine honour here do I protest.

Sat. Away, and talk not; trouble us no more.

Tam. Nay, nay, sweet emperor, we must all be friends:
The tribune and his nephews kneel for grace;   480
I will not be denied: sweet heart, look back.

Sat. Marcus, for thy sake, and thy brother's here,
And at my lovely Tamora's entreats,
I do remit these young men's heinous faults:
Stand up.   485
Lavinia, though you left me like a churl,
I found a friend, and sure as death I swore
I would not part a bachelor from the priest.
Come, if the emperor's court can feast two brides,
You are my guest, Lavinia, and your friends.   490
This day shall be a love-day, Tamora.

Tit. To-morrow, and it please your majesty
To hunt the panther and the hart with me,

---

474. *Luc.*] *Rowe; Q1 continues to Tamora; Q2 indents but without new prefix; All. Q3;
Son. F.*   477. do I] I doe *Q2-3,F.*   485-6. Stand . . . churl] *divided by Capell;
one line Qq,F; Pope makes* 'Stand up' S.D.   487. swore] sware *F.*

475-6. *mildly . . . Tend'ring*] done as
mildly as we could, consistently with
our concern for. For 'mildly' when an
adjective would be more normal (or,
put another way, for the ellipse of
'done') cf. iv. iv. 76: 'That Lucius'
banishment was wrongfully'.

481. *sweet heart*] Normally spelt as
two words, even when, as here, the
sense is much the same as that of the
modern *sweetheart*. The old spelling is
a better guide to the rhythm here.

485. *Stand up*] Pope's conjecture is
very plausible.

487. *sure as death*] This is the earliest
occurrence of this expression known to
Tilley, D136.

488. *part*] depart.

491. *love-day*] a day appointed to
settle disputes, no doubt (Wilson) with
a quibble on the sense 'a day given up
to love'. The word is exhaustively discussed by Josephine W. Bennett,
Speculum, 32 (1958), 351-70.

With horn and hound we'll give your grace bonjour.
Sat. Be it so, Titus, and gramercy too.   495
                    [*Sound trumpets. Exeunt all but Aaron.*

495. *Sound . . . Aaron*] *Exeunt.* | *sound trumpets, manet* Moore. *Qq; Exeunt F.*

494. *bonjour*] good-day (Fr.).
495. *gramercy*] thanks (Fr. *grand merci*).
S.D. Sound . . . Aaron.] The Q

S.D. shows that II. i is continuous in action with Act I. F's 'Flourish', after 'Actus Secunda' [*sic*] is clearly misplaced from the end of Act I.

ACT II

SCENE I

Aaron alone.

Aar. Now climbeth Tamora Olympus' top,
    Safe out of fortune's shot, and sits aloft,
    Secure of thunder's crack or lightning flash,
    Advanc'd above pale envy's threat'ning reach.
    As when the golden sun salutes the morn,   5
    And, having gilt the ocean with his beams,
    Gallops the zodiac in his glistering coach,
    And overlooks the highest-peering hills;
    So Tamora.
    Upon her wit doth earthly honour wait,   10
    And virtue stoops and trembles at her frown.
    Then, Aaron, arm thy heart, and fit thy thoughts,
    To mount aloft with thy imperial mistress,
    And mount her pitch whom thou in triumph long

ACT II

Scene 1

Act II Scene i] *Rowe; Actus Secunda. Flourish. F.*   Aaron *alone.*] *Enter Aaron alone. F; not in Qq.*   4. above] about *F.*   reach.] reach, *Qq;* reach: *F.* 8. highest-peering] *Theobald;* highest piering *Qq,F.*   hills;] hills. *Qq;* hills: *F.* 9.] *Centred in Qq.*   13. mount] soar *W. S. Walker.*

3. *of*] from.

4. *reach.*] I have with some hesitation adopted the usual modern punctuation, based on F. Qq make ll. 5–8 subordinate to ll. 1–4. This can scarcely be right, as *As* in l. 5 must surely be answered by *So* in l. 9, but it is possible that ll. 5–8 look backwards as well as forwards. Similarly, though I have retained the full-stop in l. 9 after *Tamora,* I think that line (separated in Qq from what precedes as well as from what follows by full-stops) may look

forward as well as backward, and should perhaps be followed by a colon, which Camb. prints.

7. *Gallops*] gallops through. Cf. Peele, *Anglorum Feriae,* l. 24: 'Gallops the zodiac in his fiery wain' (Verity).

8. *overlooks*] looks down upon from above.

14. *mount her pitch*] rise to the highest point of her flight (a technical term of falconry). Note that in l. 11 *stoop,* though not so used there, is a word technically used in falconry: a falcon

Hast prisoner held, fett'red in amorous chains,   15
And faster bound to Aaron's charming eyes
Than is Prometheus tied to Caucasus.
Away with slavish weeds and servile thoughts!
I will be bright, and shine in pearl and gold,
To wait upon this new-made empress.   20
To wait, said I? to wanton with this queen,
This goddess, this Semiramis, this nymph,
This siren that will charm Rome's Saturnine,
And see his shipwrack and his commonweal's.
Holla! what storm is this?   25

Enter CHIRON *and* DEMETRIUS, *braving.*

Dem. Chiron, thy years wants wit, thy wits wants edge,
And manners, to intrude where I am grac'd,
And may, for aught thou knowest, affected be.
Chi. Demetrius, thou dost overween in all,
And so in this, to bear me down with braves.   30

---

18. servile] idle *Q3,F.*   20. empress] Emperesse *Qq.*   22. nymph] Queene
Q3,F.   26. years wants] years want *F2.*   wits] wit *Q2–3,F.*   wants] want
Wilson.   28. knowest] know'st *F.*

'stoops' to strike its prey when it is at
its 'pitch'. Such an associative link
would be characteristic of Shakespeare.

16. *charming*] casting a spell. The
modern enfeebled sense makes the line
sound rather absurd.

17. *Prometheus*] The resemblance of
ll. 16–17 to two separate lines in Peele's
Edward I is noteworthy: 'To tie Prometheus' limbs to Caucasus' (iv. 21)
and 'Fast to those looks are all my
fancies tied' (x. 201). It is certainly
easiest to believe that 'Peele, writing
the two plays about the same time,
used up his own rhetoric twice over'
(J. M. Robertson, *Introduction to the
Study of the Shakespeare Canon*, p. 178;
cited by Baldwin (1959), p. 413).

19. *I . . . gold*] Adapted by Clown in
Heywood and Rowley, *Fortune by Land
and Sea* (c. 1607), III. iv (Sh. Soc. ed.,
1845, p. 47): 'he might go brave and
shine in pearl and gold'; Heywood has

a less close echo in *Fair Maid of the West*
(a. 1631), Pt II, Act IV (Sh. Soc. ed.,
1850, p. 148): 'That all our Court may
shine in gold and pearl'.

22. *Semiramis*] a beautiful, ambitious, and lustful (mythical) Assyrian
queen, wife of Ninus.

25. S.D. *braving*] swaggering de-
fiantly.

26. *wants*] It is never easy to decide
when to retain the inflection '-s' with a
plural subject. Its occurrence twice in
the one line makes it rash to alter it
here: moreover it seems appropriate in
a jingling phrase with a semi-proverbial ring (cf. 'as sure as eggs is eggs').
In general, see Abbott §§333–7, Franz
§§155, 673, 679.

27. *grac'd*] received with favour.

28. *affected*] loved: this meaning has
survived in the noun 'affection'.

29. *overween*] be presumptuous.

30. *braves*] blustering threats: cf. the
verb in l. 25 S.D.

'Tis not the difference of a year or two
Makes me less gracious or thee more fortunate:
I am as able and as fit as thou
To serve, and to deserve my mistress' grace;
And that my sword upon thee shall approve,   35
And plead my passions for Lavinia's love.

Aar. Clubs, clubs! these lovers will not keep the peace.

Dem. Why, boy, although our mother, unadvis'd,
Gave you a dancing-rapier by your side,
Are you so desperate grown to threat your friends?   40
Go to; have your lath glued within your sheath
Till you know better how to handle it.

Chi. Meanwhile, sir, with the little skill I have,
Full well shalt thou perceive how much I dare.

Dem. Ay, boy, grow ye so brave?   [*They draw.*

Aar.   Why, how now, lords!   45
So near the emperor's palace dare ye draw,
And maintain such a quarrel openly?
Full well I wot the ground of all this grudge:
I would not for a million of gold
The cause were known to them it most concerns;   50
Nor would your noble mother for much more
Be so dishonoured in the court of Rome.
For shame, put up.

Dem.   Not I, till I have sheath'd
My rapier in his bosom, and withal

---

32. o*r*] *om.* Hanmer.   37. *Aar.*] *Moore. Qq* (*so ll. 45, 60, 75, 90, 95, 97*).   46. ye] you *Q2–3,F.*

---

32. *gracious*] See on I. i. 11. The word is here trisyllabic, and the line an Alexandrine. Hanmer's emendation is unnecessary.

35. *approve*] prove.

36. *passions*] ardent desires.

37. *Clubs, clubs*] The cry raised at a London brawl for the watch to come and separate the combatants with clubs, cf. *1H6*, I. iii. 85: 'I'll call for clubs if you will not away.' The cry was in particularly frequent use for calling out the London prenti..s: so Dekker, *Shoemaker's Holiday*, v. ii (Mermaid edition, p. 71): 'Cry clubs for

prentices!' In such passages the purpose of the clubs does not seem to be so much to restore the peace as to take sides with one of the contesting parties.

38. *unadvis'd*] unwisely.

39. *dancing-rapier*] 'sword worn only for ornament in dancing' (On.).

41. *lath*] 'property sword' (Ridley), perhaps with special reference to the sword carried by the Vice in the Morality plays (Witherspoon), cf. *Tw.N.*, IV. ii. 138 ff.: 'Like to the old Vice, / Your need to sustain; / Who with dagger of lath, / In his rage and his wrath, / Cries, Ah, ah! to the devil'.

Thrust those reproachful speeches down his throat   55
That he hath breath'd in my dishonour here.

Chi. For that I am prepar'd and full resolv'd,
Foul-spoken coward, that thund'rest with thy tongue,
And with thy weapon nothing dar'st perform!

Aar. Away, I say!   60
Now, by the gods that warlike Goths adore,
This petty brabble will undo us all.
Why, lords, and think you not how dangerous
It is to jet upon a prince's right?
What, is Lavinia then become so loose,   65
Or Bassianus so degenerate,
That for her love such quarrels may be broach'd
Without controlment, justice, or revenge?
Young lords, beware, and should the empress know
This discord's ground, the music would not please.   70

Chi. I care not, I, knew she and all the world:
I love Lavinia more than all the world.

Dem. Youngling, learn thou to make some meaner choice:
Lavinia is thine elder brother's hope.

---

55. those] these *Q3,F.*   62. petty] pretty *F.*   64. jet] set *F.*   66. Bassianus]
Bascianus Q1–2.   70. discord's] discord *F.*

61. *Now ... adore*] Add to Wilson's
quotations for Shakespeare's use of
now 'as introductory flourish to a mild
oath' (p. xxiv) the even closer parallel,
Lucr., 1835: 'Now, by the Capitol that
we adore'.
62. *brabble*] quarrel.
64. *jet*] encroach.
68. *controlment*] check.
69. *and ... know*] H. T. Price, *Papers
of the Michigan Academy*, 21 (1935), 505,
argues that the usual interpretation of
and = 'if' is impossible, since the word-
order *should ... know* already expresses the condition. I think he is right.
For the 'emphatic *and*' he compares
l. 63 of this speech, to which add l.
99.
70. *ground*] reason, with a play on the
musical sense, 'bass on which a descant
is "raised"' (On.).
71. *care ... knew*] I do not care if she

knew—a natural mixture of tenses.
I, ... world:] Qq,F have commas
after 'I' and 'world', leaving the
attachment of 'knew ... world' uncertain. Editors have generally, and I
believe rightly, joined it to what precedes. Certainly Sisson, who removes
the comma after 'world', has no
grounds for his implied claim (*New
Readings*, II. 137) that he is more faithful to the original than 'recent
editors'.
72. *I ... world*] Probably an echo of
Kyd, *Spanish Tragedy*, II. vi. 5–6: 'On
whom I doted more then all the world,
/ Because she lou'd me more then all
the world.'
73. *Youngling*] A contemptuous expression also in *Shr.*, II. i. 331: 'Youngling, thou canst not love so dear as I',
where the retort is: 'Greybeard, thy
love doth freeze' (Delius).

Aar. Why, are ye mad? or know ye not in Rome   75
    How furious and impatient they be,
    And cannot brook competitors in love?
    I tell you, lords, you do but plot your deaths
    By this device.

Chi.   Aaron, a thousand deaths
    Would I propose, to achieve her whom I love.   80

Aar. To achieve her! how?

Dem.   Why makes thou it so strange?
    She is a woman, therefore may be woo'd;
    She is a woman, therefore may be won;
    She is Lavinia, therefore must be lov'd.
    What, man! more water glideth by the mill   85
    Than wots the miller of; and easy it is
    Of a cut loaf to steal a shive, we know:
    Though Bassianus be the emperor's brother,
    Better than he have worn Vulcan's badge.

Aar. [*Aside.*] Ay, and as good as Saturninus may.   90

Dem. Then why should he despair that knows to court it

---

75. Why,] *Theobald;* Why *Qq,F.*   Rome] *F3;* Rome, *Qq,F.*   79–80. Aaron
... love] *divided by Hanmer; Qq,F give two lines, divided after* propose.   80. love]
do loue *Q3,F.*   81. her! how?] her how? *Qq;* her, how? *F.*   makes] mak'st *F.*
90. [*Aside.*]] *Theobald; not in Qq,F.*   Saturninus] *Saturnine Q3; Saturnius F.*

---

75. *in Rome*] With *be* in l. 76.

80. *propose*] 'be ready to meet'
(Schmidt, On.) rather than 'propose
to carry out' (Wilson).

81. *To ... how?*] Takes up the previous speaker's word, as in I. i. 285.
This being so, I retain the usual editorial punctuation (Alexander has
her—) rather than return to Qq with
Wilson. Qq spell *atchiue*, which could
be cited in support of *griude* against my
emendation in II. iii. 260.

81. *makes ... strange*] *makes* is phon-
etically easier than *mak'st*, especially as
the next word begins with *th*. See
Franz §152. The whole phrase means
'seem to be surprised or shocked'
(On.). Cf. Lyly, *Euphues* (ed. R. W.
Bond, I. 231): 'loue hath as well
inueigled me as others, which make it
as straunge as I'.

82–3. *She ... won*] See *O.D.E.P.*,

p. 723, where the earliest quotation
is from Greene's *Perimedes* (1588):
'Melissa was a woman, and therefore to be woone.' Tilley, W681,
quotes 'there is no woeman but shee
will yeelde in time' from Lyly's
Euphues (1578). Cf. also *1H6*, v. iii.
78–9.

85–6. *more ... of*] See *O.D.E.P.*,
p. 694, and Tilley, W99, where the
earliest quotation is from Heywood's
Dialogue (1546).

86–7. *easy ... shive*] This is the
earliest quotation in *O.D.E.P.*, p. 582,
and in Tilley, T34. *Shive* = slice.

89. *worn ... badge*] been cuckolded
(as Vulcan by Venus). *Worn* is disyllabic, cf. on I. i. 127.

91. *court it*] play the suitor. For this
use of *it* cf. Abbott §226, Franz §295,
who compares modern colloquial
phrases like 'do it in style'.

With words, fair looks, and liberality?
What, hast not thou full often stroke a doe,
And borne her cleanly by the keeper's nose?

Aar. Why, then, it seems some certain snatch or so   95
　　Would serve your turns.

Chi.　　　　　　　　　Ay, so the turn were served.

Dem. Aaron, thou hast hit it.

Aar.　　　　　　　　　Would you had hit it too!
Then should not we be tir'd with this ado.
Why, hark ye, hark ye, and are you such fools
To square for this? would it offend you then   100
That both should speed?

Chi. Faith, not me.

Dem.　　　　　　　Nor me, so I were one.

Aar. For shame, be friends, and join for that you jar:
'Tis policy and stratagem must do
That you affect; and so must you resolve,   105
That what you cannot, as you would, achieve,

---

93. What,] *Pope;* What *Qq,F.*　　stroke] strooke *Q2;* strucke *Q3,F.*　　101.] *not in F.*

---

93. *stroke*] Cf. i. i. 364.

95. *snatch*] swift catch. Wilson compares *N.E.D.* 6b for the specifically sexual sense, subordinate to the meaning 'hasty meal, snack'. A. Forbes Sieveking, *Shakespeare's England,* ii. 369, sees in it a coursing metaphor, comparing *H5,* i. ii. 143: 'the coursing snatchers', and referring to 'the sudden snatch of the greyhound as he comes up with the quarry'. Tilley, S587, quotes 'a snatche and to go' as a proverbial phrase from Bale's *Three Laws* (1547), and from Heywood's *If You Know Not Me,* Part ii (1605): 'cannot a snatch and away serve your turn' (*Sh. Soc.* ed., 1851, p. 129), which, unless it echoes our passage, suggests that the whole phrase is proverbial.

96. *serve . . . turns*] 'serve the turn' (cf. *Ant.,* ii. v. 59: 'the best turn i' the bed') and 'hit' are both common in bawdy word-play.

100. *square*] quarrel.

102. *so*] provided that (as in l. 96); very common from early times, and still occasionally used. *So that* and (rarer) *so as* are also found.

103. *for . . . jar*] for what you quarrel for. A common type of ellipsis, cf. *3H6,* ii. v. 39: 'Pass'd over to the end they were created'. For the jingle, *join . . . jar,* A. Koszul, *Etudes Anglaises,* 7 (1954), 325, refers to *N.E.D. jar* 13, Sylvester, 'We build and balter, ioyne and iarre.'

104. *policy*] With the usual Elizabethan sense of 'Machiavellian' unscrupulousness.

105. *That*] See on i. i. 408.

affect] aim at.

106-7. *That . . . may*] See *O.D.E.P.,* p. 148, where the earliest quotation is from Heywood (1546). The ultimate source is Terence, *Andria,* iv. vi. 10: 'ut quimus, aiunt, quando ut volumus non licet,' whose form shows it was already proverbial. Tilley cites this passage under M554, but the Hey-

You must perforce accomplish as you may.
Take this of me: Lucrece was not more chaste
Than this Lavinia, Bassianus' love.
A speedier course than ling'ring languishment   110
Must we pursue, and I have found the path.
My lords, a solemn hunting is in hand;
There will the lovely Roman ladies troop:
The forest walks are wide and spacious,
And many unfrequented plots there are   115
Fitted by kind for rape and villainy:
Single you thither then this dainty doe,
And strike her home by force, if not by words:
This way, or not at all, stand you in hope.
Come, come, our empress, with her sacred wit   120
To villainy and vengeance consecrate,
Will we acquaint withal what we intend;
And she shall file our engines with advice,
That will not suffer you to square yourselves,

110. than] *Rowe;* this *Qq,F.*   122. withal] withall *Q1;* with all *Q2–3,F.*
what] that *Q2–3,F.*

wood one under M769. For the earlier history of the saying in Greek, see Plato, *Hippias Major* 301c, with note in D. Tarrant's edition (1928).

108. *Lucrece*] Killed herself after being raped by Tarquin. The story, which has obvious analogies with this play, is told at length by Shakespeare in *The Rape of Lucrece.*

110. *than*] This emendation is probably correct, *this* having crept in from the previous line. *Lingering languishment* then means 'a long sentimental courtship' (Baildon). But Steevens's interpretation of the original text is perhaps just possible: 'we must pursue by a speedier course *this coy laughing dame, this piece of reluctant softness.*'

112. *solemn*] ceremonial; cf. (Wilson) *Mac.,* III. i. 14: 'a solemn supper'. The phrase *a solemn hunting* occurs also in Chapman, *The Gentleman Usher* (*Comedies*, ed. Parrott), III. ii. 297, and in R. Wilson, *The Cobbler's Prophecy* (1594), Malone Soc. Reprint, l. 716.

115. *plots*] spots. The other sense of

plot may have contributed to its use in this context.

116. *kind*] nature: cf. II. iii. 281.

117. *Single*] A hunting term for selecting an animal from the herd in order to hunt it, cf. II. iii. 69.

120. *sacred*] Whether or not this is (Wilson, comparing *Arraignment of Paris,* IV. i. 285) 'a Peele automatism', one may agree that it is something of a cliché here: certainly not (Malone) 'accursed'.

122. *acquaint withal*] inform; cf. *All's W.,* I. iii. 126 (Munro). So Sisson; *with all what,* which I read in 1953, is unobjectionable, but unnecessary.

123. *file our engines*] sharpen our wits.

124. *square yourselves*] quarrel with each other. But the reflexive is not found elsewhere. Wilson suggests as an alternative 'settle matters with each other', which is equally without parallel and gives less appropriate sense. The context seems to demand something like 'thwart yourselves, and each other, by quarrelling'.

But to your wishes' height advance you both.   125
The emperor's court is like the house of Fame,
The palace full of tongues, of eyes and ears:
The woods are ruthless, dreadful, deaf, and dull:
There speak, and strike, brave boys, and take your
        turns;
There serve your lust, shadowed from heaven's eye,   130
And revel in Lavinia's treasury.

Chi. Thy counsel, lad, smells of no cowardice.

Dem. Sit fas aut nefas, till I find the stream
   To cool this heat, a charm to calm these fits,
   Per Stygia, per manes vehor.   [*Exeunt.*   135

---

127. and] of *Q3,F.*   130. lust] lusts *F.*   shadowed] shadow'd *F.*   133.
stream] streames *F.*   134. these] their *Q3,F.*   135. *Stygia*] *Styga F4.*

---

126. *house of Fame*] Perhaps a direct allusion to Chaucer's poem, but J. A. K. Thomson, *Shakespeare and the Classics* (1952), p. 54, suggests Ovid, *Met.*, XII. 39 ff., as more relevant. In any case, *Fame* has the Chaucerian sense of *rumour*, personified also in *Ado*, II. i. 223: 'Lady Fame'.

133. Sit . . . nefas] be it right or wrong.

135. Per . . . vehor] I am borne through the Stygian (i.e. infernal regions, i.e. I am in hell: cf. *3H6*, I. iii. 32–3: 'And till I root out their accursed line, / And leave not one alive, I live in hell.' The words are an adaptation of Seneca, *Phaedra*, 1180: 'per Styga, per amnes igneos amens sequar,' i.e. 'I [Phaedra] as a demented spirit will follow thee [Hippolytus] over Styx and over the fiery rivers.' The context and the detailed meaning are thus quite different from Shakespeare's. Editors have (*a*) read *Styga* with F4; (*b*) interpreted 'I am ready for anything.' Against (*a*) it may be argued that the original text gives perfectly good sense and that the emendation introduces a metrical anomaly (against which Horace, *Ars Poetica*, 257–8, gives a warning; this precept is also to be found in Fabricius, *De Re Poetica* (1560): G. Gregory Smith, *Elizabethan Critical Essays*, quotes the Latin text (I. 419) and Webbe's version of it (I. 294)): a resolved spondee (*Stўgă pēr*) in an even foot of a senarius, where only an iamb is admitted—it was for this 'smal faulte' that, according to Ascham (Gregory Smith, I. 24) 'M. Watson . . . would neuer suffer yet his *Absalon* to go abroad'; against (*b*) that it makes much less apt sense than the interpretation given above.

SCENE II

Enter TITUS ANDRONICUS, *and his three sons, making a noise*
with hounds and horns, and MARCUS.

Tit. The hunt is up, the morn is bright and grey,
    The fields are fragrant and the woods are green.
    Uncouple here and let us make a bay,
    And wake the emperor and his lovely bride,
    And rouse the prince, and ring a hunter's peal,   5
    That all the court may echo with the noise.
    Sons, let it be your charge, as it is ours,
    To attend the emperor's person carefully:
    I have been troubled in my sleep this night,
    But dawning day new comfort hath inspir'd.   10

Here a cry of hounds, and wind horns in a peal, then enter
SATURNINUS, TAMORA, BASSIANUS, LAVINIA, CHIRON,
DEMETRIUS, *and their Attendants.*

    Many good morrows to your majesty;
    Madam, to you as many and as good:
    I promised your grace a hunter's peal.
Sat. And you have rung it lustily, my lords;

Scene II

Scene II] *Rowe; not in Qq,F.*   *and* MARCUS] *not in Qq.*   1. morn] Moone *Q 1–2.*
11. Many] *Qq,F repeat speech-heading.*   14. lords] lord *Dyce.*

S.D. and Marcus] An alternative to
this addition by F would be to read
Martius for *Marcus* at l. 20. But since
Marcus takes part in the hunt (sc. iv),
F is probably right.

    1. *up*] on foot.

    grey] Cf. 'grey-ey'd morn' in *Rom.*,
II. iii. 1. On.'s statement that this, and
the substantival use of *grey* to mean
'the cold sunless light of early morning', are not pre-Shakespearian is misleading. The normal *adjectival* use of
grey in this sense goes back to the four-
teenth century (*N.E.D.* 5; and cf. J. M.
Robertson, *Introduction to the Study of the
Shakespeare Canon*, p. 95). But though
the phrase is not specifically Shakespearian, the 'exact duplication of

rhythm and structure' (Robertson) in
Peele's *Old Wife's Tale*, 350–1: 'The
day is clear, the welkin bright and
grey, / The lark is merry and records
her notes' may be due to imitation of
Titus by Peele, or, indeed, by the
reporter of that sadly mangled text,
which is dated between Jan. 1593 and
May 1594 by T. Larsen, *Modern Philology*, 30 (1932–3), 28.

    3. *bay*] deep prolonged barking.

    5. *hunter's peal*] 'horn-blowing which
set the hounds' tongues into activity,
and produced a pleasing din' (J. W.
Fortescue in *Shakespeare's England*, II.
347).

    10. S.D. cry] deep barking in
unison.

Somewhat too early for new-married ladies.   15
Bass. Lavinia, how say you?
Lav.   I say, no;
    I have been broad awake two hours and more.
Sat. Come on then; horse and chariots let us have,
    And to our sport. Madam, now shall ye see
    Our Roman hunting.
Marc.   I have dogs, my lord,   20
    Will rouse the proudest panther in the chase,
    And climb the highest promontory top.
Tit. And I have horse will follow where the game
    Makes way, and run like swallows o'er the plain.
Dem. Chiron, we hunt not, we, with horse nor hound,   25
    But hope to pluck a dainty doe to ground.   [*Exeunt.*

SCENE III

Enter AARON, *alone.*

Aar. He that had wit would think that I had none,
    To bury so much gold under a tree,
    And never after to inherit it.
    Let him that thinks of me so abjectly
    Know that this gold must coin a stratagem,   5
    Which, cunningly effected, will beget
    A very excellent piece of villainy:

16–17.] *So F;* I . . . more *one line in Qq.*   17. broad] *not in F.*   24. run] *F2;*
runnes *Qq,F.*   like] likes *F.*

Scene III

Scene III] *Capell; not in Qq,F.*

18. *horse*] An archaic plural here and in l. 23: a use to be distinguished from the collective sense (*horse and foot*), cf. Franz §191.

21. *chase*] hunting-ground.

24. *run*] In 1953 I retained *runs*, but it is better to emend; *runs* could have arisen from *makes*.

Scene III

1 ff.] For the burying of gold to incriminate an innocent person, cf. the story of Ulysses and Palamedes, referred to in Ovid, *Met.*, XIII. 60 (G. K. Hunter).

3. *inherit*] enjoy the possession of.

4. *thinks . . . abjectly*] thinks of me as contemptible; cf. N. Field, *Woman is a Weathercock*, II. i. 273–4, 'Ile thinke / As abjectly of thee', and *Tim.*, III. iii. 18, 'think so backwardly of me', with my *New Shakespeare* note.

And so repose, sweet gold, for their unrest
That have their alms out of the empress' chest.

Enter TAMORA *alone to the Moor.*

Tam. My lovely Aaron, wherefore look'st thou sad　　10
　　When everything doth make a gleeful boast?
　　The birds chant melody on every bush,
　　The snake lies rolled in the cheerful sun,
　　The green leaves quiver with the cooling wind,
　　And make a chequer'd shadow on the ground;　　15
　　Under their sweet shade, Aaron, let us sit,
　　And, whilst the babbling echo mocks the hounds,
　　Replying shrilly to the well-tun'd horns,
　　As if a double hunt were heard at once,
　　Let us sit down and mark their yellowing noise;　　20
　　And after conflict, such as was suppos'd
　　The wand'ring prince and Dido once enjoyed,
　　When with a happy storm they were surpris'd,
　　And curtain'd with a counsel-keeping cave,
　　We may, each wreathed in the other's arms,　　25

9. *alone*] *not in* F.　　13. *snake*] snakes *Q1-2*.　　20. *yellowing*] ye¹ping F.
22. *enjoyed*] enioy'd *F*.

8. *repose . . . unrest*] The original
source of expressions of this type (cf.
IV. ii. 31 and *R3*, IV. iv. 29: 'Rest thy
unrest on England's lawful earth')
seems to be Kyd, *Spanish Tragedy*, I.
iii. 5: 'Then rest we heere a while in
our unrest.' Delius on IV. ii. 31 quoted
both the passages in this play. Steevens
had already quoted *Spanish Tragedy*,
III. xiii. 29, 'Thus therefore will I rest
me in unrest.'

9. *That . . . chest*] 'who are to come at
this gold' (Johnson).

11. *boast*] display (Wilson).

12-15.] Herford, Introduction, p.
292, compares this with Seneca,
Phaedra, 508-9, 'hinc aves querulae
fremunt / ornique ventis lene per-
cussae tremunt.'

13. *snake lies*] I do not think *snakes
lies* can be right (but see on II. i. 26).
If the Q3 correction is accepted, the Q1
compositor must be supposed to have

set up *snakes* for *snake* under the
influence of *birds* and *leaves*.

17. *babbling echo*] Echo is 'the babbling gossip of the air' in *Tw.N.*, I. v.
294, and the two passages are linked
by IV. ii. 152 below, where 'babbling
gossip' occurs in another connection.
Wilson quotes Sidney, *Arcadia*, I. x, as
a source for the whole passage, and for
other hunting passages in Shakespeare. The resemblance is not striking. The closest parallel in Shakespeare to the present passage is (as
Parrott, p. 27, noted) *Ven.*, 695-6:
'Thus do they spend their mouths:
Echo replies, / As if another chase were
in the skies.'

20. *yellowing*] 'app. extension of *yell*
on the analogy of *bell, bellow*' (*N.E.D.*).

21-4. *And . . . cave*] On Dido and
Aeneas, see Virgil, *Aen.* IV.

23. *with*] by: Abbott §193, Franz
§535. So in l. 78.

Our pastimes done, possess a golden slumber,
Whiles hounds and horns and sweet melodious birds
Be unto us as is a nurse's song
Of lullaby to bring her babe asleep.

Aar. Madam, though Venus govern your desires,   30
Saturn is dominator over mine:
What signifies my deadly-standing eye,
My silence and my cloudy melancholy,
My fleece of woolly hair that now uncurls
Even as an adder when she doth unroll   35
To do some fatal execution?
No, madam, these are no venereal signs:
Vengeance is in my heart, death in my hand,
Blood and revenge are hammering in my head.
Hark, Tamora, the empress of my soul,   40
Which never hopes more heaven than rests in thee,
This is the day of doom for Bassianus;
His Philomel must lose her tongue to-day,
Thy sons make pillage of her chastity,
And wash their hands in Bassianus' blood.   45
Seest thou this letter? take it up, I pray thee,

---

32. deadly-standing] *Theobald;* deadlie standing *Qq,F.*   34. woolly] wollie *Q1.*

27–9. *Whiles . . . asleep*] Parrott (p. 28) compares *Ven.*, 973–4: 'By this, far off she hears some huntsman hollo;/ A nurse's song ne'er pleas'd her babe so well.'

31. *dominator*] 'a planet or sign supposed [in astrology] to dominate a particular person' (*N.E.D.*). For the influence of Saturn, see *N.E.D.*, *saturnine*, defined as 'sluggish, cold and gloomy in temperament', and D. C. Allen, *The Star-crossed Renaissance* (1941), p. 172. Oppel (p. 24) notes the contrast between Aaron's cold plans for revenge and Tamora's hot love. See also McKerrow's Nashe, IV. 117–18 (G. K. Hunter).

32. *deadly-standing*] fixed in a death-dealing—rather than a deathly (On.) or deathlike (Wilson)—stare. Cf. *2H6*, V. ii. 9, where 'deadly-handed' means murderous. (Wilson quotes this, though it tells against his interpreta-

tion, as does *R3*, I. iii. 225: 'No sleep close up that deadly eye of thine.') The implied comparison is with the basilisk or cockatrice, cf. *R3*, IV. i. 54–5: 'A cockatrice hast thou hatch'd to the world, / Whose unavoided eye is murderous' (quoted by P. Robinson, *Contemporary Review* (1894), 406).

37. *venereal*] connected with love (Venus).

39. *Blood . . . head*] Apparently echoed by Giles Fletcher (the elder) in 'The Rising to the Crowne of Richard the Third', printed in *Licia* (?1593), sig. M3v (p. 158 of Grosart's edition, 1871): 'Blood and revenge did hammer in my head, / Vnquiet thoughts did gallop in my braine.' As the preface *To the Reader* is dated 8 September 1593, Shakespeare could just be the debtor on a very late dating of *Titus*. I owe this reference to Mr E. Honigmann.

And give the king this fatal-plotted scroll.
Now question me no more; we are espied;
Here comes a parcel of our hopeful booty,
Which dreads not yet their lives' destruction.   50

Enter BASSIANUS *and* LAVINIA.

Tam. Ah, my sweet Moor, sweeter to me than life.
Aar. No more, great empress; Bassianus comes:
        Be cross with him; and I'll go fetch thy sons
        To back thy quarrels, whatsoe'er they be.   [*Exit.*
Bass. Who have we here? Rome's royal empress,   55
        Unfurnish'd of her well-beseeming troop?
        Or is it Dian, habited like her,
        Who hath abandoned her holy groves
        To see the general hunting in this forest?
Tam. Saucy controller of my private steps!   60
        Had I the pow'r that some say Dian had,
        Thy temples should be planted presently
        With horns, as was Actæon's; and the hounds
        Should drive upon thy new-transformed limbs,
        Unmannerly intruder as thou art.   65
Lav. Under your patience, gentle empress,
        'Tis thought you have a goodly gift in horning,

47. fatal-plotted] *Theobald;* fatall plotted *Qq,F.*   48. more;] more *Q1;* more,
Q2–3,F.   50. *Enter . . .* LAVINIA.] *after l. 54 Pope.*   52. Bassianus] *Bascianus*
Q1–2 (and in l. 50 S.D.).   54. quarrels] quarrell *Q3,F.*   55. Who] Whom *F.*
56. her] our *Q3,F.*   60. my] our *Q3,F.*   61. pow'r] *Alexander;* powre *Q1;*
power *Q2–3,F.*   64. drive] dine *Collier (2nd ed.).*   thy] his *Q3,F.*

49. *parcel . . . booty*] part of the vic-
tims we expect.
    50. Enter . . . LAVINIA.] Wilson
rightly restores the Qq,F placing of
this entrance, which Pope had post-
poned till after l. 54. He writes that
'Bassianus and Lavinia are clearly
intended to overhear Tamora's en-
dearments.'
    53. *Be cross*] pick a quarrel.
    55. *empress*] See on I. i. 89.
    60. *controller*] 'censorious critic'
(On.).
    62. *presently*] immediately: a fre-
quent Elizabethan use.
    63. *Actæon's*] He was transformed

into a stag and killed by his own
hounds, as a punishment for seeing
Diana and her nymphs bathing. The
point here is, of course, to lead up
to the never-failing joke about the
cuckold's horns in l. 67. The cuckold's
horns are called '*Actæons* ornament' by
Sidney, *Arcadia*, Bk. III (*Works*, ed.
Feuillerat, II. 70), and 'Actaeon's
badge' in *The Batchelars Banquet* (1603),
ed. F. P. Wilson, p. 51.
    64. *drive*] rush.
    66. *empress*] See on I. i. 89.
    67. *gift in*] So always in Shakespeare
(e.g. *MND.*, III. ii. 301) where modern
English would have 'gift for'. *N.E.D.*

And to be doubted that your Moor and you
Are singled forth to try experiments.
Jove shield your husband from his hounds to-day!   70
'Tis pity they should take him for a stag.

Bass. Believe me, queen, your swart Cimmerian
Doth make your honour of his body's hue,
Spotted, detested, and abominable.
Why are you sequest'red from all your train,   75
Dismounted from your snow-white goodly steed,
And wand'red hither to an obscure plot,
Accompanied but with a barbarous Moor,
If foul desire had not conducted you?

Lav. And, being intercepted in your sport,   80
Great reason that my noble lord be rated
For sauciness. I pray you, let us hence,
And let her joy her raven-coloured love;
This valley fits the purpose passing well.

Bass. The king my brother shall have note of this.   85

Lav. Ay, for these slips have made him noted long:
Good king, to be so mightily abused!

Tam. Why, I have patience to endure all this.

69. try experiments] trie thy experimens *Q1*.   72. swart] *Capell;* swartie *Q1–2;*
swarty *Q3;* swarth *F*.   78. but] *not in Q3,F*.   85. note] *Pope;* notice *Qq,F*.
88. Why, I have . . . this.] *Alexander;* Why I haue . . . this. *Qq;* Why I haue . . .
this? *F;* Why haue I . . . this? *F2*.

gives an instance as late as 1710.

69. *singled*] See on II. i. 117.

to try experiments] to experiment. Cf.
to try conclusions in *Ham.*, III. iv. 195. For
the spelling *experimens* (if not a misprint) cf. Wyld, p. 302.

72. *swart*] Closer to the Q spelling
(probably *swarte* misread) than F's
swarth.

Cimmerian] A people thought to live
away from the light of the sun: hence
'Cimmerian darkness'.

75. *sequest'red*] Stressed on the first
syllable, as in *Oth.*, III. iv. 41: 'a
sequester from liberty'.

78. *with*] See on l. 23.

79. *had*] A mixed construction, as if
'why would you have been seques-
tered' had preceded; so *R3*, II. ii. 5–7
(Folio): 'Why do you look on us, and

shake your head, / And call us orphans,
wretches, castaways, / If that our
noble father were alive?'

83. *joy*] enjoy: a parallel, not a
shortened, form.

86. *long*] Johnson noted the incongruity of this when 'he had been mar-
ried but one night'. In its rudimentary
way, this line suggests the 'double
time' which is customarily attributed
to *Othello*.

88. *Why . . . this*] I take it that
Tamora is claiming to be unmoved by
the taunts hurled at her, in order to
deceive Bassianus and Lavinia. This
makes her change of attitude in l. 91
more dramatic. This interpretation
makes it unnecessary to accept the
emendation of F2, as Alexander,
Sisson, and Munro agree.

Enter CHIRON *and* DEMETRIUS.

Dem. How now, dear sovereign, and our gracious mother!
        Why doth your highness look so pale and wan?   90
Tam. Have I not reason, think you, to look pale?
        These two have tic'd me hither to this place:
        A barren detested vale you see it is;
        The trees, though summer, yet forlorn and lean,
        Overcome with moss and baleful mistletoe: 95
        Here never shines the sun: here nothing breeds,
        Unless the nightly owl or fatal raven:
        And when they show'd me this abhorred pit,
        They told me, here, at dead time of the night,
        A thousand fiends, a thousand hissing snakes,   100
        Ten thousand swelling toads, as many urchins,
        Would make such fearful and confused cries,
        As any mortal body hearing it

92. tic'd] ticed *Qq*.   95. Overcome] Orecome *Q2–3,F.*

92. *tic'd*] enticed.

93 ff.] Richard Hurd in his 'Discourse on Poetical Imitation' (*Q. Horatii Flacci Epistolae*, etc., ed. 3 (1757), II. 115) cites this passage as 'an *Anti-tempe*'.

93. *barren*] monosyllabic, cf. *2H6*, II. iv. 3: 'Barren winter, with his wrathful nipping cold'. R. A. Law, *S.P.* 40 (1943), 149, suggests that this whole description is indebted to Virgil, *Aen.*, VII. 561–71. The resemblance does not seem to me very close. In its rather melodramatic horror it has some likeness to Seneca, *Thyestes*, 650 ff., as Kittredge notes (p. 972).

95. *Overcome*] overgrown. The Q1 spelling probably goes back to the MS., and is quite compatible with normal scansion: monosyllabic *never* is common in Shakespeare.

97. *fatal*] ominous, cf. *Mac.*, I. v. 39–40: 'The raven himself is hoarse / That croaks the fatal entrance of Duncan'. The earliest quotation given by Tilley, R33, for the ominous character of the raven is Marlowe, *Jew of Malta*, 640–1 (II. i. 1–2): 'the sad presaging Rauen that tolls / The sicke mans passeport

in her hollow beake'. The equally ominous night-raven, or night-crow, is a different species of bird: see *N.E.D.*

99. *dead . . . night*] The meaning seems to be exactly that of present-day *at dead of night*. I think the basic meaning is 'a time at which nothing is going on', though Shakespeare exploits contextual suggestions here, as in *Ham.*, I. i. 65: 'jump at this dead hour', and *R2*, IV. i. 10: 'In that dead time when Gloucester's death was plotted', where Wilson's note 'fatal (or "gloomy") period' concentrates on the suggestion at the expense of the primary meaning. Professor Ellis-Fermor compares 'dead water' (between two tides), and suggests that the 'dead time' is when time itself seems to stand still.

101. *urchins*] 'hedgehogs' or 'goblins'? Wilson gives the former meaning, but notes 'gen. associated with witchcraft or devils', and compares *Tp.*, I. ii. 326 (which On. glosses *goblin*) and *hedge-pig* in *Mac.*, IV. i. 2. P. Robinson, *Contemporary Review* (1894), 397–9, argues strongly that 'goblin' is the only Shakespearian sense for the word and its compounds.

    Should straight fall mad, or else die suddenly.
    No sooner had they told this hellish tale   105
    But straight they told me they would bind me here
    Unto the body of a dismal yew,
    And leave me to this miserable death.
    And then they called me foul adulteress,
    Lascivious Goth, and all the bitterest terms   110
    That ever ear did hear to such effect;
    And had you not by wondrous fortune come,
    This vengeance on me had they executed.
    Revenge it, as you love your mother's life,
    Or be ye not henceforth call'd my children.   115
Dem. This is a witness that I am thy son.   [*Stab him.*
Chi. And this for me, struck home to show my strength.
Lav. Ay, come, Semiramis, nay, barbarous Tamora,
    For no name fits thy nature but thy own.
Tam. Give me the poniard; you shall know, my boys,   120
    Your mother's hand shall right your mother's wrong.
Dem. Stay, madam, here is more belongs to her:
    First thrash the corn, then after burn the straw.
    This minion stood upon her chastity,
    Upon her nuptial vow, her loyalty,   125
    And with that painted hope braves your mightiness:
    And shall she carry this unto her grave?

---

110. Lascivious] Lauicious *Q1-2*.   115. ye] *not in Capell*.   henceforth] from henceforth *Pope*.   call'd my children] my children call'd *Wilson*.   118. Ay,] *Hanmer;* I, *Theobald;* I *Qq,F*.   120. the] thy *Q3,F*.   126. painted] pall'd *A. Walker conj.*   braves] she braves *F2*.

104. *Should*] would. The modern 'Standard' distinctions had not yet been established in Shakespeare's day, cf. Abbott §322, Franz §612.

  straight] immediately, so in l. 106.

110. *lascivious Goth*] Possibly (though not necessarily), as Herford suggests, with the same pun on *Goth* and *goat* as in *AYL.*, III. iii. 7–9: 'I am here with thee and thy goats as the most capricious poet, honest Ovid, was among the Goths.' Goats are proverbially lustful, cf. *Oth.*, III. iii. 404: 'as prime as goats'.

115. *Or . . . children*] Best read as a headless line with a strong stress on *Or*. If any alteration is required, Capell's is the best (with *children* trisyllabic). Wilson's transposition is arbitrary.

118. *Semiramis*] See on II. i. 22.

124. *minion stood upon*] saucy creature made much of.

126. *painted hope*] Metre and sense awkward. A. Walker's *pall'd* = 'weakened' (*R.E.S.*, n.s. 6, 1955, 81) implies a misreading of 'pauled'; cf. *Ant.*, II. vii. 87, 'Thy paul'd Fortunes'.

Chi. And if she do, I would I were an eunuch.
    Drag hence her husband to some secret hole,
    And make his dead trunk pillow to our lust.   130
Tam. But when ye have the honey we desire,
    Let not this wasp outlive, us both to sting.
Chi. I warrant you, madam, we will make that sure.
    Come, mistress, now perforce we will enjoy
    That nice-preserved honesty of yours.   135
Lav. O Tamora, thou bearest a woman's face,—
Tam. I will not hear her speak; away with her!
Lav. Sweet lords, entreat her hear me but a word.
Dem. Listen, fair madam: let it be your glory
    To see her tears; but be your heart to them   140
    As unrelenting flint to drops of rain.
Lav. When did the tiger's young ones teach the dam?
    O, do not learn her wrath; she taught it thee;

---

131. we] ye *F2*.   132. outlive, us] *Theobald;* out liue us *Q1;* out-liue vs *Q2–3,F;* outlive ye *Dyce (2nd ed.);* o'erlive, us *Maxwell conj.*   135. nice-preserved] nice preserued *Qq.*   136. bearest] bear'st *F.*   woman's] woman *F.*

129–30. *Drag . . . lust*] J. D. Ebbs, *Modern Language Notes,* 66 (1951), 480–1, notes the resemblance of this to Nashe, *Unfortunate Traveller* (in *Works,* ed. McKerrow, II. 226): 'Her husbands dead bodie he made a pillow to his abhomination.' Nashe's novel was completed 27 June 1593, registered 17 September 1593, and printed 1594. Since Chiron and Demetrius do not in fact do what they here propose, it might be argued that these lines are a last-minute addition by Shakespeare to his text.

131. *we*] I retain this, with some hesitation, but encouraged by the example of Alexander, on the hypothesis that Tamora is entering wholeheartedly into her sons' plans, so that the desire is hers as well as theirs.

132. *outlive . . . sting*] A very awkward line. Theobald's punctuation seems to be the only way to make sense of it, but *outlive* intransitively in the sense of survive is unparalleled. *O'erlive* would be easier, and if Shakespeare spelt mono-

syllabic *over* as *our* the corruption would not be difficult (admittedly *ore* is the normal spelling but we have the spelling *moreour* at *Tw.N.,* I. iii. 39). There is one other passage where a similar corruption is not unlikely: at *2H6,* IV. viii. 27, *given out* occurs in the unparalleled sense of 'surrendered' or 'abandoned', and Walker's conjecture *given over* is attractive. In the present passage it is tempting to accept Dyce's *outlive ye* (= survive your attack).

133. *make that sure*] make sure of that, with the special implication of rendering harmless, cf. l. 187. The phrase is used in *1H4,* V. iii. 47–8: 'I have paid Percy, I have made him sure,' leading to a play in the retort on *sure* = *safe.*

138. *entreat . . . hear*] The infinitive without *to* after verbs of asking is commoner in Shakespeare than in modern English, cf. Abbott §§349–50, Franz §650.

143. *learn*] teach: acceptable Elizabethan English, though now a vulgarism.

The milk thou suck'st from her did turn to marble;
Even at thy teat thou hadst thy tyranny.   145
Yet every mother breeds not sons alike:
Do thou entreat her show a woman's pity.
Chi. What, would'st thou have me prove myself a bastard?
Lav. 'Tis true the raven doth not hatch a lark:
Yet have I heard—O, could I find it now!—   150
The lion mov'd with pity did endure
To have his princely paws par'd all away.
Some say that ravens foster forlorn children,
The whilst their own birds famish in their nests:
O, be to me, though thy hard heart say no,   155
Nothing so kind, but something pitiful.
Tam. I know not what it means; away with her!
Lav. O, let me teach thee! for my father's sake,

---

144. suck'st] suck'dst *Rowe (3rd ed.)* (*Ravenscroft*).   147. woman's] woman
Q2–3,F.   151. mov'd] moued *Qq.*   158. thee!] thee: *Theobald;* thee *Qq,F.*

144. *suck'st*] instead of the unpronounceable *suckdst*: so in *1H6*, v. iv. 28,
Cor., III. ii. 129: see on I. i. 317. Tilley,
E198, cites from Elyot's *Governour*
(1531): 'often times the childe souk-
ethe the vice of his nouryse with the
milk of her pappe'; so Lyly, *Euphues,*
ed. Bond, I. 266; and, for more detail
about the belief, Burton, *Anatomy of
Melancholy* 1, 2, 4, 1. Shakespeare
alludes to the notion again in *R3*, II. ii.
30: 'Yet from my dugs he drew not
this deceit'.
    148. *What . . . bastard?*] The logic of
this leaves something to be desired.
Grant White asks: 'how was he to
prove himself a *bastard* by being unlike
his mother?' But the whole line is only a
rhetorical way of asking: 'would you
have me false to my parentage?'
    149. *raven . . . lark*] Verity compares
Horace, *Odes,* IV. iv. 31–2: 'neque im-
bellem feroces / progenerant aquilae
columbam' ('nor do fierce eagles
bring forth an unwarlike dove'). The
earliest English quotation in Tilley,
E2, is from Pettie's *Civile Conversation*
(1581).
    151–2. *The lion . . . away*] The fable

is that of the Lion as Suitor. The Latin
version of Camerarius (1573) and
Bullokar's English (1584) are quoted
by A. Yoder, *Animal Analogy in Shakespeare's Character Portrayal* (1947), pp.
82–3, and Camerarius also in Baldwin, I. 631–2. Camerarius' *ungues
praecidi . . . patitur* might seem to support the emendation *claws* for *paws,*
but the corruption would not be easy,
and Shakespeare is no doubt 'hunting
the letter'. Cf., moreover, Marlowe,
1 Tamb., I. ii. 52–3: 'As princely lions
when they rouse themselves, / Stretching their paws', which Shakespeare
may be echoing.
    152. *paws par'd*] Cf. T. Fuller, *Com-
ment . . . St. Matthew's Gospel* (1652),
p. 28, 'Christ's innocence . . . pared the
Lions paws'. Versions of the proverb
'Leonem ex unguibus aestimare'
vary between *claws* and *paws* (Tilley,
L313).
    154. *birds*] young ones (the original
sense, and still in dialect).
    156. *Nothing . . . pitiful*] not, indeed,
as kind as the raven, but showing some
pity.
    157. *it*] the word 'pity'.

That gave thee life when well he might have slain thee,
Be not obdurate, open thy deaf ears. 160
Tam. Hadst thou in person ne'er offended me,
Even for his sake am I pitiless.
Remember, boys, I pour'd forth tears in vain
To save your brother from the sacrifice,
But fierce Andronicus would not relent: 165
Therefore away with her, and use her as you will:
The worse to her, the better lov'd of me.
Lav. O Tamora, be call'd a gentle queen,
And with thine own hands kill me in this place,
For 'tis not life that I have begg'd so long; 170
Poor I was slain when Bassianus died.
Tam. What begg'st thou then, fond woman? let me go.
Lav. 'Tis present death I beg; and one thing more
That womanhood denies my tongue to tell.
O, keep me from their worse than killing lust, 175
And tumble me into some loathsome pit,
Where never man's eye may behold my body:
Do this, and be a charitable murderer.
Tam. So should I rob my sweet sons of their fee:
No, let them satisfice their lust on thee. 180
Dem. Away! for thou hast stay'd us here too long.
Lav. No grace? no womanhood? Ah, beastly creature,
The blot and enemy to our general name!
Confusion fall—
Chi. Nay, then I'll stop your mouth. Bring thou her husband:

160. ears] yeares *Q1–2.* 171. Bassianus] *Bascianus Q1–2; Bussianus Q3.*
172. then, . . . woman? . . . go.] *Chambers (1907);* then . . . woman . . . goe?
Qq; then? . . . woman . . . go? *F.* 180. satisfice] satisfie *Q2–3,F.* 184. fall—]
Q3,F; fall *Q1;* fall. *Q2.*

160. *ears*] For the phonetic spelling *years* cf. Wyld, p. 308. At *1H4,* I. ii. 148, *Yedward* is a familiar form for *Edward; yer* for *ere* is regular in Holinshed.

172. *What . . . go?*] A better rhythm, I think, than the F punctuation usually adopted.

174. *denies*] does not allow.

179. *So*] if I did that.

180. *satisfice*] Q1 reads either this or *satisfiee.* Even if it is the latter, it is probably only a 'foul case' error for *satisfice,* a well-authenticated sixteenth-century form, influenced by the Latin, and by the analogy of *suffice.*

183. *our general name*] the name of woman, which is common (general) to our sex.

184. *Confusion fall—*] Q1's omission of punctuation after *fall* is a customary way of indicating a broken-off speech, cf. Simpson, p. 98.

This is the hole where Aaron bid us hide him.   186
   [*Exeunt* CHIRON *and* DEMETRIUS *with* LAVINIA.
Tam. Farewell, my sons: see that you make her sure.
  Ne'er let my heart know merry cheer indeed
  Till all the Andronici be made away.
  Now will I hence to seek my lovely Moor,   190
  And let my spleenful sons this trull deflower.   [*Exit.*

   Enter AARON, *with two of Titus' sons.*

Aar. Come on, my lords, the better foot before:
  Straight will I bring you to the loathsome pit
  Where I espied the panther fast asleep.
Quint. My sight is very dull, whate'er it bodes.   195
Mart. And mine, I promise you: were it not for shame,
  Well could I leave our sport to sleep awhile.
Quint. What, art thou fallen? What subtle hole is this,
  Whose mouth is covered with rude-growing briers,
  Upon whose leaves are drops of new-shed blood   200
  As fresh as morning dew distill'd on flowers?
  A very fatal place it seems to me.
  Speak, brother, hast thou hurt thee with the fall?
Mart. O brother, with the dismall'st object hurt
  That ever eye with sight made heart lament.   205
Aar. Now will I fetch the king to find them here,
  That he thereby may have a likely guess
  How these were they that made away his brother. [*Exit.*

186. *Exeunt . . .* LAVINIA.] *not in Qq,F; Exeunt F2.* 191. *Exit.*] *not in Qq.* 198.
What,] *F4*; What *Qq,F.* 199. rude-growing] *Pope;* rude growing *Qq,F.*
201. morning] mornings *Q3,F.* 204. hurt] *not in Q3,F.* 208. *Exit*] *after l.*
207 *in Q1; Exit Aaron F.*

186. *bid*] An unusual but not unparalleled form of the past indicative
(it occurs at i. i. 338 and v. iii. 165 as a
past participle), found as late as Emily
Brontë. See Wyld, p. 351, or *N.E.D.*,
for the blending of two O.E. verbs in
bid, and the borrowing of certain
forms from O.E. Class I.

 187. *make her sure*] See on l. 133.

 189. *made away*] killed, cf. l. 208.

 191. *spleenful*] lustful. The spleen
was considered the seat of the passions
in general, cf. On.

trull] harlot.

 192. *the . . . before*] Tilley, F570,
quotes 'set out the better leg' from
Medwall's *Nature* (c. 1500) and 'set
forth the better foote' from Golding's
Abraham's Sacrifice (1577).

 202. *fatal*] ill-omened. Cf. *Mac.*,
i. v. 40; 'the fatal entrance of Duncan'.

 205. *That . . . lament*] that ever eye
made heart lament to see. On the
ellipse of *of* after *sight* see on II. i. 103.

 208. *made away*] See on l. 189.

Mart. Why dost not comfort me, and help me out
　　　From this unhallow'd and blood-stained hole?　　　210
Quint. I am surprised with an uncouth fear;
　　　A chilling sweat o'er-runs my trembling joints:
　　　My heart suspects more than mine eye can see.
Mart. To prove thou hast a true-divining heart,
　　　Aaron and thou look down into this den,　　　215
　　　And see a fearful sight of blood and death.
Quint. Aaron is gone, and my compassionate heart
　　　Will not permit mine eyes once to behold
　　　The thing whereat it trembles by surmise.
　　　O, tell me who it is; for ne'er till now　　　220
　　　Was I a child to fear I know not what.
Mart. Lord Bassianus lies beray'd in blood,
　　　All on a heap, like to a slaughtered lamb,
　　　In this detested, dark, blood-drinking pit.
Quint. If it be dark, how dost thou know 'tis he?　　　225
Mart. Upon his bloody finger he doth wear
　　　A precious ring, that lightens all this hole,
　　　Which, like a taper in some monument,

---

210. unhallow'd] vnhollow *Qq*.　　214. true-divining] *Theobald;* true diuining *Qq,F*.　　220. who] how *Q3,F*.　　222. beray'd] *Wilson;* bereaud *Q1;* embrewed *Q2–3,F;* bedaub'd *or* bedew'd *Bolton conj.*　　in blood] heere *Q2–3,F*.　　223. to a] to the *F*.　　227. this] the *Q3,F*.

210. *unhallow'd*] Wilson suggests that the MS. had *unhallowd* misread by the Q1 compositor as *unhollowe*. This is no doubt correct for the *d* : *e* corruption, but the *o* may represent a phonetic spelling by Shakespeare, for whom *a* and *o* (partly unrounded) were closer than they are now: cf. Wyld, pp. 240–2. In *Ham.*, III. ii. 11, where F reads *tatters*, Q2 (set up from Shakespeare's MS.) and Q1 (representing what was heard on the stage) both read *totters*.

211. *surprised*] bewildered.
uncouth] uncanny.
219. *by surmise*] when it only imagines it.
222. *beray'd*] Probably, as Wilson suggests, Q1's text represents a misreading of *bereied* as *bereud*. Bolton's conjectures are published in *P.M.L.A.*,

44 (1929), 769. *Bedew'd* (which might have been spelt *bedeaud* in the MS.) is not impossible. If Q2's *embrewed* is a mere conjecture, as it presumably is, it is odd that *in blood* was altered, since *embrewde in blood* would have restored both sense and metre. An early owner of the copy of Q1 has emended to 'heere reav'd of lyfe', perhaps with the help of l. 282.

223. *on a heap*] prostrate, cf. *Tim.*, IV. iii. 101: 'laid proud Athens on a heap'.

227. *ring . . . hole*] An allusion to the belief that carbuncles emitted (Johnson) 'not reflected but native light'. Johnson notes that Boyle, the pioneer of modern chemistry, still believed this. The same property is attributed to the Moonstone of Wilkie Collins's novel, First Period, ch. 9.

Doth shine upon the dead man's earthy cheeks,
And shows the ragged entrails of this pit: 230
So pale did shine the moon on Pyramus
When he by night lay bath'd in maiden blood.
O brother, help me with thy fainting hand,
If fear hath made thee faint, as me it hath,
Out of this fell devouring receptacle,   235
As hateful as Cocytus' misty mouth.
Quint. Reach me thy hand, that I may help thee out,
Or, wanting strength to do thee so much good,
I may be pluck'd into the swallowing womb
Of this deep pit, poor Bassianus' grave.   240
I have no strength to pluck thee to the brink.
Mart. Nor I no strength to climb without thy help.
Quint. Thy hand once more; I will not loose again,
Till thou art here aloft, or I below.

---

229. earthy] earthly *Q3,F*.   230. this] the *F*.   231. Pyramus] Priamus *Q1*.
235. fell devouring] fell-devouring *W. S. Walker*.   236. Cocytus'] *F2* (*Cocitus*);
Ocitus Qq,F.   243. more;] *Theobald;* more, *Qq,F;* more *Pope*.

230. *ragged entrails*] rugged interior.
231. *Pyramus*] See *M.N.D.*, v. i, for the story of Pyramus and Thisbe. The Q2 correction of *Priamus* to *Piramus* shows some knowledge and intelligence. There is always the possibility (on which in general see W. W. Greg, *The Editorial Problem in Shakespeare*, p. 87, n. 4) that the corrections had been made during printing in the copy of Q1 from which Q2 was printed; cf. v. i. 141. I would agree with Greg (see review cited on p. viii above) that the supposition of a lost corrected state of Q1 is probably otiose.
235. *receptacle*] See on I. i. 92.
236. *Cocytus' misty mouth*] Probably (Wilson) Cocytus, properly a river of Hell, is here used generally for Hell, and its mouth is simply the entrance to Hell. Wilson's supposition that this is a 'confused memory' of *Locrine*, IV. v. 44–5: 'Backe will I post to hell mouth *Taenarus*, / And passe *Cocitus*, to the Elysian fields' is more hazardous, but possible. The mouth of Cocytus would more strictly be the point at which it

flows into Acheron. They are the first two rivers to be crossed in the underworld—in which order, authorities are not agreed.
238–9. *Or . . . pluck'd*] or that, if I want strength, I may be plucked. This must be a subordinate clause parallel to 'that . . . out'. It is not clear why Quintus should be so gloomily resigned, but it is even harder to make sense of the usual editorial punctuation (contrary to Qq,F) with a semi-colon after *out*, which presumably means that this is a principal clause.
239. *swallowing womb*] Wilson (on v. ii. 192 with a cross-reference from this line) compares *Rom.*, II. iii. 9: 'The earth that's nature's mother is her tomb', and *R2*, II. i. 82–3: 'a grave, / Whose hollow womb inherits nought but bones'.
244. *aloft*] Qq spell *a loft* (and Q1 *a liue* in l. 257), as often. Here the spelling corresponds to the derivation (*on + loft*) but it often occurs without any such justification, as in *a leauen* (= eleven), *Ham.* (Q2), I. ii. 251.

Thou canst not come to me: I come to thee.   [*Falls in.*

Enter the Emperor and AARON *the Moor.*

Sat. Alone with me: I'll see what hole is here,   246
  And what he is that now is leapt into it.
  Say, who art thou that lately didst descend
  Into this gaping hollow of the earth?
Mart. The unhappy sons of old Andronicus;   250
  Brought hither in a most unlucky hour,
  To find thy brother Bassianus dead.
Sat. My brother dead! I know thou dost but jest:
  He and his lady both are at the lodge
  Upon the north side of this pleasant chase;   255
  'Tis not an hour since I left them there.
Mart. We know not where you left them all alive;
  But, out alas! here have we found him dead.

Enter TAMORA, ANDRONICUS, *and* LUCIUS.

Tam. Where is my lord the king?
Sat. Here, Tamora; though grip'd with killing grief.   260
Tam. Where is thy brother Bassianus?
Sat. Now to the bottom dost thou search my wound:
  Poor Bassianus here lies murthered.
Tam. Then all too late I bring this fatal writ,

245. *Falls in*] *Pope; Boths fall in* F; *not in* Qq. *Emperor and*] *Emperour,* Q3,F.
251. sons] sonne *Q2–3,*F. 256. them] him *Q3,*F. 257. them] him F.
260. *Sat.*] *King.* Qq,F (*and throughout scene*). grip'd] *Maxwell;* griude Q1;
greeu'd (-ie-) *Q2–3,*F; gnaw'd *W. S. Walker.*

255. *chase*] See on II. ii. 21.
  256. *hour*] Disyllabic, see on I. I. 127.
  258. *out*] This interjection, 'expressing abhorrence, reproach, or indig-
nation' (On.) here reinforces *alas*.
  260. *grip'd*] seized, cf. *3H6,* I. iv. 171:
'inly sorrow gripes his soul' and *Rom.,*
IV. v. 129: 'griping grief'. Q1's *griude*
is not an inconceivable spelling for
griev'd (cf. the spelling *griue* in *Per.*
(Q1), I. ii. 100, and the rhyme *grife /
life* in Daye's translation of *Daphnis and
Chloe* (ed. 1890), p. 37), though Shakespeare elsewhere has only *grieu'* or
greeu'd, but 'griev'd with grief' is surely

too careless for him to have written.
I cannot recall an instance of the corruption *p* : *u,* but it would be possible
with the 'stumpy *p*' which occurs a
number of times in the Shakespearian
three pages of *Sir Thomas More:* see
E. M. Thompson, *Shakespeare's Hand-
writing* (Oxford, 1916), p. 49. In *Err.,*
v. i. 121, there is an *a* : *p* error (*death*
misread as *depth*). The spelling *gripde*
postulated for the MS. would be possible, though perhaps less usual than
gripte, as Dr Alice Walker has pointed
out to me.
  262. *search*] probe.

The complot of this timeless tragedy;   265
And wonder greatly that man's face can fold
In pleasing smiles such murderous tyranny.
               [She giveth Saturnine a letter.

Sat. *And if we miss to meet him handsomely,*
    Sweet huntsman, Bassianus 'tis we mean,
    Do thou so much as dig the grave for him: 270
    Thou know'st our meaning; look for thy reward
    Among the nettles at the elder-tree
    Which overshades the mouth of that same pit
    Where we decreed to bury Bassianus:
    Do this, and purchase us thy lasting friends.   275
O Tamora, was ever heard the like?
This is the pit, and this the elder-tree.
Look, sirs, if you can find the huntsman out
That should have murthered Bassianus here.

---

268. *Sat.*] *Saturninus reads the letter.* Qq,F *(centred)*.   271. *meaning;*] *meaning: Pope; meaning Q1; meaning,* Q2–3,F.   *reward*] *reward,* Q1–2; *reward.* Q3.   276. O] *Theobald; King.* O Qq,F.

265. *complot*] This word is found in most of the senses of plot, which is (*N.E.D.*) perhaps an abbreviation of it. Hence it seems to me probable that there is here a pun on the special theatrical sense of *plot* (or *plat*): 'a skeleton outline of the action' hung up at some convenient place, perhaps 'in the centre of the tiring-house' (Chambers, I. 123–4). The 'writ' gives, as it were, the outline of the tragedy. I think this sense may be present in the rather odd pun in Kyd's *Spanish Tragedy* (ed. Boas), IV. ii. 12–13: 'No, not an herb within this garden Plot— / Accursed complot of my miserie': the garden where her son has been hanged is, as it were, an epitome of her misery. I doubt whether Boas's suggestion of 'part-plotter' covers even part of the sense. The dramatic implications of the word are more evident in *Arden of Feversham* (in *Sh. Apocrypha*, ed. Tucker Brooke), v. i. 103–4: 'will you two performe / The complot that I laid?' For an extensive survey of Shakespeare's imagery drawn from the stage, see E. K. Chambers, *Shakespearean Gleanings* (Oxford, 1944), pp. 43–8. Sir Edmund quotes the present passage. Among his other quotations, the nearest parallel is *2H6*, III. i. 152–3: 'For thousands more that yet suspect no peril / Will not conclude their plotted tragedy.'

timeless] untimely.

266. *fold*] conceal (Wilson). But there is also surely, as Dr B. L. Joseph has pointed out to me, a suggestion of the wrinkles of a false smile. An interesting parallel is *Meas.*, v. i. 118–19: 'Unfold the evil which is here wrapp'd up / In countenance', where the primary meaning of *countenance* is 'authority' or 'worldly credit', but where the literal sense of 'face' is present—the set, mask-like, false expression is to be ironed out.

268. handsomely] conveniently.

272. elder-tree] An ill-omened tree: 'Judas was hanged on an elder' (*LLL.*, v. ii. 606–7).

275. purchase] win.

279. *should have*] was to have

Aar. My gracious lord, here is the bag of gold.   280
Sat. Two of thy whelps, fell curs of bloody kind,
    Have here bereft my brother of his life.
    Sirs, drag them from the pit unto the prison:
    There let them bide until we have devis'd
    Some never-heard-of torturing pain for them.   285
Tam. What, are they in this pit? O wondrous thing!
    How easily murder is discovered!
Tit. High emperor, upon my feeble knee
    I beg this boon, with tears not lightly shed,
    That this fell fault of my accursed sons,   290
    Accursed, if the fault be prov'd in them,—
Sat. If it be prov'd! you see it is apparent.
    Who found this letter? Tamora, was it you?
Tam. Andronicus himself did take it up.
Tit. I did, my lord: yet let me be their bail;   295
    For by my fathers' reverent tomb I vow
    They shall be ready at your highness' will
    To answer their suspicion with their lives.

---

285. torturing] *F3;* tortering *Qq,F.*   286. What,] *Rowe (3rd ed.);* What *Qq,F.*
291. fault] *Theobald (Ravenscroft);* faults *Qq,F.*   296. fathers'] *Delius;* fathers
Qq,F; father's *Rowe.*

(according to the 'complot'), and
presumably has.

    281. *kind*] natural disposition.

    285. *torturing*] Qq,F's *tortering* is
phonetic, cf. *2H6,* I. ii. 42: 'ill-
nurter'd', and Wyld, p. 265 and
(examples) p. 277.

    287.] Cf. Tilley, M1315, 'Murder
will out', citing this and other Shakespeare passages.

    easily] Disyllabic; this common pro-
nunciation is often in sixteenth-
century English represented by the
spelling 'easely'.

    291–2. *Accursed . . . apparent*] Cf. *R3,*
III. iv. 72–3: 'Hast. If they have done
this thing my noble lord,— / Glo. If!
thou protector of this damned strumpet.' H. F. Brooks points out this ex-
change goes back to More (in a
passage which is the first quotation in
Tilley, I16, 'If's and and's'). He also
quotes the interruption in Kyd,

Spanish Tragedy, II. i. 76–7, 'If Madame
Bel-imperia be in love— / What,
Villaine, ifs and ands?'

    292. *apparent*] manifest; more usual
in Shakespeare than the modern sense
in which the apparent is contrasted
with the real.

    294.] As Delius noted, this is in con-
flict with the plan outlined at l. 46,
unless Tamora deliberately dropped
the letter again. This is the sort of
anomaly that could survive in foul
papers but would be cleared up in
production.

    296. *reverent*] Used interchangeably
with *reverend,* cf. III. i. 23, v. iii. 137, and
1H6, III. i. 49–50: 'Win. Unreverent
Gloucester! Glo. Thou art reverent /
Touching thy spiritual function, not
thy life,' where the word-play requires
both identity of form and diversity of
meaning.

    298. *their suspicion*] the suspicion

Sat. Thou shalt not bail them: see thou follow me.
    Some bring the murthered body, some the
        murtherers:
    Let them not speak a word; the guilt is plain;   301
    For, by my soul, were there worse end than death,
    That end upon them should be executed.
Tam. Andronicus, I will entreat the king:
    Fear not thy sons, they shall do well enough.   305
Tit. Come, Lucius, come; stay not to talk with them.

                                  [Exeunt.

SCENE IV

Enter the empress' sons, with LAVINIA, *her hands cut off,
and her tongue cut out, and ravish'd.*

Dem. So, now go tell, and if thy tongue can speak,
    Who 'twas that cut thy tongue and ravish'd thee.
Chi. Write down thy mind, bewray thy meaning so,
    And if thy stumps will let thee play the scribe.
Dem. See how with signs and tokens she can scrowl.   5
Chi. Go home, call for sweet water, wash thy hands.
Dem. She hath no tongue to call, nor hands to wash;
    And so let's leave her to her silent walks.
Chi. And 'twere my cause, I should go hang myself.
Dem. If thou hadst hands to help thee knit the cord.   *[Exeunt.*

306. Exeunt.] *not in Qq.*

Scene IV

Scene IV.] *Dyce; not in Qq,F.*   4. thee] thee, *Rowe (Ravenscroft).*   5. scrowl]
scowle *F.*   10. Dem.] *Dmet. Q1.*   Exeunt.] *not in Qq.*

under which they lie. For this 'objective genitive' cf. Franz §322.

305. *Fear not*] do not be afraid for. Cf. *1H4*, IV. i. 24: 'he was much fear'd by his physicians' (Delius).

Scene IV

3. *bewray*] make known.

4. *And if*] if, as in l. 1. To treat *And* as connective, and place a comma after *thee*, is much less satisfactory.

5. *See . . . scrowl*] An ironic anticipation of the final disclosure, which Witherspoon compares with the anticipation by Gloster (*Lr.*, III. vii. 56–7) of the torture he himself undergoes immediately after. *Scrowl* is apparently (On.) 'a form of "scrawl", to gesticulate, with a play on "scroll", to write down.'

6. *sweet*] perfumed.

9. *cause*] case, perhaps with a suggestion of the specific sense of 'disease'.

Enter MARCUS, *from hunting.*

Marc. Who is this? my niece, that flies away so fast!   11
  Cousin, a word; where is your husband?
  If I do dream, would all my wealth would wake me!
  If I do wake, some planet strike me down,
  That I may slumber an eternal sleep!   15
  Speak, gentle niece, what stern ungentle hands
  Hath lopp'd and hew'd and made thy body bare
  Of her two branches, those sweet ornaments,
  Whose circling shadows kings have sought to sleep in,
  And might not gain so great a happiness   20
  As half thy love? Why dost not speak to me?
  Alas, a crimson river of warm blood,
  Like to a bubbling fountain stirr'd with wind,
  Doth rise and fall between thy rosed lips,
  Coming and going with thy honey breath.   25
  But, sure, some Tereus hath deflow'red thee,

10. S.D. *Enter . . . hunting*] *Winde Hornes. Enter . . . hunting, to Lauinia F.*   11]
this? . . . fast!] this, . . . fast, *Q1–2;* this . . . fast? *Q3;* this, . . . fast? *F.*   15. an,
in *Q2–3,F.*   21. half] have *Theobald.*

10. S.D. from hunting] H. T. Price, *J.E.G.P.,* 42 (1943), 61, compares Marcus' entry 'in that mood of hearty cheerfulness which is always produced by a day's hunting in the forest', only to find Lavinia in her sorry plight, with Lear's entry from hunting in *Lr.,* I. iv, to face a comparable disaster.

12. *Cousin*] 'collateral relative more distant than brother or sister' (On.).

14. *some . . . down*] Cf. *Ham.,* I. i. 162: 'The nights are wholesome; then no planets strike.' Shakespeare refers to the astrological influence of adverse planets also in *Oth.,* II. iii. 184, and *Cor.,* II. ii. 118–19 (Tilley, P389).

17. *Hath*] Not uncommon with a plural subject, cf. Abbott §334, Franz §156.

21. *half*] This makes tolerable sense and the conjecture *have* is weak. But *Lr.,* I. i. 104, where the point of *half* is much more obvious, does not support it very strongly.

22–5. *Alas . . . breath*] Parrott, p. 29 compares *Lucr.,* 1734–8: 'And from the purple fountain Brutus drew / The murderous knife, and as it left the place, / Her blood, in poor revenge, / held it in chase; / And bubbling from her breast, it doth divide / In two slow rivers.' Wilson (pp. liii–liv) holds, unconvincingly, it seems to me, that Shakespeare is here caricaturing what he had treated seriously in *Lucr.*

26. *Tereus*] The story of Tereus is constantly in Shakespeare's mind in *Titus.* Tereus raped his wife's sister Philomela, and cut out her tongue and immured her in a tower. She succeeded in depicting her fate in a tapestry (l. 39), which she had conveyed to her sister Progne, who released her, and revenged her by killing Itylus, her own son by Tereus, and serving him to his father at a meal. Philomela then threw the head on the table. The gods thereupon changed Tereus to a hoopoe, Philomela to a

And, lest thou should'st detect him, cut thy tongue.
Ah, now thou turn'st away thy face for shame,
And, notwithstanding all this loss of blood,
As from a conduit with three issuing spouts,   30
Yet do thy cheeks look red as Titan's face
Blushing to be encount'red with a cloud.
Shall I speak for thee? shall I say 'tis so?
O, that I knew thy heart, and knew the beast,
That I might rail at him to ease my mind.   35
Sorrow concealed, like an oven stopp'd,
Doth burn the heart to cinders where it is.
Fair Philomel, why, she but lost her tongue,
And in a tedious sampler sew'd her mind:
But, lovely niece, that mean is cut from thee;   40

27. him] *Rowe (Ravenscroft);* them *Qq,F.*   30. three] *Hanmer;* their *Qq,F.*
33. thee?...so?] thee?...so. *Q1–2;* thee,...so? *Q3.*   38. Philomel] *Camb.;*
Philomela Qq,F.   why] *not in Q3,F.*   39. sew'd] *Pope;* sowed *Qq,F (so*
l. 43).

nightingale, Progne to a swallow, and
Itylus to a pheasant.

27. *him*] The reading *them* may have
been due to the compositor's belief
that *Tereus* was plural (for *hath* with a
plural subject see on l. 17). Plural pro-
nouns after *no, every, any* are found
in sixteenth-century English (Franz
§353), but not after *some* with singular
reference, as in mod. colloquial English, and (after *another*) as early as
Bunyan (*Holy War,* Cambridge English Classics, p. 217).

30. *three*] Hanmer's correction is excellent. The MS. probably had *thre,*
misread as *ther.*

31. *Titan*] See on I. i. 226.

32. *Blushing . . . cloud*] Wilson (and
earlier E. Koeppel, *Englische Studien,*
35 (1905), 124) compares the development of this image in *R2,* III. iii. 63–6:
'As doth the blushing discontented
sun / From out the fiery portal of the
east, / When he perceives the envious
clouds are bent / To dim his glory'.

34. *heart*] Virtually, 'what is in your
mind'. The heart was the seat of
thought, not only of emotion; cf. T.

Starkey, *Dialogue between Pole and Lupset*
(ed. K. M. Burton, 1948), p. 57: 'all
wit, reason and sense, life and all other
natural power springeth out of the
heart.' Rolfe cites *Ado,* III. ii. 13–14:
'what his heart thinks his tongue
speaks.' Failure to realize this led to
the conjecture *hurt* (W. S. Walker).

36–7. *Sorrow . . . is*] Particularly
close (Parrott, p. 29) to *Ven.,* 331–3:
'An oven that is stopp'd, or river
stay'd, / Burneth more hotly, swelleth
with more rage: / So of concealed
sorrow may be said.' Baldwin, II. 435–
6, claims that the *Ven.* lines are the
earlier, on grounds that are not clear to
me. For the general notion cf. *Gorboduc,*
III. i. 101–2: 'The fire not quenched,
but kept in close restraint, / Fedde still
within, breakes forth with double
flame' (quoted Tilley, F265).

37. *where*] in which. This use is in
modern English confined to compounds such as *wherein,* and even they
are felt as stilted if not archaic.

38. *Philomel*] See on l. 26.

39. *tedious*] laboriously executed
(Wilson).

A craftier Tereus, cousin, hast thou met,
And he hath cut those pretty fingers off,
That could have better sew'd than Philomel.
O, had the monster seen those lily hands
Tremble like aspen-leaves upon a lute,　　　　　　45
And make the silken strings delight to kiss them,
He would not then have touch'd them for his life.
Or had he heard the heavenly harmony
Which that sweet tongue hath made,
He would have dropp'd his knife, and fell asleep,　　50
As Cerberus at the Thracian poet's feet.
Come, let us go, and make thy father blind,
For such a sight will blind a father's eye:
One hour's storm will drown the fragrant meads;
What will whole months of tears thy father's eyes?　　55
Do not draw back, for we will mourn with thee:
O, could our mourning ease thy misery!　　　　[*Exeunt.*

41. cousin] *not in Q3,F.*　　met] met withall *F.*

45. *like aspen-leaves*] This comparison
is found as early as Chaucer, *Troilus,*
III. 1200. There is a curious series of
verbal resemblances between these
lines and Spenser, *Amoretti,* I. 1–4:
'Happy ye leaues when as those lilly
hands, / which hold my life in their
dead doing might, / shall handle you
and hold in loues soft bands, / lyke
captiues trembling at the victors
sight.' It is probably a coincidence; if
not, Spenser must presumably have
seen the printed text of *Titus. Amoretti*
was entered on the Stationers' Register
on 19 November 1594, and published
1595, and this introductory sonnet
might be expected to be among the
last written. (Against the view that a
version found in MS. in a copy of the

Faerie Queene, 1590, represents an
earlier draft, see A. C. Judson, *Modern
Language Notes,* 58 (1943), 548–50.)

48–51. *Or . . . feet*] Wilson, following
Parrott, compares *Lucr.,* 552–3: 'So
his unhallowed haste her words delays, / And moody Pluto winks while
Orpheus plays,' and notes that nowhere but in these two passages is the
story of Orpheus linked with a situation in which 'a brutal ravisher is
stayed by the charm of his victim's
voice'.

50. *fell*] For the use of the past indicative form for past participle cf.
Franz §167.

51. *Cerberus*] the three-headed dog
that guarded the entrance to hell.

54. *hour's*] See on I. i. 127.

ACT III

SCENE I

Enter the Judges and Senators, with Titus' two sons, bound, passing on the stage to the place of execution, and TITUS *going before, pleading.*

Tit. Hear me, grave fathers! noble tribunes, stay!
For pity of mine age, whose youth was spent
In dangerous wars, whilst you securely slept;
For all my blood in Rome's great quarrel shed,
For all the frosty nights that I have watch'd,   5
And for these bitter tears, which now you see
Filling the aged wrinkles in my cheeks,
Be pitiful to my condemned sons,
Whose souls is not corrupted as 'tis thought.
For two and twenty sons I never wept,   10
Because they died in honour's lofty bed:
        [*Andronicus lieth down, and the Judges pass by him.*
For these, tribunes, in the dust I write
My heart's deep languor and my soul's sad tears.
Let my tears staunch the earth's dry appetite;
My sons' sweet blood will make it shame and blush.   15
O earth, I will befriend thee more with rain,
That shall distil from these two ancient urns,

ACT III

Scene I

ACT III Scene 1] *Rowe; Actus Tertius. F; not in Qq.*   4. Rome's] Roomes *Q1.*
9. is] are *F2.*   12. these,] these, these *F2;* these, these, *F4.*   13. tears] cares
Hudson.   17. urns] *Hanmer;* ruines *Qq,F.*

2. *mine . . . youth*] See on I. i. 5: the construction is not common in the first and second persons.

  9. *is*] See on II. i. 26.

  10. *two and twenty*] See on I. i. 80.

  12. *For . . . write*] A headless line: but the F2 supplement is plausible.

  14. *staunch*] satisfy.

  15. *shame*] be ashamed; cf. *AYL.,* IV. iii. 137: 'I do not shame / To tell you what I was.'

  17. *urns*] water-jugs. An excellent correction by Hanmer of a minim error—*urnes* corrupted to *ruines.*

Than youthful April shall with all his show'rs:
In summer's drought I'll drop upon thee still;
In winter with warm tears I'll melt the snow,   20
And keep eternal spring-time on thy face,
So thou refuse to drink my dear sons' blood.

Enter LUCIUS, *with his weapon drawn.*

O reverent tribunes! O gentle aged men!
Unbind my sons, reverse the doom of death;
And let me say, that never wept before,   25
My tears are now prevailing orators.

Luc. O noble father, you lament in vain:
The tribunes hear you not, no man is by;
And you recount your sorrows to a stone.

Tit. Ah, Lucius, for thy brothers let me plead: 30
Grave tribunes, once more I entreat of you,—

Luc. My gracious Lord, no tribune hears you speak.

Tit. Why, 'tis no matter, man: if they did hear,
They would not mark me, or if they did mark,
They would not pity me, yet plead I must,   35
And bootless unto them.

22. sons'] *Theobald (2nd ed.);* sonnes *Qq,F;* Son's *F4.*   23. gentle aged men]
gentle-aged men *W. S. Walker;* gentle-aged-men *Boswell.*   28. you] *not in F.*
34. or] *not in Q1;* oh *F.*   did mark] did heare *F.*   35. *not in Q3.*   35–6. yet
. . . them] *not in F.*

19. *still*] all the time. Seldom used by
Shakespeare in the modern sense.

22. *So*] on condition that. The figure
in this line is Biblical as Noble points
out, comparing Hebrews, vi. 7, and
Genesis, iv. 11: 'the earth which hath
opened her mouth to receive thy
brother's blood'.

23. *reverent*] See on II. iii. 296.

33–6.] Cf. Kyd, *Sp. Trag.* I. iii. 23–6.

36. *And . . . them*] Probably a false
start which Shakespeare omitted to de-
lete in his MS. Q3 and F get into curious tangles, of which the only interest
is that F restores part of a line omitted
altogether in Q3, and must therefore
have consulted some other source of
information, presumably the prompt-
copy, which would in all probability

have eliminated the unsatisfactory
'And . . . them'. But why should 'yet
. . . must' not have been in the prompt-
copy? And is it any more than coincidence that F should here introduce
two new errors, 'oh' for 'or' and
'heare' (from the previous line) for
'marke'? It is worth noting that 'or'
(though almost certainly correct) does
not go back to Q1, and 'oh' may be an
alternative prompt-book reading, independent of the later Quartos.
Bolton's suggestion of 'a happy guess
on the part of the Folio editors'
(*P.M.L.A.*, 44 (1929), 770, n. 14) does
not carry conviction, but the whole
passage raises problems which I cannot solve. On this problem see W. W,
Greg, *The Shakespeare First Folio* (1955).

Therefore I tell my sorrows to the stones,
Who, though they cannot answer my distress,
Yet in some sort they are better than the tribunes,
For that they will not intercept my tale.   40
When I do weep, they humbly at my feet
Receive my tears, and seem to weep with me;
And were they but attired in grave weeds,
Rome could afford no tribunes like to these.
A stone is soft as wax, tribunes more hard than stones;
A stone is silent, and offendeth not,   46
And tribunes with their tongues doom men to death.
But wherefore stand'st thou with thy weapon drawn?
Luc. To rescue my two brothers from their death;
For which attempt the judges have pronounc'd   50
My everlasting doom of banishment.
Tit. O happy man! they have befriended thee.
Why, foolish Lucius, dost thou not perceive
That Rome is but a wilderness of tigers?
Tigers must prey, and Rome affords no prey   55
But me and mine: how happy art thou then,

---

37. to] bootles to *Q3,F.*   44. tribunes] Tribune *Q2–3,F.*   45. soft as] as soft *F.*

pp. 206–7. Greg suggests that F got the words not in Q3 from an annotated copy of Q2 used as prompt-book, by which a scribe corrected the copy of Q3 from which F was set up. He assumes, what is less than certain, that F's 'oh' in l. 34 is a misprint for 'or' and not of independent origin. He is unwilling to admit a manuscript prompt-book, which would have made possible the correction of Q2 corruptions (p. 205), but admits that a corrector would not necessarily have accepted the prompt-book readings (p. 209, note E); the same, surely, applies to the variant stage-directions at v. iii. 26, where there would be no strong inducement to reinstate 'the dishes' for Q2's 'The meate on the table', which Greg (p. 209, Note C) calls spurious, but which might have commended itself as more explicit. Even if, as Greg thinks, the company

was using an annotated Q2 as a prompt-book, and this was all that was available for correction of the copy of Q3 used by the printer of F, it would be rash to assume that *no* authoritative corrections were made to that copy of Q2, which must on any showing have been accompanied by the manuscript from which F printed III. ii. See especially I. i. 398, and v. ii. 18 (where, *pace* Greg, I still believe that F has the true text).

40. *intercept*] interrupt; cf. *1H4*, I. iii. 150–1: 'his Irish expedition, / From which he intercepted did return'.

54. *Rome . . . tigers*] Cf. *Tim.*, IV. I. 1–2: 'O thou wall / That girdles in those wolves'. Wilson justly notes that 'Shakespeare thought of a wilderness or desert chiefly as a place where neither law nor mercy held sway', and quotes *Lucr.*, 544: 'a wilderness where no laws'.

From these devourers to be banished!
But who comes with our brother Marcus here?

Enter MARCUS *with* LAVINIA.

Marc. Titus, prepare thy aged eyes to weep;
  Or if not so, thy noble heart to break: 60
  I bring consuming sorrow to thine age.
Tit. Will it consume me? let me see it then.
Marc. This was thy daughter.
Tit.   Why, Marcus, so she is.
Luc. Ay me, this object kills me!
Tit. Faint-hearted boy, arise, and look upon her.   65
  Speak, Lavinia, what accursed hand
  Hath made thee handless in thy father's sight?
  What fool hath added water to the sea,
  Or brought a faggot to bright-burning Troy?
  My grief was at the height before thou cam'st,   70
  And now like Nilus it disdaineth bounds.
  Give me a sword, I'll chop off my hands too;
  For they have fought for Rome, and all in vain;
  And they have nurs'd this woe, in feeding life;
  In bootless prayer have they been held up,   75
  And they have serv'd me to effectless use.
  Now all the service I require of them
  Is that the one will help to cut the other.
  'Tis well, Lavinia, that thou hast no hands,
  For hands to do Rome service is but vain.   80

---

58. *with*] *and Q3,F.*   59. aged] noble *Q3,F.*   69. bright-burning] *F3;* bright
burning *Qq,F.*

64. *Ay*] So spelt in the old editions
where the meaning is, as here, *alas.*
Contrast *ay* = yes, which is invariably
spelt *I.*
  object] 'spectacle. Lit. something
presented to the sight' (Wilson).
  66. *Speak . . . hand*] A headless line.
  68. *What . . . sea*] See *O.D.E.P.*,
p. 695, and Tilley, W106, where the
first quotation in approximately this
form is from Barclay's *Ship of Fools*
(1509).

71. *disdaineth bounds*] Wilson quotes
from C. Spurgeon, *Shakespeare's Imagery*,
pp. 93–4, to the effect that flood
images are much commoner in Shakespeare than in Peele, Greene, Heywood, or Kyd.
  76. *effectless*] fruitless. The whole
phrase is an oxymoron.
  80. *is*] See on II. i. 26. This example
is perhaps easier than some, since the
virtual subject is 'the doing of service
to Rome by hands'.

Luc. Speak, gentle sister, who hath mart'red thee?
Marc. O, that delightful engine of her thoughts,
    That blabb'd them with such pleasing eloquence,
    Is torn from forth that pretty hollow cage,
    Where like a sweet melodious bird it sung   85
    Sweet varied notes, enchanting every ear.
Luc. O, say thou for her, who hath done this deed?
Marc. O, thus I found her straying in the park,
    Seeking to hide herself, as doth the deer
    That hath receiv'd some unrecuring wound.   90
Tit. It was my dear, and he that wounded her
    Hath hurt me more than had he kill'd me dead:
    For now I stand as one upon a rock
    Environ'd with a wilderness of sea,
    Who marks the waxing tide grow wave by wave,   95
    Expecting ever when some envious surge
    Will in his brinish bowels swallow him.
    This way to death my wretched sons are gone;
    Here stands my other son, a banish'd man,
    And here my brother, weeping at my woes: 100
    But that which gives my soul the greatest spurn
    Is dear Lavinia, dearer than my soul.
    Had I but seen thy picture in this plight
    It would have madded me: what shall I do
    Now I behold thy lively body so?   105
    Thou hast no hands to wipe away thy tears,
    Nor tongue to tell me who hath mart'red thee:

---

81. mart'red] martred *Q1–2;* marterd *Q3;* martyr'd *F* (*so l. 107*).   86. Sweet
varied] Sweet-varied *W. S. Walker.*

81. *mart'red*] disfigured.

82. *engine*] instrument. The whole phrase again in *Ven.*, 367.

89. *deer*] All the early editions spell *Deare* both here and in l. 91, thus emphasizing the pun. Tilley, D189, quotes Surrey's *Faithful Lover* (*a.* 1547), l. 35: 'Then as the stricken deer withdraws him selfe alone'.

90. *unrecuring*] incurable.

96. *Expecting . . . when*] waiting for the time when. Also Spenser, *F.Q.*, III. xii. 1, 9; Jonson, *Cat.*, III. 562; *N.E.D.* first in 1687, and as late as

Godwin (1794). 'Look . . . when' is recorded from 1568. Later examples: Scott, *Redgauntlet*, ch. I, 'expecting any moment when he would start off'; Carlyle, *French Revolution*, III. iv. 6 (Temple Classics ed., III. 235), 'expecting when the end will be'; Tennyson, *The Vision of Sin*, l. 8, 'Expecting when a fountain should arise'.

envious] malignant: 'the most frequent Shakespearian sense' (On.).

101. *spurn*] contemptuous stroke or thrust (On.).

105. *lively*] living.

Thy husband he is dead, and for his death
Thy brothers are condemn'd, and dead by this.
Look, Marcus! ah, son Lucius, look on her!   110
When I did name her brothers, then fresh tears
Stood on her cheeks, as doth the honey-dew
Upon a gath'red lily almost withered.

Marc. Perchance she weeps because they kill'd her husband;
Perchance because she knows them innocent.   115

Tit. If they did kill thy husband, then be joyful,
Because the law hath ta'en revenge on them.
No, no, they would not do so foul a deed;
Witness the sorrow that their sister makes.
Gentle Lavinia, let me kiss thy lips,   120
Or make some sign how I may do thee ease.
Shall thy good uncle, and thy brother Lucius,
And thou, and I, sit round about some fountain,
Looking all downwards to behold our cheeks
How they are stain'd, like meadows yet not dry,   125
With miry slime left on them by a flood?
And in the fountain shall we gaze so long
Till the fresh taste be taken from that clearness,
And made a brine-pit with our bitter tears?
Or shall we cut away our hands like thine?   130
Or shall we bite our tongues, and in dumb shows
Pass the remainder of our hateful days?
What shall we do? let us that have our tongues
Plot some device of further misery,
To make us wonder'd at in time to come.   135

Luc. Sweet father, cease your tears; for at your grief
See how my wretched sister sobs and weeps.

Marc. Patience, dear niece. Good Titus, dry thine eyes.

Tit. Ah, Marcus, Marcus! brother, well I wot
Thy napkin cannot drink a tear of mine,   140

---

115. them] him Q3,F.   121. sign] signes F.   125. like] Q1 (Rowe); in Q2–3,F.
134. misery] miseries F.

109. *by this*] by this time.

113. *Upon . . . withered*] An alexandrine.

121. *do thee ease*] help, or relieve, thee.

129. *And made*] i.e. and it (the 'clearness', or clear pool) made. Cf. on v. iii. 101.

140. *napkin*] handkerchief. The form *napking*, which Q1 prints at l. 146

For thou, poor man, hast drown'd it with thine own.

Luc. Ah, my Lavinia, I will wipe thy cheeks.

Tit. Mark, Marcus, mark! I understand her signs:
　　Had she a tongue to speak, now would she say
　　That to her brother which I said to thee:　　　　　　145
　　His napkin, with his true tears all bewet,
　　Can do no service on her sorrowful cheeks.
　　O, what a sympathy of woe is this;
　　As far from help as limbo is from bliss.

Enter AARON *the Moor, alone.*

Aar. Titus Andronicus, my lord the emperor　　　　　150
　　Sends thee this word: that, if thou love thy sons,
　　Let Marcus, Lucius, or thyself, old Titus,
　　Or any one of you, chop off your hand
　　And send it to the king: he for the same
　　Will send thee hither both thy sons alive,　　　　　155
　　And that shall be the ransom for their fault.

Tit. O gracious emperor! O gentle Aaron!
　　Did ever raven sing so like a lark
　　That gives sweet tidings of the sun's uprise?
　　With all my heart I'll send the emperor my hand.　160
　　Good Aaron, wilt thou help to chop it off?

Luc. Stay, father, for that noble hand of thine,
　　That hath thrown down so many enemies,
　　Shall not be sent; my hand will serve the turn,
　　My youth can better spare my blood than you,　　165
　　And therefore mine shall save my brothers' lives.

Marc. Which of your hands hath not defended Rome,

146. with his] *F4;* with her *Qq,F.*　　150. *Aar.*] *Moore. Qq,F (so l. 174).*

is probably Shakespeare's own. Cf.
Wyld, p. 290.
　　141. *drown'd*] saturated.
　　149. *As far . . . bliss*] Wilson quotes
Err., IV. ii. 32: 'he's in Tartar limbo,
worse than hell', and notes that limbo,
the abode of the unbaptized, was further from salvation than hell. But the
meaning may be vaguer here.
　　151–2. *that . . . Let*] The same irregularity in *H5,* IV. iii. 34–6: 'proclaim
it . . . / That he which hath no stomach

to this fight, / Let him depart.' In the
light of the present passage, the alternative explanation of the other becomes doubly improbable: that *that he*
means 'that man'. Cf. Abbott §415. Cf.
also *Tim.,* v. i. 206–8: 'Tell Athens . . .
that whoso please / To stop affliction,
let him take his haste.'
　　160. *With . . . hand*] Many editors
since Steevens have printed *my hand* as
a separate line. But alexandrines are
common in this play.

And rear'd aloft the bloody battle-axe,
Writing destruction on the enemy's castle?
O, none of both but are of high desert: 170
My hand hath been but idle; let it serve
To ransom my two nephews from their death;
Then have I kept it to a worthy end.

Aar. Nay, come, agree whose hand shall go along,
For fear they die before their pardon come.   175

Marc. My hand shall go.

Luc.   By heaven, it shall not go!

Tit. Sirs, strive no more: such with'red herbs as these
Are meet for plucking up, and therefore mine.

Luc. Sweet father, if I shall be thought thy son,
Let me redeem my brothers both from death.   180

Marc. And for our father's sake, and mother's care,
Now let me show a brother's love to thee.

Tit. Agree between you; I will spare my hand.

Luc. Then I'll go fetch an axe.

Marc. But I will use the axe.   [*Exeunt.*   185

Tit. Come hither, Aaron; I'll deceive them both:
Lend me thy hand, and I will give thee mine.

Aar. [*Aside.*] If that be call'd deceit, I will be honest,
And never whilst I live deceive men so:
But I'll deceive you in another sort,   190
And that you'll say ere half an hour pass.
                        [*He cuts off Titus' hand.*

Enter LUCIUS *and* MARCUS *again.*

Tit. Now stay your strife; what shall be is dispatch'd.
Good Aaron, give his majesty my hand:
Tell him it was a hand that warded him
From thousand dangers, bid him bury it;   195
More hath it merited; that let it have.
As for my sons, say I account of them

---

169. enemy's] *Capell conj.;* enemies' *Theobald;* enemies *Qq,F.*   177. with'red]
withred *Qq;* withered *F.*   188. [*Aside.*]] *Rowe; not in Qq,F.*

169. *castle*] There is no reason to
think that this is corrupt, or that it has
any but the normal meaning. Robertson aptly quotes Greene, *Orlando Furi-*

oso, I. ii. 370–1: 'on this Castle wall /
Ile write my resolution with my blood'.
179. *shall*] am to; cf. Abbott §315.
191. *hour*] See on I. i. 127.

As jewels purchas'd at an easy price;
And yet dear too, because I bought mine own.
Aar. I go, Andronicus; and for thy hand   200
　　Look by and by to have thy sons with thee.
　　[*Aside.*] Their heads, I mean. O, how this villainy
　　Doth fat me with the very thoughts of it!
　　Let fools do good, and fair men call for grace,
　　Aaron will have his soul black like his face.   [*Exit.* 205
Tit. O, here I lift this one hand up to heaven,
　　And bow this feeble ruin to the earth:
　　If any power pities wretched tears,
　　To that I call, What, would'st thou kneel with me?
　　Do then, dear heart; for heaven shall hear our prayers,
　　Or with our sighs we'll breathe the welkin dim,   211
　　And stain the sun with fog, as sometime clouds
　　When they do hug him in their melting bosoms.
Marc. O brother, speak with possibility,
　　And do not break into these deep extremes.   215
Tit. Is not my sorrows deep, having no bottom?
　　Then be my passions bottomless with them.
Marc. But yet let reason govern thy lament.
Tit. If there were reason for these miseries,
　　Then into limits could I bind my woes: 220
　　When heaven doth weep, doth not the earth o'erflow?
　　If the winds rage, doth not the sea wax mad,
　　Threat'ning the welkin with his big-swol'n face?
　　And wilt thou have a reason for this coil?

202. [*Aside.*]] *Rowe; not in Qq,F.*   209. would'st] would *Q2–3;* wilt *F.*   214.
possibility] possibilities *Q3,F.*   216. Is . . . sorrows] *Dyce (2nd ed.) conj.;* Is . . .
sorrow *Qq,F;* Are . . . sorrows *Heath.*

201. *Look*] expect.
203. *fat*] nourish, i.e. delight. Comparable is *Mer.V.*, I. iii. 48: 'I will feed fat the ancient grudge I bear him.'
207. *ruin*] mutilated body. Wilson compares *Cym.*, IV. ii. 354, where *ruin* is used of Cloten's headless body.
211. *breathe . . . dim*] Verity compares Marlowe's *Faustus* (ed. Boas), I. iii. 4: 'dims the welkin with her pitchy breath'.
212. *sometime*] Interchangeable in Shakespeare's English with *sometimes.*

216. *Is . . . sorrows*] See on II. i. 26. A singular verb in a question before a plural subject is particularly common. This seems to me the easiest correction of the Qq,F reading if it is admitted, as I think it must be, that *them* in l. 217 makes *sorrows* necessary here.
217. *passions*] passionate outbursts.
220. *bind*] confine.
221. *o'erflow*] become flooded.
224. *coil*] ado; cf. *John*, II. i. 165: 'I am not worth this coil that's made for me.'

I am the sea. Hark how her sighs doth blow;   225
She is the weeping welkin, I the earth:
Then must my sea be moved with her sighs;
Then must my earth with her continual tears
Become a deluge, overflow'd and drown'd;
For why my bowels cannot hide her woes,   230
But like a drunkard must I vomit them.
Then give me leave, for losers will have leave
To ease their stomachs with their bitter tongues.

Enter a Messenger with two heads and a hand.

Mess. Worthy Andronicus, ill art thou repaid
For that good hand thou sent'st the emperor.   235
Here are the heads of thy two noble sons,
And here's thy hand, in scorn to thee sent back:
Thy grief their sports, thy resolution mock'd;
That woe is me to think upon thy woes,
More than remembrance of my father's death.   [*Exit.*
Marc. Now let hot Etna cool in Sicily,   241
And be my heart an ever-burning hell!
These miseries are more than may be borne.
To weep with them that weep doth ease some deal,
But sorrow flouted at is double death.   245
Luc. Ah, that this sight should make so deep a wound,
And yet detested life not shrink thereat;
That ever death should let life bear his name,

225. doth] doe *Q2-3,F.*   blow] *F2;* flow *Qq,F.*   229. overflow'd] ouer-
flowed *Qq.*   drown'd] drowned *Q2-3.*   230. her] their *Theobald conj.*
238. grief] griefe, *Q1-2;* griefes *Q3;* griefes, *F;* grief's (*and* sport *for* sports) *Pope.*
240. Exit.] *not in Q1.*

225. *doth*] See on II. iv. 17.
230. *For why*] because.
232-3. *losers . . . tongues*] See
O.D.E.P., p. 386, and Tilley, L458,
where the first quotation is from More
.(1533).
238. *grief*] I do not think this need be
changed to *griefs.* Titus' grief is the
sport of each one of them. If a change
were to be made I should rather read
sport.
239. *That*] so that, cf. *Mac.,* II. ii.

6-7: 'I have drugg'd their possets, /
That death and nature do contend
about them.'
woe is me] In such expressions, *me* is
originally a dative, cf. *methinks.*
244. *To . . . that weep*] Cf. Romans,
XII. 15: 'weep with them that weep.'
245. *flouted at*] mocked.
247. *shrink*] slip away (*N.E.D.* 6),
rather than 'wither away' (Wilson).
248. *bear his name*] i.e. still be called
'life'.

Where life hath no more interest but to breathe!

[Lavinia kisses Titus.

Marc. Alas, poor heart, that kiss is comfortless   250
    As frozen water to a starved snake.
Tit. When will this fearful slumber have an end?
Marc. Now farewell, flatt'ry: die, Andronicus;
    Thou dost not slumber: see thy two sons' heads,
    Thy warlike hand, thy mangled daughter here;   255
    Thy other banish'd son, with this dear sight
    Struck pale and bloodless; and thy brother, I,
    Even like a stony image, cold and numb.
    Ah, now no more will I control thy griefs.
    Rent off thy silver hair, thy other hand   260
    Gnawing with thy teeth; and be this dismal sight
    The closing up of our most wretched eyes.
    Now is a time to storm; why art thou still?
Tit. Ha, ha, ha!
Marc. Why dost thou laugh? it fits not with this hour.   265
Tit. Why, I have not another tear to shed:
    Besides, this sorrow is an enemy,
    And would usurp upon my wat'ry eyes,
    And make them blind with tributary tears:
    Then which way shall I find Revenge's cave?   270

---

249. *Lavinia . . . Titus.*] *Johnson; not in Qq,F.*   253. flatt'ry] *Kittredge;* flattrie *Q1;* flattery (-ie) *Q2–3,F.*   255. hand] hands *F.*   256. son] sonnes *F.*   259. thy] *Q1 (Theobald);* my *Q2–3,F.*

250 ff. *Alas . . .*] 'The behaviour of all these personages upon this dreadful occasion is singularly proper, and the horrid "laugh" [l. 264] of the father has something great in it even for Shakespeare' (Capell).

251. *starved*] numbed, cf. *Cym.,* I. iv. 187: 'catch cold and starve'. The phrase 'starved snake' is semi-proverbial: Parrott quotes *2H6,* III. i. 343, to which add Jonson, *Poetaster,* III. iv. 329.

256. *dear*] grievous. See On. on the distinction between this and the more common word *dear* (= beloved).

259. *control*] check: a slightly different sense from that of I. i. 420.

260. *Rent*] A common alternative form of *rend.*

263. *Now . . . still?*] With Titus' momentary silence at the supreme moment of grief, E. Wolff, *Die Antike,* 20 (1944), 143–4, compares Hecuba's behaviour as described in Ovid, *Met.,* XIII, esp. l. 538: 'Troades exclamant, obmutuit illa dolore.' The resemblance is not very close, though both characters go on to plan revenge. The Hecuba story has already been referred to at I. i. 136–8 (see note).

264. *Ha, ha, ha!*] Wilson compares Hieronymo's laughter in *Spanish Tragedy* (ed. Boas), III. xi. 30.

For these two heads do seem to speak to me,
And threat me I shall never come to bliss
Till all these mischiefs be return'd again
Even in their throats that hath committed them.
Come, let me see what task I have to do.   275
You heavy people, circle me about,
That I may turn me to each one of you,
And swear unto my soul to right your wrongs.
The vow is made. Come, brother, take a head;
And in this hand the other will I bear.   280
†And, Lavinia, thou shalt be employ'd in these arms:†
Bear thou my hand, sweet wench, between thy teeth.
As for thee, boy, go get thee from my sight;
Thou art an exile, and thou must not stay:
Hie to the Goths, and raise an army there;   285
And if ye love me, as I think you do,
Let's kiss and part, for we have much to do.   [*Exeunt.*

Luc. Farewell, Andronicus, my noble father;
The woefull'st man that ever liv'd in Rome.
Farewell, proud Rome, till Lucius come again;   290
He loves his pledges dearer than his life.
Farewell, Lavinia, my noble sister;

---

274. hath] haue *Q2–3,F.*   281. And] *not in F2.*   arms] things *F.*   in these
arms] in this *Lettsom conj.*   286. ye] you *Q2–3,F.*   287. *Exeunt.*] *Exeunt. Manet*
Lucius F.   290. Rome, . . . again;] Rome . . . againe, *Qq;* Rome, . . . againe. *F;*
Rome! . . . again, *Rowe.*   291. loves] leaves *Rowe;* loans *Ridley conj.*

---

274. *hath*] See on II. iv. 17.
276. *heavy*] sorrowful.
281. *And . . . arms*] I leave this line as
hopelessly corrupt. Lettsom's conjecture gives good sense, and could be
used to modify a hypothesis of Camb.
The latter suggests that *armes* was
added above *teeth* as a substitute and
was mistaken for the end of l. 281, and
then assumes that *in these* was added by
the printer to incorporate *armes* into
the line, which it reconstructs in its
original form as: *And thou, Lavinia, shalt*
be employ'd. But equally easily *this*
could have been corrupted to *these*
with the same effect, as Lettsom's conjecture presupposes. The *And* at the
beginning of the line is metrically awk-

ward, and may have been repeated
from the previous line (Malone).

291. *loves*] I now (1961) accept the
original text; l. 291 gives Lucius'
ground for asserting that he is sure to
return (Baildon): so Sisson, *New Read-*
ings in Shakespeare (1956), II. 140, 'I will
carry out my vow and return even at
the risk of my life.' Rowe's correction,
though graphically easy—*leues : loues*
(cf. J. Dover Wilson, *The Manuscript of*
Shakespeare's Hamlet, pp. 109–10)—is
thus unnecessary; Ridley's is unduly
commercial: *pledges* here corresponds
to Latin *pignora* for 'dear ones'. Even
with Rowe's emendation, his change
of punctuation would be unnecessary.

O, would thou wert as thou tofore hast been!
But now nor Lucius nor Lavinia lives
But in oblivion and hateful griefs.   295
If Lucius live, he will requite your wrongs,
And make proud Saturnine and his empress
Beg at the gates like Tarquin and his queen.
Now will I to the Goths, and raise a pow'r,
To be reveng'd on Rome and Saturnine.   [Exit Lucius.

SCENE II.—A Banket.

Enter ANDRONICUS, MARCUS, LAVINIA, and the Boy.

Tit. So, so; now sit; and look you eat no more
     Than will preserve just so much strength in us
     As will revenge these bitter woes of ours.

297. empress] Emperesse Q1.   298. like] likes F.   299. pow'r] Kittredge;
powre Q1; power Q2–3,F.

Scene II
Scene II] Capell; not in F (which first prints the scene).   Banket] Bnaket F; Banquet
F2.

293. tofore] formerly. Two words in Qq,F.

297. and his empress] See on I. i. 89. And his should be pronounced and 's.

Scene II
Scene II] Only in F. In my 1953 edition, I dismissed too hastily the possibility that this scene is a later addition. E. K. Chambers, William Shakespeare, I. 316, had noted the 'distinct scribal origin' reflected in the S.D. forms 'Andronicus' and 'Tamira'. Moreover, as N. S. Brooke has pointed out to me—and as I now find C. M. Haines had noted in 'The "Law of Re-entry" in Shakespeare' (R.E.S., I (1925), 449–50)—the end of III. ii is the only place in the play where characters exit to re-enter immediately; whereas the end of III. i makes a natural break, and points forward to the revenge theme. Is it a serious objection that without sc. ii the Folio Act III would be only 300 lines long? As Greg points out, the Folio act-division is certainly wrong at the end of Act I (The Shakespeare First Folio (1955), p. 205). Altogether, the date of the scene remains very much an open question—it would be convenient, but hazardous, to make its addition the justification for Henslowe's 'ne' of 24 January 1594 —and if so, its authorship must also be uncertain. There is no positive reason to deny it to Shakespeare, or to attach much weight to the 'fancy' Chambers records having had that it is by Webster (William Shakespeare, I. 321).

Banket] A common sixteenth-century form, also in Q1, v. ii. 76, 194 and (Qq,F) 203.

Andronicus] So for Titus at S.D. II. iii. 258. In this scene, and only in it, the speech-prefix is An.

Marcus, unknit that sorrow-wreathen knot:
Thy niece and I, poor creatures, want our hands,   5
And cannot passionate our ten-fold grief
With folded arms. This poor right hand of mine
Is left to tyrannize upon my breast;
Who when my heart, all mad with misery,
Beats in this hollow prison of my flesh,   10
Then thus I thump it down.
Thou map of woe, that thus dost talk in signs,
When thy poor heart beats with outrageous beating
Thou canst not strike it thus to make it still.
Wound it with sighing, girl, kill it with groans;   15
Or get some little knife between thy teeth,
And just against thy heart make thou a hole,
That all the tears that thy poor eyes let fall
May run into that sink, and soaking in,
Drown the lamenting fool in sea-salt tears.   20

Marc. Fie, brother, fie! teach her not thus to lay
Such violent hands upon her tender life.

Tit. How now! has sorrow made thee dote already?
Why, Marcus, no man should be mad but I.
What violent hands can she lay on her life?   25
Ah, wherefore dost thou urge the name of hands,
To bid Æneas tell the tale twice o'er,

9. Who] And *Rowe.*   14. still.] still? *F.*

6. *passionate*] express with appropriate feeling: Steevens quotes Spenser, *F.Q.*, I. xii. 16. 1–2: 'Great pleasure
mixt with pittifull regard, / That godly
King and Queene did passionate.'
B. L. Joseph, *Elizabethan Acting* (London, 1951), p. 73, comments on this
passage as an example of the notion
that folded arms symbolize inexpres-
siveness: 'whilst they feel more than a
dull grief, their mutilations do not
allow the expression of what is really
within.'

9. *Who*] Probably used for *which*
(Abbott §264, Franz §335), with *hand*
as antecedent. Then *I* is substituted as
subject in l. 11. Rowe's emendation
cuts the knot but does not explain the
F reading.

12. *map*] image, embodiment.

15. *Wound . . . sighing*] Sighs were
thought to drain the heart of blood; cf.
2H6, III. i. 61, 63, *3H6*, IV. iv. 22
(Verity; Stoll).

20. *fool*] This word often has an
affectionate implication, most notably
in *Lr.*, v. iii. 307: 'my poor fool is
hang'd.'

27–8. *To . . . miserable*] A reminiscence (Lee) of Virgil, *Aen.*, II. 2:
'infandum, regina, iubes renovare
dolorem'. This is such a commonplace
that Wilson's parallel from *Troublesome Reign of King John*, Part I, x. 27–8:
'Must I discourse? let Dido sigh and
say / She weepes againe to hear the
wrack of Troy?' is of no significance.

How Troy was burnt and he made miserable?
O, handle not the theme, to talk of hands,
Lest we remember still that we have none.   30
Fie, fie, how franticly I square my talk,
As if we should forget we had no hands,
If Marcus did not name the word of hands!
Come, let's fall to; and, gentle girl, eat this:
Here is no drink? Hark, Marcus, what she says;   35
I can interpret all her martyr'd signs:
She says she drinks no other drink but tears,
Brew'd with her sorrow, mesh'd upon her cheeks.
Speechless complainer, I will learn thy thought;
In thy dumb action will I be as perfect   40
As begging hermits in their holy prayers:
Thou shalt not sigh, nor hold thy stumps to heaven,
Nor wink, nor nod, nor kneel, nor make a sign,
But I of these will wrest an alphabet,
And by still practice learn to know thy meaning.   45
Boy. Good grandsire, leave these bitter deep laments:
Make my aunt merry with some pleasing tale.
Marc. Alas, the tender boy, in passion mov'd,
Doth weep to see his grandsire's heaviness.

38. Brew'd] Breu'd *F.*   39. complainer, I] *Capell;* complainet, I *F;* complaint,
O I *F2.*

29–33. *handle . . . hands*] Here, as in
IV. i. 70 (see note), Shakespeare may
owe something to the story of Io in
Ovid, *Met.*, I, where ll. 635–6 run 'Illa
etiam supplex Argo cum bracchia
vellet / Tendere, non habuit quae
bracchia tenderet Argo', which Golding translates: 'when she did devise, /
To *Argus* for to lift her hands in meeke
and humble wise, / She saw she had no
hands at all.'

30. *still*] See on III. i. 19.

31. *square*] regulate.

36. *martyr'd signs*] 'the signs the poor
martyr makes' (Wilson). I doubt
whether Wilson is right in seeing 'an
allusion to signs made by those burnt
at the stake'.

37. *drinks . . . tears*] Biblical, cf.
Psalm lxxx. 5: 'and givest them

plenteousness of tears to drink'
(Prayer Book version).

38. *mesh'd*] Lit. 'mixed with water
to form wort' (On.); here a rhetorical variation of *brew'd*; cf. *mash* (dial.)
(tea).

39. *complainer*] F's 'complainet'
arises from a misunderstood attempt at
proof-correction of the uncorrected
'complaine'.

40. *perfect*] as in 'word-perfect'. The
epithet can be applied either (as here)
to the person who knows a lesson perfectly, or to the lesson ('the lesson . . .
once made perfect', *Ven.*, 407–8), or to
the knowledge ('a perfect thought',
John, v. vi. 6).

45. *still*] constant; cf. *Lucr.*, 702:
'comprehend in still imagination'.

48. *passion*] See on I. i. 106.

Tit. Peace, tender sapling; thou art made of tears,   50
  And tears will quickly melt thy life away.
                    [*Marcus strikes the dish with a knife.*
  What dost thou strike at, Marcus, with thy knife?
Marc. At that that I have kill'd, my lord; a fly.
Tit. Out on thee, murderer! thou kill'st my heart;
  Mine eyes are cloy'd with view of tyranny: 55
  A deed of death done on the innocent
  Becomes not Titus' brother. Get thee gone;
  I see thou art not for my company.
Marc. Alas, my lord, I have but kill'd a fly.
Tit. 'But'? How if that fly had a father and mother?   60
  How would he hang his slender gilded wings,
  And buzz lamenting doings in the air!
  Poor harmless fly,
  That, with his pretty buzzing melody,
  Came here to make us merry, and thou hast kill'd him.
Marc. Pardon me, sir; it was a black ill-favour'd fly   66
  Like to the empress' Moor; therefore I kill'd him.
Tit. O, O, O!
  Then pardon me for reprehending thee,
  For thou hast done a charitable deed.   70
  Give me thy knife, I will insult on him;
  Flattering myself as if it were the Moor

---

52. thy] *not in F.*   54. thee] *F3;* the *F.*   55. are] *not in F.*   60. 'But'?]
But? *F.*   How if] *F3;* How: if *F.*   62. doings] dolings *Theobald.*

---

54. *thee, murderer*] The F1 reading as an exclamation not directly addressed to Marcus, is perhaps defensible, but seems awkward after l. 52 and before the second half of this line. *The* for *thee* was a common sixteenth-century spelling, and sometimes leads to confusion.

62. *lamenting doings*] An odd phrase, that seems to mean little more than 'lamentations'.

71. *insult on*] triumph over; cf. *R3*, II. iv. 51: 'Insulting tyranny'.

72. *as if*] with the thought that (perhaps following the similar use of *tamquam, quasi* in Silver Latin: see J. D. Duff on Juvenal, III. 222). This usage

is not uncommon in Shakespeare's time; Raleigh, *History of the World* (Selections ed. by G. E. Hadow, p. 139): 'The *Illyrian* Queen was secure of the *Romans*, as if they would not dare to stirre against her'; Sidney, *Arcadia*, I. xiii. 1 (ed. Feuillerat, p. 85): 'thus did I flatter my selfe, as though my wound had bene no deeper'; *ibid.*, II. xx. 4 (p. 280): 'she founde meanes to have us accused to the King, as though we went about some practise to overthrowe him'; Bunyan, *Holy War*, Advertisement to the Reader: 'Insinuating as if I would shine'. Cf. IV. iv. 53n.; Milton, *Comus*, 763.

Come hither purposely to poison me.
There's for thyself, and that's for Tamora.
Ah, sirrah!   75
Yet, I think, we are not brought so low,
But that between us we can kill a fly
That comes in likeness of a coal-black Moor.
Marc. Alas, poor man! grief has so wrought on him,
He takes false shadows for true substances.   80
Tit. Come, take away. Lavinia, go with me:
I'll to thy closet, and go read with thee
Sad stories chanced in the times of old.
Come, boy, and go with me: thy sight is young,
And thou shalt read when mine begin to dazzle.   85
                                                        [*Exeunt.*

---

74. Tamora] *Tamira F.*   75. *as separate line Capell; with l. 74 F; with l. 76
Steevens (1778).*   85. begin] begins *Rowe (3rd ed.).*

80. *shadows . . . substances*] The *substance/shadow* antithesis is very common in Shakespeare; this instance is particularly close to Ovid, *Met.*, III. 417 (Narcissus), 'corpus putat esse quod umbra est.'

81. *take away*] clear the table.

82–3. *read . . . old*] Cf. *R2*, III. ii. 155–6: 'For God's sake, let us sit upon the ground / And tell sad stories of the death of kings.' Parrott, p. 32, notes that the parallel is more than verbal: in both passages the 'sad stories' are a consolation for present sorrow.

85. *begin*] If this is right, the virtual subject is 'eyes', understood from *sight* (Dyce).

ACT IV

SCENE I

Enter Lucius' son, and LAVINIA *running after him, and the boy flies from her with his books under his arm. Enter* TITUS *and* MARCUS.

Boy. Help, grandsire, help! my aunt Lavinia
    Follows me everywhere, I know not why.
    Good uncle Marcus, see how swift she comes:
    Alas, sweet aunt, I know not what you mean.
Marc. Stand by me, Lucius; do not fear thine aunt.   5
Tit. She loves thee, boy, too well to do thee harm.
Boy. Ay, when my father was in Rome she did.
Marc. What means my niece Lavinia by these signs?
Tit. Fear her not, Lucius: somewhat doth she mean.
Marc. See, Lucius, see how much she makes of thee;   10
    Somewhither would she have thee go with her.
    Ah, boy, Cornelia never with more care
    Read to her sons than she hath read to thee
    Sweet poetry and Tully's Orator.
    Canst thou not guess wherefore she plies thee thus?   15

ACT IV

Scene i

Act IV Scene i] *Rowe; Actus Quartus. F; not in Qq.*   Lucius' son] *young Lucius F.*   1. *Boy*] *Puer Qq (so throughout).*   5. thine] *thy F.*   9. her] *not in F.*   10. *Marc.* See] *W. S. Walker; See Qq,F.*   11. Somewhither] *Some whither Q1;* *Some whether Q2–3,F.*   12. Ah,] *A Q1–2.*   15. Canst] *Marc. Canst Capell.*

10. Marc.] L. 18 shows that the boy's reply is addressed to Marcus, not to Titus. In view of the occurrence of *Lucius* both in l. 9 and in l. 10, it seems more likely that the change of speaker takes place here than at l. 15.

12. *Cornelia*] the mother of the Gracchi (second century B.C.). Wilson's objection that 'Cicero's *De*

Oratore was not written until fifty years after their death' rests on a misinterpretation of l. 13, where *Read to* means 'gave lessons to' (*N.E.D.* 12) and does not govern 'Sweet . . . Orator.'

14. *Tully's Orator*] Either Cicero's *De Oratore* or, more probably, his *ad M. Brutum Orator.*

Boy. My lord, I know not, I, nor can I guess,
          Unless some fit or frenzy do possess her;
          For I have heard my grandsire say full oft,
          Extremity of griefs would make men mad;
          And I have read that Hecuba of Troy   20
          Ran mad for sorrow; that made me to fear,
          Although, my lord, I know my noble aunt
          Loves me as dear as e'er my mother did,
          And would not, but in fury, fright my youth;
          Which made me down to throw my books and fly,   25
          Causeless perhaps, but pardon me, sweet aunt;
          And, madam, if my uncle Marcus go,
          I will most willingly attend your ladyship.
Marc. Lucius, I will.
Tit. How now, Lavinia! Marcus, what means this?   30
          Some book there is that she desires to see.
          Which is it, girl, of these? Open them, boy.
          But thou art deeper read, and better skill'd;
          Come, and take choice of all my library,
          And so beguile thy sorrow, till the heavens   35
          Reveal the damn'd contriver of this deed.
          Why lifts she up her arms in sequence thus?
Marc. I think she means that there were more than one
          Confederate in the fact: ay, more there was;
          Or else to heaven she heaves them for revenge.   40
Tit. Lucius, what book is that she tosseth so?
Boy. Grandsire, 'tis Ovid's Metamorphosis;
          My mother gave it me.
Marc.   For love of her that's gone,

---

21. for] through *Q3,F.*   36.] *F adds in separate line* What booke?   38. were]
was *Q3,F.*   40. for] to *F.*

---

20. *have read*] Probably, as H. Nørgaard, *Eng. Studies*, 45 (1964), 139,
suggests, from T. Cooper, *Thesaurus*,
s.v. *Hecuba*.

24. *but in fury*] except in a fit of
madness.

26. *causeless*] 'without reasonable
cause' (Wilson).

33. *deeper*] i.e. than to read boys'
schoolbooks (Delius; Wilson).

36 (app. crit.). What booke?] The

insertion of this in F seems to be a compositor's vagary. Professor Dover
Wilson tells me that he withdraws the
suggestion that it is a relic of a par-
tially deleted passage in the MS.

39. *fact*] crime, as always in Shakespeare.

41. *tosseth*] turns over the leaves of.

42. *Metamorphosis*] I retain this
spelling, which is, as Wilson notes, that
of Golding's translation.

  Perhaps, she cull'd it from among the rest.

Tit. Soft, so busily she turns the leaves!   45
  Help her: what would she find? Lavinia, shall I read?
  This is the tragic tale of Philomel,
  And treats of Tereus' treason and his rape;
  And rape, I fear, was root of thy annoy.

Marc. See, brother, see! note how she quotes the leaves. 50

Tit. Lavinia, wert thou thus surpris'd, sweet girl,
  Ravish'd and wrong'd, as Philomela was,
  Forc'd in the ruthless, vast, and gloomy woods?
  See, see!
  Ay, such a place there is, where we did hunt,— 55
  O, had we never, never hunted there,—
  Pattern'd by that the poet here describes,
  By nature made for murthers and for rapes.

Marc. O, why should nature build so foul a den,
  Unless the gods delight in tragedies?   60

Tit. Give signs, sweet girl, for here are none but friends,
  What Roman lord it was durst do the deed:
  Or slunk not Saturnine, as Tarquin erst,
  That left the camp to sin in Lucrece' bed?

Marc. Sit down, sweet niece: brother, sit down by me. 65
  Apollo, Pallas, Jove, or Mercury,
  Inspire me, that I may this treason find!
  My lord, look here; look here, Lavinia:

---

45. so] see how *Rowe.* 46.] *so Qq,F; two lines divided after* her *Capell.* Help
her] S.D. *Dyce conj.* 49. thy] thine *Q2–3,F.* 50. quotes] coats *Q1.* 54–5.]
so Pope; one line in Qq,F. 63. slunk] slonke *Q1.*

46. *Help her*] Very likely (Dyce) a S.D.

47. *Philomel*] See on II. iv. 26.

50. *quotes*] marks, observes.

53. *vast*] desolate.

57. *pattern'd by*] on the pattern of; cf. *Meas.*, II. i. 30: 'Let mine own judgment pattern out my death.'

here] In *Met.*, VI. 520–1: 'rex Pandione natam / In stabula alta trahit, silvis obscura vetustis.' Golding translates: 'king *Terew* tooke the ladie by the hand, / And led hir to a pelting grange that peakish-ly did stand / In woods forgrowne.'

62. *What Roman lord*] Wilson (on l. 36) finds this inconsistent with ll. 38–40, which he therefore thinks 'perhaps a second-thought insertion'. But (i) there might have been 'more than one / Confederate in the fact' and yet only one actual ravisher, (ii) in any case l. 40 offers an alternative interpretation of Lavinia's gestures.

63. *slunk*] Q1's spelling *slonke* is only graphic, to avoid a confusing run of minims, as in *son.* Cf. v. i. 9, where Q1 has *sprong*, and v. iii. 163 (*Song*).

This sandy plot is plain; guide, if thou canst,
This after me.   [*He writes his name with his staff*
                          and guides it with feet and mouth.

           I have writ my name   70
Without the help of any hand at all.
Curs'd be that heart that forc'd us to this shift!
Write thou, good niece, and here display at last
What God will have discovered for revenge.
Heaven guide thy pen to print thy sorrows plain,   75
That we may know the traitors and the truth!
                          [*She takes the staff in her mouth, and*
                          guides it with her stumps, and writes.
O, do ye read, my lord, what she hath writ?
Tit. Stuprum. Chiron. Demetrius.
Marc. What, what! the lustful sons of Tamora
Performers of this heinous, bloody deed?   80
Tit. Magni dominator poli,
Tam lentus audis scelera? tam lentus vides?

---

70. [*He . . . mouth.*]] *here Collier; after l. 68 Qq,F.*   me. I] me, I *Qq,F;* me. See, I
Keightley.   72. this] that *F.*   77. O] *Titus.* Oh *Q3,F; Boy.* Oh *Capell conj.*
78. *Tit.*] *Maxwell; not in Qq,F.*   81. *Magni*] *Magne Theobald.*

---

70. *after me*] as I have done. Ovid
may have afforded a hint for the
writing of the name (which, however,
is in the chap-book version). When Io
has been transformed into a cow, she
first tries to tell her father who she is,
but cannot any longer speak; then
'Littera pro verbis, quam pes in pul-
vere duxit, / Corporis indicium mutati
triste peregit' (*Met.*, I. 649–50); Golding translates: 'But for because she
could not speake she printed in the
sand / Two letters with hir foot, where-
by was given to vnderstand / The sor-
rowfull changing of hir shape.' See
also J. G. McManaway, *R.E.S.*, n.s. 9
(1958), 172–3.

    72. *forc'd . . . shift*] See on IV. ii.
177.

    78. *Tit.*] I think this is the best solu-
tion of the problem of attribution at
this point. Q1–2 continue ll. 77–8 to
Marcus, but give a fresh prefix for
Marcus at l. 79. Q3 transfers ll. 77–8 to

Titus, but he never addresses Marcus
as 'Lord' whereas Marcus so addresses
him several times (I. i. 355, 391; III. ii.
53; IV. i. 83, iii. 69). It was to Capell's
credit that, without knowledge of
Q1–2, he proposed to transfer both
lines to the Boy, but I think it is more
dramatic to let Titus himself read
the fatal message. 'Stuprum' =
rape.

    81–2. Magni . . . vides?] 'Ruler of
the great heavens, art thou so slow to
hear and to see crimes?' From Seneca,
Phaedra, 672–1, where the first half-line
reads *Magne regnator deum.* At l. 1159,
the beginning of the speech echoed
above at II. i. 135, we have *saeve*
dominator freti. J. A. K. Thomson,
Shakespeare and the Classics (1952), p. 52,
points out that Seneca, *Epistle*, 107, in a
translation from Cleanthes, has 'parens
celsique dominator poli', and that the
conflation suggests a good knowledge
of Seneca. I allow this parallel to

Marc. O, calm thee, gentle lord, although I know
          There is enough written upon this earth
          To stir a mutiny in the mildest thoughts   85
          And arm the minds of infants to exclaims.
          My lord, kneel down with me; Lavinia, kneel;
          And kneel, sweet boy, the Roman Hector's hope;
          And swear with me, as with the woeful fere
          And father of that chaste dishonoured dame,   90
          Lord Junius Brutus sware for Lucrece' rape,
          That we will prosecute by good advice
          Mortal revenge upon these traitorous Goths,
          And see their blood, or die with this reproach.

Tit.   'Tis sure enough, and you knew how;   95
          But if you hunt these bear-whelps, then beware:
          The dam will wake, and if she wind ye once:
          She's with the lion deeply still in league,
          And lulls him whilst she playeth on her back,
          And when he sleeps will she do what she list.   100
          You are a young huntsman, Marcus, let alone;
          And come, I will go get a leaf of brass,
          And with a gad of steel will write these words,
          And lay it by: the angry northen wind
          Will blow these sands like Sibyl's leaves abroad,   105

---

88. hope] hop (*or* l op, *slipping out of line*) *Q1*.   91. sware] *F3;* sweare *Qq,F*.
97. wake, ... once:] *Staunton;* wake ... once, *Q1;* wake, ... once, *Q2–3,F;* wake;
... once, *Theobald*.   ye] you *Q2–3,F*.   101. let] let it *Q3,F*.   104. northen]
Northerne *Q3;* northern *F*.

decide in favour of retaining 'Magni'
instead of Theobald's 'Magne', though
it is metrically objectionable (see on
II. i. 235).

86. *exclaims*] outcries, protests; so
R2, I. ii. 2.

89. *fere*] husband.

92. *by good advice*] 'by well-considered means' (Hudson).

96. *bear-whelps*] Noble notes that 'the
ferocity of the she-bear bereft of her
whelps is a frequent figure in the Old
Testament. See *Hos*., xiii. 8; *2 Sam*.
xvii. 8, *Prov*. xvii. 12.'

97. *and if*] if. This seems better than
to take *and* as connective, punctuate
heavily after *wake* and lightly after

once, and make the *if*-clause dependent
on l. 99.

wind] get wind of.

98. *still*] See on III. i. 19.

101. *let alone*] = let it alone. Cf.
Wint., II. ii. 53: 'le't not be doubted'
and Furness's note on *Wint*., II. i. 18.

102. *leaf of brass*] Recurs in *The
Welsh Embassador* (Malone Society
Reprint), l. 976, which quotes v. ii. 9
(see note).

103. *gad*] 'sharp spike; applied to a
stylus' (On.).

104. *northen*] See *N.E.D.* for this
fairly common form.

105. *Sibyl's leaves*] The prophecies of
the Sibyl were written on leaves which

And where's our lesson then? Boy, what say you?

Boy. I say, my lord, that if I were a man
　　　Their mother's bedchamber should not be safe
　　　For these base bondmen to the yoke of Rome.

Marc. Ay, that's my boy! thy father hath full oft   110
　　　For his ungrateful country done the like.

Boy. And, uncle, so will I and if I live.

Tit. Come, go with me into mine armoury:
　　　Lucius, I'll fit thee; and withal, my boy,
　　　Shalt carry from me to the empress' sons   115
　　　Presents that I intend to send them both:
　　　Come, come; thou'lt do my message, wilt thou not?

Boy. Ay, with my dagger in their bosoms, grandsire.

Tit. No, boy, not so: I'll teach thee another course.
　　　Lavinia, come. Marcus, look to my house;   120
　　　Lucius and I'll go brave it at the court:
　　　Ay, marry, will we, sir; and we'll be waited on. [*Exeunt.*

Marc. O, heavens, can you hear a good man groan
　　　And not relent, or not compassion him?
　　　Marcus, attend him in his ecstasy,   125

---

106. our] you *Q2;* your *Q3,F.*　　109. base] bad *Q2–3,F.*　　114. withal, . . .
boy,] *Capell;* withall . . . boy *Qq,F.*　　115. Shalt] *Capell;* Shall *Qq,F.*　　117.
my] *Q1 (Rowe);* thy *Q2–3,F.*　　123. good man] goodman *Q1.*

---

were frequently blown away before
there was time to collect them.
Steevens quotes Virgil, *Aen.*, VI. 74–5:
'Foliis tantum ne carmina manda, /
Ne turbata volent rapidis ludibria
ventis.'—'But, oh! commit not thy
prophetic mind / To flitting leaves, the
sport of every wind, / Lest they disperse in air our empty tale' (Dryden).

114. *fit thee*] furnish you with what
you need.

114–15. *withal . . . Shalt*] Lucius is the
only boy in question, hence *my boy*
must be vocative, and should be set off
by commas. I also accept Capell's
shalt. It would easily be corrupted
when the construction was misunderstood, and though *shall* for *shalt* is
sometimes found (Franz §152) it
would be very odd with unexpressed
subject. *Shalt* for *thou shalt* is, on the
other hand, common (Franz §306,

Abbott §401). Editors except Capell
seem to have gone to sleep over this
passage. It is true that the third person
can be used as virtually equivalent to
the second; see *Lr.*, I. i. 69: 'What says
our second daughter?' But I doubt
whether a parallel could be found for
a transition from the second to the
third person, and then back again within the same sentence to the second.

121. *brave it*] See on II. i. 91.

122. *be waited on*] 'i.e. not ignored as
hitherto' (Wilson).

123. *good man*] Munro, *T.L.S.*,
10 June 1949, p. 385, would retain the
Q1 spelling *goodman* and interpret 'a
fellow being and a kinsman smitten by
suffering'. I find this forced: certainly
goodman sometimes means simply *good
man*, as in the F text of *Lr.*, IV. iv. 18.

125. *ecstasy*] fit of madness; cf. *Ham.*,
II. i. 102: 'the very ecstasy of love'.

That hath more scars of sorrow in his heart
Than foemen's marks upon his batt'red shield,
But yet so just that he will not revenge.
Revenge the heavens for old Andronicus!   [*Exit.*

SCENE II

Enter AARON, CHIRON *and* DEMETRIUS *at one door, and at the other door, young* LUCIUS *and another, with a bundle of weapons, and verses writ upon them.*

Chi. Demetrius, here's the son of Lucius;
    He hath some message to deliver us.
Aar. Ay, some mad message from his mad grandfather.
Boy. My lords, with all the humbleness I may,
    I greet your honours from Andronicus;   5
    [*Aside.*] And pray the Roman gods confound you both.
Dem. Gramercy, lovely Lucius: what's the news?
Boy. [*Aside.*] That you are both decipher'd, that's the news,
    For villains mark'd with rape. [*Aloud.*] May it
        please you,
    My grandsire, well-advis'd, hath sent by me   10
    The goodliest weapons of his armoury

---

127. batt'red] battred *Qq;* batter'd *F.*   129. the] ye *Johnson conj.*

Scene II
Scene II] *Pope; not in Qq,F.*   the other] another *Q2–3,F.*   6. [*Aside.*]] *Capell (so ll. 8, 17); not in Qq,F.*   7. Gramercy] Gramarcie *Q1–2.*   8.] *not in F.*

129. *Revenge the heavens*] let the heavens revenge. Marcus credits Titus with adherence to the stock text on this subject, Romans, xii. 19: 'Vengeance is mine; I will repay, saith the Lord.'

Scene II
7. *Gramercy*] The Q1–2 spelling represents the habitual pronunciation of *e* before *r*, which has survived in a few words like *clerk*: see Wyld, pp. 212–22.
8. *decipher'd*] detected. The F omis-sion results from the ending of ll. 7 and 8 with the same two words; cf. l. 76.

10. *well-advis'd*] in his right mind; as Wilson says, this is meant to contra-dict what Aaron has said in l. 3. Cf. *Err.*, II. ii. 217: 'mad or well-advis'd'. Not pre-Shakespearian in *N.E.D.*, but Palsgrave, *Acolastus* (E.E.T.S.), 26. 34, translates 'male sanus' by 'not wel advysed'; Cooper, *Thesaurus*, s.v. *sanus, pro sano aliquid facere*, 'To doe a thing as it becometh one well advised or in his right minde'.

To gratify your honourable youth,
The hope of Rome, for so he bid me say;
And so I do, and with his gifts present
Your lordships, that, whenever you have need,   15
You may be armed and appointed well.
And so I leave you both, [*Aside.*] like bloody villains.

[*Exeunt Boy and Attendant.*

Dem. What's here? a scroll; and written round about;
Let's see:

Integer vitae, scelerisque purus,   20
Non eget Mauri iaculis, nec arcu.

Chi. O, 'tis a verse in Horace; I know it well:
I read it in the grammar long ago.
Aar. Ay, just; a verse in Horace; right, you have it.
[*Aside.*] Now, what a thing it is to be an ass!   25
Here's no sound jest! the old man hath found their
guilt,
And sends them weapons wrapp'd about with lines,
That wound, beyond their feeling, to the quick;
But were our witty empress well afoot,
She would applaud Andronicus' conceit: 30

13. bid] bad *Q3,F.*   15. that] *Pope; not in Qq,F.*   17. *Exeunt . . . Attendant*]
Capell; Exit Qq,F.   18. about;] about, *Qq;* about? *F.*   20–1.] *one line in Qq;*
two lines (prose) in F.   arcu] *Q1 (F2); arcus Q2–3,F.*   25. [*Aside.*]] *Johnson (so,*
unnecessarily, l. 48); not in Qq,F.   27. them] the *Q3,F.*

13. *bid*] See on II. iii. 186.
14. *his gifts*] I cannot see what is
wrong with these words, for which
Wilson proposes *his gift.*
17. *like . . . villains*] Q1 indicates the
aside by a capital for *Like*, preceded by
a rather long space and a colon after
both.
18. *round about*] all round; appropriate for a scroll. Not quite the same
as v. ii. 98, with which Wilson links it,
glossing both 'all over'.
20–1. Integer . . . arcu.] Horace,
Odes, I. xxii. 1–2: 'the man who is upright in life and free from crime does
not need the javelins or bow of the
Moor.' Possibly chosen in part with a
glance at Aaron the Moor.
23. *grammar*] Lily's Latin Grammar,
the standard text-book, in which the

quotation occurs twice, once with
Horace's name mentioned (H. R. D.
Anders, *Shakespeare's Books*, Berlin,
1904, p. 16). This second mention
is in the section on prosody, usually
begun (Baldwin, I. 579) in the fourth
form.
24. *just*] precisely, as often in expressions of assent, cf. *Meas.*, III. i. 65–6:
'*Claud.* Perpetual durance? | *Isab.* Ay,
just; perpetual durance.'
26. *Here's . . . jest!*] Ironical; see
Jonson, *E.M.I.*, IV. ii. 17, 'here's no
fopperie!'
28. *wound . . . quick*] A deliberate
paradox: they are wounded to the
quick though, because of their stu-
pidity, they do not feel it.
29. *witty*] quick-witted.
afoot] up and about (On.).

But let her rest in her unrest awhile.—
And now, young lords, was't not a happy star
Led us to Rome, strangers, and more than so,
Captives, to be advanced to this height?
It did me good before the palace gate   35
To brave the tribune in his brother's hearing.
Dem. But me more good, to see so great a lord
Basely insinuate and send us gifts.
Aar. Had he not reason, Lord Demetrius?
Did you not use his daughter very friendly?   40
Dem. I would we had a thousand Roman dames
At such a bay, by turn to serve our lust.
Chi. A charitable wish and full of love.
Aar. Here lacks but your mother for to say amen.
Chi. And that would she for twenty thousand more.   45
Dem. Come, let us go and pray to all the gods
For our beloved mother in her pains.
Aar. Pray to the devils; the gods have given us over.
                                    [*Trumpets sound.*
Dem. Why do the emperor's trumpets flourish thus?
Chi. Belike for joy the emperor hath a son.   50
Dem. Soft, who comes here?

Enter Nurse, with a blackamoor Child.

Nurse.   God morrow, lords.
O, tell me, did you see Aaron the Moor?

---

48. *Trumpets sound*] *Flourish* F.   51. God . . . lords] *so* F; *with l*. 52 *Qq*.   God]
Good *Q3,F*.

---

31. *rest . . . unrest*] See on II. iii. 8.

35-6. This has not happened in the play, as E. S. Brubaker notes in *Shakespeare Quarterly*, 3 (1952), 140. But it need not go back to an earlier version, as he conjectures.

38. *insinuate*] curry favour.

42. *At . . . bay*] cornered like that. A common metaphor from a hunted animal turning to face its pursuers.

43. *charitable . . . love*] Cf. Romans, xiii. 9–10. The collocation of *charitable* and *love* seems to reflect the controversy on the relative merits of *love* and

charity to render the Greek 'αγάπη. This is more clearly echoed in *LLL.*, IV. iii. 127 ('thy love is far from charity') and 365 ('who can sever love from charity?'). Of the main sixteenth-century versions, only the Bishops' Bible read *charity*. See Noble, pp. 140, 146.

45. *more*] i.e. more Roman dames.

50. *Belike*] probably.

51. *God morrow*] the full expression is '(God) give you good-morrow', which is variously contracted. Cf. *Godden* (IV. iv. 42).

Aar. Well, more or less, or ne'er a whit at all,
  Here Aaron is; and what with Aaron now?
Nurse. O gentle Aaron, we are all undone!   55
  Now help, or woe betide thee evermore!
Aar. Why, what a caterwauling dost thou keep!
  What dost thou wrap and fumble in thy arms?
Nurse. O, that which I would hide from heaven's eye,
  Our empress' shame, and stately Rome's disgrace.   60
  She is delivered, lords, she is delivered.
Aar. To whom?
Nurse.   I mean she is brought a-bed.
Aar. Well, God give her good rest! What hath he sent her?
Nurse. A devil.
Aar. Why, then she is the devil's dam: a joyful issue.   65
Nurse. A joyless, dismal, black, and sorrowful issue.
  Here is the babe, as loathsome as a toad
  Amongst the fair-fac'd breeders of our clime;
  The empress sends it thee, thy stamp, thy seal,
  And bids thee christen it with thy dagger's point.   70
Aar. 'Zounds, ye whore! is black so base a hue?
  Sweet blowse, you are a beauteous blossom, sure.
Dem. Villain, what hast thou done?
Aar. That which thou canst not undo.
Chi. Thou hast undone our mother.   75
Aar. Villain, I have done thy mother.

---

58. thy] thine *Q2–3,F.*   65.] Why . . . dam: (*with l. 64*) / A . . . issue. *Hanmer.*
68. fair-fac'd] *N.E.D.;* fairfast *Q1–2;* fairest *Q3,F.*   71. 'Zounds, ye] Out you
F.   76.] *not in F.*

53. *more*] With a pun on *Moor*, cf.
Mer.V., III. v. 44–5: 'It is much that the
Moor should be more than reason'
(Delius).
  65. *devil's dam*] See Tilley, D225.
  67. *loathsome as a toad*] See Tilley,
T361.
  68. *fair-fac'd*] For the Q1 spelling cf.
Q1 of *LLL.,* v. ii. 836: *smothfast.*
  71. *'Zounds*] The substitution of *Out*
in the Folio is the only trace in that
text of the influence of the 1606 Act
against profanity on the stage, for
which see Chambers, I. 238. The omission of l. 76 might also look like

bowdlerization, but must be acci-
dental: two successive lines end with
mother, and l. 77 is pointless without
l. 76; cf. l. 8.
  72. *blowse*] Normally 'a ruddy fat-
faced wench' (Johnson, *Dict.*). The
application to a black male baby is no
doubt a mere joke.
  76. *done*] had sexual intercourse
with. Puns on this are common. Cf.
Meas., I. ii. 93–4: 'What has he done?
—A woman' (Delius) and Mistress
Overdone in the same play. Tilley,
T200, quotes 'the thynge that is done
can not be undone' from Taverner's

Dem. And therein, hellish dog, thou hast undone her.
    Woe to her chance, and damn'd her loathed choice!
    Accurs'd the offspring of so foul a fiend!
Chi. It shall not live.   80
Aar. It shall not die.
Nurse. Aaron, it must; the mother wills it so.
Aar. What, must it, nurse? then let no man but I
    Do execution on my flesh and blood.
Dem. I'll broach the tadpole on my rapier's point: 85
    Nurse, give it me; my sword shall soon dispatch it.
Aar. Sooner this sword shall plough thy bowels up.
    Stay, murtherous villains! will you kill your brother?
    Now, by the burning tapers of the sky
    That shone so brightly when this boy was got,   90
    He dies upon my scimitar's sharp point
    That touches this my first-born son and heir.
    I tell you, younglings, not Enceladus,
    With all his threat'ning band of Typhon's brood,
    Nor great Alcides, nor the god of war,   95
    Shall seize this prey out of his father's hands.
    What, what, ye sanguine, shallow-hearted boys!
    Ye white-lim'd walls! ye alehouse painted signs!
    Coal-black is better than another hue
    In that it scorns to bear another hue,   100
    For all the water in the ocean

---

77. her] *not in Q3,F.*   95. Alcides] *Alciades Q1.*   98. white-lim'd] *F3;*
whitelimde *Q1;* white limbde *Q2–3;* white-limb'd *F.*

Proverbs (1539), and *O.D.E.P.*, p. 154, analogous sayings as early as Chaucer.

    85. *broach*] 'stick on a sword's point as on a spit' (On.).

    93. *Enceladus*] One of the Titans (sons of Typhon, l. 94) who fought against the gods.

    95. *Alcides*] Heracles, grandson of Alcaeus.

    97. *sanguine*] red-faced (in contrast to black).

    98. *white-lim'd walls*] Perhaps a reference to Matthew, xxiii. 27: 'whited sepulchres'. Wilson quotes *Piers Plowman* (C), xvii. 264–7:

'Ypocrisie . . . is ylikned in Latyn . . . to a wal white-lymed and were blak with-innes.'

    alehouse . . . signs] 'crudely painted' (Wilson, quoting (after Delius) *2H6,* III. ii. 81: 'make my image but an alehouse sign').

    99–100. *Coal-black . . . hue*] See *O.D.E.P.*, p. 49: 'Black will take no other hue', first quoted from Heywood (1546). The notion that black is the best colour is found in Sandford's *Garden of Pleasure* (1573): Tilley, G172.

    101–3. *For . . . flood*] Either this, or a common proverbial source, must lie behind Heywood, *The Captives* (Malone

Can never turn the swan's black legs to white,
Although she lave them hourly in the flood.
Tell the empress from me, I am of age
To keep mine own, excuse it how she can.   105
Dem. Wilt thou betray thy noble mistress thus?
Aar. My mistress is my mistress; this my self;
The vigour and the picture of my youth:
This before all the world do I prefer;
This maugre all the world will I keep safe,   110
Or some of you shall smoke for it in Rome.
Dem. By this our mother is for ever sham'd.
Chi. Rome will despise her for this foul escape.
Nurse. The emperor in his rage will doom her death.
Chi. I blush to think upon this ignomy.   115
Aar. Why, there's the privilege your beauty bears.
Fie, treacherous hue, that will betray with
      blushing
The close enacts and counsels of thy heart!
Here's a young lad fram'd of another leer:
Look how the black slave smiles upon the father,   120
As who should say, 'Old lad, I am thine own.'
He is your brother, lords, sensibly fed
Of that self blood that first gave life to you;
And from that womb where you imprisoned were

---

115. *ignomy*] ignominie *F.*   118. *thy*] the *Q3,F.*   124. *that*] your *Q1–2.*

Soc. Reprint), 14–16, 'The stayneles swanne, / wth all the Oceans water canott wash / the blacknes ffrom her ffeete, tis borne with her.' See *O.D.E.P.*, p. 693: 'To wash a blacka-moor (Ethiopian) white', first quoted from Becon (1543).

110. *maugre*] in spite of.

111. *smoke for it*] suffer for it. *N.E.D.* 4 notes 'in early use with allusion to ac-tual burning', but links one later quo-tation with sense 2, under which Hey-wood, 1533, is specially relevant, 'When I have beten her tyll she smoke.' This may be the force of the figure here. On. glosses 'have a "warm" time of it'.

113. *escape*] 'outrageous transgres-sion' (On., who describes the sense as 'peculiarly Shakespearian'). Wilson

adds that it is used especially of sexual offences. Delius happily glosses 'faux pas'.

115. *ignomy*] This shortened form of *ignominy* is common.

118. *close enacts*] secret purposes.

119. *leer*] complexion.

122. *sensibly*] 'as a creature endowed with feeling' (On.). This is not entirely satisfactory. Wilson suggests 'plainly' as an alternative, and Ridley 'till capable of sensation', which is toler-ably good sense, but hard to get out of the word.

123. *self*] same.

124. *that womb*] I agree with Dr Alice Walker (see p. xii) that *your* which I accepted in 1953, is intoler-ably awkward.

He is enfranchised and come to light: 125
Nay, he is your brother by the surer side,
Although my seal be stamped in his face.
Nurse. Aaron, what shall I say unto the empress?
Dem. Advise thee, Aaron, what is to be done,
 And we will all subscribe to thy advice: 130
 Save thou the child, so we may all be safe.
Aar. Then sit we down, and let us all consult.
 My son and I will have the wind of you:
 Keep there; now talk at pleasure of your safety.
Dem. How many women saw this child of his?   135
Aar. Why, so, brave lords! when we join in league,
 I am a lamb; but if you brave the Moor,
 The chafed boar, the mountain lioness,
 The ocean swells not so as Aaron storms.
 But say again, how many saw the child?   140
Nurse. Cornelia the midwife, and myself,
 And no one else but the delivered empress.
Aar. The empress, the midwife, and yourself:
 Two may keep counsel when the third's away:
 Go to the empress; tell her this I said.   [*He kills her.*   145
 'Wheak, wheak!'

136. we] we all *F2.* join] are join'd *Maxwell conj.* 142. no one] none *F.*
146–7.]*so Camb.; one line Qq,F.* 146.Wheak,wheak]*N.E.D.;*Weeke,weeke*Qq,F.*

125. *enfranchised*] Baildon compares
Wint., II. ii. 59–61: 'This child
was prisoner to the womb and is /
By law and process of great nature
thence / Freed and enfranchis'd.'
 126. *surer side*] *O.D.E.P.*, p. 435, and
Tilley, M1205, quote from Hall's
Chronicle (1548), in a speech attributed
to Henry V: 'if the old and trite proverb be true that the woman's side is
the surer side'.
 130. *subscribe to*] acquiesce in.
 131. *so*] See on II. i. 102.
 133. *have the wind of*] 'keep watch
upon (as upon game when following it
down the wind)' (On.).
 136. *join*] The metrical irregularity
may be justified by a pause after *lords*
but I suspect the true reading is *are
join'd*: *ioind* might have been misread
as *ioine*, and *are* omitted in con-
sequence.

138. *chafed*] enraged, an epithet frequently used of an animal brought
to bay, as Wilson points out on *John*,
III. i. 259. But that is not to say that
it *means* 'brought to bay' as he glosses
it here.
 143. *empress*] See on I. i. 89.
 144. *Two . . . away*] See *O.D.E.P.*,
p. 330: 'Three (two) may keep counsel
if two (one) be away', first quoted from
Romance of the Rose, c. 1400. Though
this is treated as a single proverb, it is
really two proverbs, the point of
which is not the same. We can have, as
here, a proverb asserting that two can
keep a secret whereas three cannot, or
else (as in *Rom.*, II. iv. 211: 'Two may
keep counsel, putting one away') one
asserting, more ironically, that the
only safe secret is one that *no* one
shares.
 146. *Wheak*] squeak.

So cries a pig prepared to the spit.

Dem. What mean'st thou, Aaron? wherefore didst thou this?

Aar. O Lord, sir, 'tis a deed of policy:

Shall she live to betray this guilt of ours,   150
A long-tongu'd babbling gossip? no, lords, no.
And now be it known to you my full intent.
Not far, one Muly lives, my countryman;
His wife but yesternight was brought to bed.
His child is like to her, fair as you are: 155
Go pack with him, and give the mother gold,
And tell them both the circumstance of all,
And how by this their child shall be advanc'd,
And be received for the emperor's heir,
And substituted in the place of mine,   160
To calm this tempest whirling in the court;
And let the emperor dandle him for his own.
Hark ye, lords; you see I have given her physic,
And you must needs bestow her funeral;
The fields are near, and you are gallant grooms.   165
This done, see that you take no longer days,
But send the midwife presently to me.
The midwife and the nurse well made away,
Then let the ladies tattle what they please.

153. Muly lives,] *Steevens conj.; Muliteus Qq,F;* Muliteus lives, *Rowe.*   163. you] ye *Q3,F.*

149. *policy*] See on II. i. 104.

151. *babbling gossip*] See on II. iii. 17.

153. *Muly lives*] Steevens's excellent correction. The MS. probably read *Muli leues* (cf. Wilson, *The Manuscript of Shakespeare's Hamlet,* p. 105, for *live* spelt *leue* and set up as *leaue* in Q2 of *Ham.,* III. iv. 158), or conceivably, though this would be odd, *leus. Muly* as a Moorish name occurs in Peele's *Battle of Alcazar.* At the same time, very odd pseudo-classical names are not surprising in this play, and 'Muliteus my countryman his wife' for 'the wife of Muliteus my countryman' would not be an abnormal construction, so the original text may be sound. But 'not far' goes much more happily with 'lives' than with 'was brought to bed'. Qq,F do not punctuate at the end of the line, which slightly favours the original text. Alexander retains 'Muliteus' but puts a dash at the end of the line to indicate an anacoluthon, thus making the worst of both worlds.

156. *pack*] conspire, come to an arrangement.

164. *bestow*] Rare with an indirect object instead of with 'on', but also found in Swift.

165. *grooms*] fellows.

166. *days*] time. Wilson compares *Troil.,* IV. v. 12: "Tis but early days', and *nowadays* implies a similar use.

167. *presently*] immediately.

Chi. Aaron, I see thou wilt not trust the air   170
    With secrets.
Dem.   For this care of Tamora,
    Herself and hers are highly bound to thee.   [*Exeunt.*
Aar. Now to the Goths, as swift as swallow flies,
    There to dispose this treasure in mine arms,
    And secretly to greet the empress' friends.   175
    Come on, you thick-lipp'd slave, I'll bear you hence;
    For it is you that puts us to our shifts;
    I'll make you feed on berries and on roots,
    And feed on curds and whey, and suck the goat,
    And cabin in a cave, and bring you up   180
    To be a warrior, and command a camp.   [*Exit.*

SCENE III

Enter TITUS, *old* MARCUS, *young* LUCIUS, *and other Gentlemen,
with bows, and Titus bears the arrows with letters on the ends
of them.*

Tit. Come, Marcus, come; kinsmen, this is the way.
    Sir boy, let me see your archery:
    Look ye draw home enough, and 'tis there straight.

170–1. Aaron . . . secrets] *so Theobald; one line in Qq,F.*   179. feed] feast *Hanmer.*

Scene III
Scene III.] *Capell; not in Qq,F.*   ends] end *F.*   2. let] now let *F2.*

173. *as . . . flies*] The same metaphor in II. ii. 24. The comparison is already proverbial for T. Wilson, *Rule of Reason* (1551), cited by Tilley, S1023.

176. *thick-lipp'd*] A typical feature of a blackamoor also in *Oth.*, I. i. 66.

177. *puts . . . shifts*] 'bring to extremity' (*N.E.D.*): here not quite so strong, perhaps 'cause trouble'. The still more literal meaning 'cause to have recourse to stratagems' (here and in the similar phrase at IV. i. 72) makes good sense, but the idiom seems to have developed along less specific

lines. Cf. *Revenger's Tragedy*, IV. ii. 2: 'How that great villain puts me to my shifts.' The earliest *N.E.D.* quotation (1553) is antedated by one from Borde (1542), cited by F. P. Wilson, *R.E.S.*, n.s. 3 (1952), 198.

180. *cabin*] lodge.

Scene III
3. *home*] to the full extent. More common with verb of striking, and in metaphors therefrom, but here it refers to the stretching of the bow necessary to ensure that the arrow gets 'home'.

Terras Astraea reliquit: Be you rememb'red, Marcus,
She's gone, she's fled. Sirs, take you to your tools.   5
You, cousins, shall go sound the ocean,
And cast your nets;
Happily you may catch her in the sea;
Yet there's as little justice as at land.
No; Publius and Sempronius, you must do it;   10
'Tis you must dig with mattock and with spade,
And pierce the inmost centre of the earth:
Then, when you come to Pluto's region,
I pray you, deliver him this petition;
Tell him, it is for justice and for aid,   15
And that it comes from old Andronicus,
Shaken with sorrows in ungrateful Rome.
Ah, Rome! Well, well, I made thee miserable
What time I threw the people's suffrages
On him that thus doth tyrannize o'er me.   20
Go, get you gone; and pray be careful all,
And leave you not a man-of-war unsearch'd:
This wicked emperor may have shipp'd her hence;
And kinsmen, then we may go pipe for justice.
Marc. O Publius, is not this a heavy case,   25
        To see thy noble uncle thus distract?

4–8.] *Capell divides after* reliquit, fled, shall, nets, sea.   7–8.] *divided by Maxwell;*
one line in Qq,F.   8. Happily] haply *F.*   catch] finde *Q3,F.*   26. thus] this *Q2.*

4. Terras . . . reliquit] the goddess of
justice has left the earth (Ovid, *Met.*, I.
150). See F. A. Yates, 'Queen Eliza-
beth as Astraea' in *Journal of the War-
burg and Courtauld Institutes*, 10 (1947),
27–82. (I owe this reference to Mr
Peter Ure.) Miss Yates deals with the
identification of Astraea with the constellation Virgo (l. 64 below), e.g. in
Spenser, *F.Q.*, v. i. 11, VII. vii. 37,
and (p. 71) suggests that in *Titus* 'the
good empire [i.e. the golden age]
returns with Lucius' who bears the
name of the traditional first king of
England, and that 'it is perhaps
a very significant detail that it was
Lucius who hit Virgo in the shooting scene and therefore, presumably, brought her down to earth.' I

am sceptical about this last point.
Be you rememb'red] remember.
7–8. *And . . . sea*] By dividing this
line only, and leaving the earlier part
of the passage lineated as in Qq,F, I
have dealt less violently with these
lines than has been customary since
Capell.
8. *Happily*] perhaps; this form and
'haply' are interchangeable in Shakespeare's English.
11–12. *'Tis . . . earth*] Titus' behaviour in this scene recalls that of
Hieronymo in Kyd's *Spanish Tragedy*,
III. xii–xiii. Robertson quotes xii. 71–5,
xiii. 108–10.
24. *pipe for*] 'look for in vain,
"whistle for"' (On.).
26. *distract*] See on I. i. 462.

Pub. Therefore, my lords, it highly us concerns
  By day and night t' attend him carefully,
  And feed his humour kindly as we may,
  Till time beget some careful remedy.   30
Marc. Kinsmen, his sorrows are past remedy,   31
  But * * *   31*a*
  Join with the Goths, and with revengeful war
  Take wreak on Rome for this ingratitude,
  And vengeance on the traitor Saturnine.
Tit. Publius, how now! how now, my masters!   35
  What, have you met with her?
Pub. No, my good lord; but Pluto sends you word,
  If you will have Revenge from hell, you shall:
  Marry, for Justice, she is so employ'd,
  He thinks, with Jove in heaven, or somewhere else, 40
  So that perforce you must needs stay a time.
Tit. He doth me wrong to feed me with delays.
  I'll dive into the burning lake below,
  And pull her out of Acheron by the heels.
  Marcus, we are but shrubs, no cedars we;   45
  No big-bon'd men fram'd of the Cyclops' size;
  But metal, Marcus, steel to the very back,
  Yet wrung with wrongs more than our backs can bear:

---

27. lords] lord *F2*. 30. careful] cureful *Schmidt conj.;* easeful *W. S. Walker.*
31*a.*] *See note.* 32. Join] But *Q1 catchword.* 48. backs] backe *F.*

30. *careful*] 'costing trouble' (Wilson).

31*a. But*] The catchword shows that at least a line has dropped out before *Join.* I suspect that it contains the words *let us* and that *Join* is infinitive. Q1 has no punctuation at the end of l. 31.

33. *wreak*] vengeance. Wilson is mistaken in saying that the noun does not occur in Shakespeare outside this play: cf. *Cor.,* IV. v. 91.

43. *burning lake*] Probably Phlegethon, though this is properly a river. Cf. Marlowe, *Faustus* (ed. Boas), III. i. 48–9: 'the fiery lake / Of everburning Phlegethon', and Kyd, *Spanish Tragedy,* III. xii. 11: 'the lake where hell doth stand', as well as

'the burning lake' (*2H6,* I. iv. 42).

44. *Acheron*] Apparently used generally for 'hell'. Wilson considers that it is a lake here (so in Sackville, *Induction,* 480).

45. *shrubs . . . cedars*] Contrasted also in *Lucr.,* 664: 'The cedar stoops not to the base shrub's foot' (Wilson). Tilley, C208, quotes various phrases to the effect that the shrub can survive where the cedar succumbs, the earliest *c.* 1592. The cedar and the hyssop are the extremes of the vegetable kingdom in 1 Kings, iv. 33.

46. *Cyclops'*] Giants in Homer's *Odyssey* IX.

47. *steel . . . back*] *O.D.E.P.,* p. 620, and Tilley, S842, cite 'steele to the backe' from Lyly's *Euphues* (1578).

And sith there's no justice in earth nor hell,
We will solicit heaven and move the gods   50
To send down Justice for to wreak our wrongs.
Come, to this gear. You are a good archer, Marcus.
                              [*He gives them the arrows.*
Ad Jovem, that's for you: here, *Ad Apollinem*:
Ad Martem, that's for myself:
Here, boy, to Pallas: here, to Mercury: 55
To Saturn, Caius, not to Saturnine;
You were as good to shoot against the wind.
To it, boy! Marcus, loose when I bid.
Of my word, I have written to effect;
There's not a god left unsolicited.   60
Marc. Kinsmen, shoot all your shafts into the court:
    We will afflict the emperor in his pride.
Tit. Now, masters, draw. O, well said, Lucius!
    Good boy, in Virgo's lap: give it Pallas.
Marc. My lord, I aim'd a mile beyond the moon;   65
    Your letter is with Jupiter by this.

---

56. Saturn, Caius] *Capell; Saturnine* to *Caius Qq,F.*   65. aim'd] *Hudson;* aime
Qq,F.   66. Jupiter] *Iubiter Q1.*

49–50. *And . . . gods*] A reversal of
Virgil, *Aen.*, VII. 312: 'flectere si
nequeo superos, Acheronta movebo'
('If Jove and heaven my just desires
deny, / Hell shall the power of
heaven and Jove supply!' (Dryden)),
as Douce noted, *Illustrations of Shake-*
speare (1807), II. 116.

52. *gear*] business, rather than
(Ridley) 'arms'.

56. *Caius*] The corrections seem certain, cf. v. ii. 151. For the 'Saturn . . .
Saturnine' antithesis, see Introduction,
p. xxx, n. 5.

57. *were . . . shoot*] would do as much
good by shooting. The original sense
of this idiom is literally: 'it would be as
good to you', but long before Shakespeare's time the phrase had come to
be used with a personal subject.

63. *well said*] well done.

64. *Virgo*] the constellation: see on
l. 4. This passage may be indebted, as
R. A. Law suggests (*S.P.*, 40 (1943),

150–1), to the Chorus's description of
the 'disarrangement of the zodiacal
signs in view of Atreus's crime' in
Seneca, *Thyestes*, 844 ff.

65. *aim'd*] I think Hudson's correction (implying the corruption *d : e*) is
unavoidable. Cf. *O.D.E.P.*, p. 81: 'cast
beyond the moon' (i.e. 'indulge in wild
conjectures'), first quoted from Heywood (1546). Marcus expresses his
sense of the futility of Titus' actions,
while at the same time the literal
meaning of his words is calculated to
satisfy Titus.

66. *Jupiter*] Spelt *Iubiter* here and at
ll. 78, 82, 83. Only in the last of these is
it required, as a misunderstanding by
the Clown. Wilson suggests that the
other occurrences are the result of
changes 'on the press or in proof'. This
is not entirely satisfactory, and implies
more careful proof-correction than we
should expect. Moreover, the form is
not a sheer illiterate blunder, but a

Tit. Ha, ha! Publius, Publius, what hast thou done?
    See, see, thou hast shot off one of Taurus' horns.
Marc. This was the sport, my lord: when Publius shot,
    The Bull, being gall'd, gave Aries such a knock   70
    That down fell both the Ram's horns in the court;
    And who should find them but the empress' villain?
    She laugh'd, and told the Moor he should not
        choose
    But give them to his master for a present.
Tit. Why, there it goes: God give his lordship joy!   75

    Enter the Clown, with a basket, and two pigeons in it.

    News, news from heaven! Marcus, the post is come.
    Sirrah, what tidings? have you any letters?
    Shall I have justice? what says Jupiter?
Clo. Ho, the gibbet-maker? He says that he hath taken
    them down again, for the man must not be hang'd   80
    till the next week.
Tit. But what says Jupiter, I ask thee?
Clo. Alas, sir, I know not Jubiter; I never drank with
    him in all my life.
Tit. Why, villain, art not thou the carrier?   85
Clo. Ay, of my pigeons, sir; nothing else.
Tit. Why, didst thou not come from heaven?

75. his] your *Q3,F.*   76.] *so Rowe (3rd ed.); two lines divided, after* heaven, *in Qq,F.*   News] *Clowne.* Newes *Q1.*   78. Jupiter] *Iubiter Q1.*   79. Ho,] Who? *Rowe; O, Camb.*   82. Jupiter] *Iubiter Q1.*   83–4.] *prose Capell; verse, divided after* Jupiter, *Qq,F.*   83. Jubiter] *Iupiter Q2–3,F.*   87. Why,] Why *Q1.*

current spelling in Middle English and later (Wyld, pp. 312–13), and it is conceivable that Shakespeare used it throughout to lead up to the joke in l. 84. But that joke seems to depend on the Clown's pronunciation seeming odd to the audience, so that I have, with some hesitation, followed Wilson in retaining *Jubiter* only in l. 83.

    by this] Cf. III. i. 109.

68. *Taurus*] the Bull (sign of the zodiac). Aries (l. 70) is the Ram.

71. *horns*] The usual joke on cuckoldry.

72. *villain*] servant, with a play on the modern sense, as in *AYL.*, I. i. 60.

75. *there it goes*] 'the hunter's cry of encouragement' (Wilson, comparing *Tp.*, IV. i. 259).

79. *Ho*] An exclamation of mild surprise at the question seems in place, hence (with Delius and Alexander) I return to the Qq,F text.

    gibbet-maker] The same misunderstanding, also by a Clown, occurs in Heywood's *Golden Age* (*a.* 1611), Act III (Sh. Soc. ed., 1851, p. 46).

83. *Jubiter*] See on l. 66.

Clo. From heaven? alas, sir, I never came there. God
    forbid I should be so bold to press to heaven in my
    young days. Why, I am going with my pigeons to   90
    the tribunal plebs, to take up a matter of brawl be-
    twixt my uncle and one of the emperal's men.

Marc. Why, sir, that is as fit as can be to serve for your
    oration; and let him deliver the pigeons to the
    emperor from you.   95

Tit. Tell me, can you deliver an oration to the emperor
    with a grace?

Clo. Nay, truly, sir, I could never say grace in all my
    life.

Tit. Sirrah, come hither: make no more ado,   100
    But give your pigeons to the emperor:
    By me thou shalt have justice at his hands.
    Hold, hold; meanwhile here's money for thy charges.
    Give me pen and ink.   104
    Sirrah, can you with a grace deliver up a supplication?

Clo. Ay, sir.

---

88. From . . . there] *prose Pope; separate line of verse Qq,F.*   90. Why] *begins new line in Qq.*   92. emperal's] Emperialls *Q2–3,F.*   105. up] *not in Q2–3,F.*

88–90. *God . . . days*] Greg, *The Shakespeare First Folio* (1955), pp. 203–4, taking up a suggestion he first made in *The Library*, 4 ser. 13 (1922–3), 141, notes that 'the typographical arrangement [as a separate paragraph] suggests that this unquestionably Shakespearian sally was a marginal addition.'

91–2. *tribunal plebs . . . emperal's*] Malapropisms for *tribunus plebis* and *emperor's*. Wilson (who compares Launce's 'Imperial court', *Gent.*, II. iii. 5, already cited by Delius) notes that 'the Clown is also seeking for justice', but, more realistically than Titus, 'with a bribe'.

91. *take up*] settle (amicably).

92. *emperal's*] This malapropism recurs in Beaumont and Fletcher, *Knight of the Burning Pestle*, II. i (ed. Waller, VI. 183).

96–7. *Tell . . . grace?*] Wilson notes

that this question is virtually repeated at l. 106, and suggests 'duplication owing to revision', with ll. 94–100 and ll. 101–7 as alternatives, the latter being the later 'because it is not, like the other, detachable from the text'. It looks to me more like 'foul papers' not finally tidied up—the dividing line between this and revision is never easy to draw. The lines that could be most easily dispensed with are ll. 97–100: the pun on *grace* may be an afterthought, to which the rest of the passage was not adjusted. I cannot see that Marcus' speech, ll. 94–6, goes any more closely with ll. 97–100 than with what follows.

103. *Hold*] here you are.

meanwhile] Rather obscure whether it is taken (Qq,F and most editors) with what follows or (Delius) with *Hold*. Perhaps it means 'to keep you going until you get justice'.

Tit. Then here is a supplication for you. And when you
    come to him, at the first approach you must kneel;
    then kiss his foot; then deliver up your pigeons; and
    then look for your reward. I'll be at hand, sir; see   110
    you do it bravely.
Clo. I warrant you, sir; let me alone.
Tit. Sirrah, hast thou a knife? Come, let me see it.
    Here Marcus, fold it in the oration;
    For thou hast made it like an humble suppliant: 115
    And when thou hast given it to the emperor,
    Knock at my door, and tell me what he says.
Clo. God be with you, sir; I will.   [*Exit.*
Tit. Come, Marcus, let us go. Publius, follow me.   [*Exeunt.*

SCENE IV

*Enter Emperor and Empress and her two sons; the Emperor brings the
arrows in his hand that Titus shot at him.*

Sat. Why, lords, what wrongs are these! Was ever seen
    An emperor in Rome thus overborne,
    Troubled, confronted thus; and, for the extent

115. For] So, *Maxwell conj.*   116. to] *not in Q3,F.*

Scene IV

Scene IV.] *Capell; not in Qq,F.*

111. *bravely*] in good style (Rolfe,
who compares *Tp.*, III. iii. 83–4:
'Bravely the figure of this harpy hast
thou / Perform'd').

112. *let me alone*] See on I. i. 449.

115. *For . . . suppliant*] I do not understand this. Is 'it' the knife or the oration? If the latter, we have the difficulty noted by Wilson that this 'seems
to imply that Marcus wrote the letter',
which disagrees with l. 105. (I cannot
see why Wilson thinks it is even in
agreement with ll. 94–6.) In either
case, what is the point of 'for'? I am
tempted to suggest that between ll. 115
and 116 Marcus does as Titus has
asked him, and that Titus then says:

'So [i.e. 'that's good', as in *H8*, IV. ii.
3–4: 'Reach a chair: / So'], thou hast
etc.' ('For' and 'So' are confused in
Donne's *Extasie*, l. 59.) With this interpretation, 'it' would be 'the knife
wrapped in the oration'. Or, with the
same interpretation, we could read
'Now'. The only permissible alternative, which seems very weak but
does give a meaning to 'for', is to take
'it' as the oration (with the difficulties
mentioned), and to suppose Titus to be
asking Marcus to fold the knife in it in
order that it may *no longer* be a humble
suppliant.

Scene IV

3. *extent*] exercise.

Of egal justice, us'd in such contempt?
My lords, you know, as know the mightful gods,   5
However these disturbers of our peace
Buzz in the people's ears, there nought hath pass'd
But even with law against the wilful sons
Of old Andronicus. And what and if
His sorrows have so overwhelm'd his wits?   10
Shall we be thus afflicted in his wreaks,
His fits, his frenzy, and his bitterness?
And now he writes to heaven for his redress:
See, here's to Jove, and this to Mercury;
This to Apollo; this to the god of war;   15
Sweet scrolls to fly about the streets of Rome!
What's this but libelling against the senate,
And blazoning our injustice every where?
A goodly humour, is it not, my lords?
As who would say, in Rome no justice were.   20
But if I live, his feigned ecstasies
Shall be no shelter to these outrages;
But he and his shall know that justice lives
In Saturninus' health; whom, if she sleep,
He'll so awake, as she in fury shall   25

5. know, as know] *Camb.;* know *Qq,F.*   18. unjustice] Iniustice *F.*   24.
whom] who (*retaining* he . . . he) *Capell.*   she] *Rowe;* he *Qq,F.*   25. she]
Rowe; he *Qq,F.*

4. *egal*] equal: this form, through
French instead of direct from Latin,
was still common.

8. *even*] 'in exact agreement' (On.).

11. *wreaks*] 'vindictive acts' (On.);
cf. on IV. iii. 33.

17. *libelling*] making libellous state-
ments. This line may be echoed in
Marlowe's *Edward II* (ed. Charlton
and Waller), II. ii. 34–5: 'What call
you this but private libelling / Against
the earl of Cornwall and my brother?'
(cited by Verity).

18. *blazoning*] proclaiming; a metaphor from heraldry.

20. *were*] For subjunctive *be* and
were after *say, think* etc., see Franz §640,
Abbott §§299, 301; cf. *1H4,* II. i. 15–16:
'I think this be the most villainous

house in all London road for fleas';
1H6, II. i. 46: 'I think this Talbot be a
fiend of hell.'

21. *feigned ecstasies*] Baildon notes
that Saturninus alone, being 'of a suspicious and cowardly temperament',
seems to suspect that Titus' madness
is not genuine. On *ecstasies*, cf. IV. i.
125.

25. *she*] Almost certainly correct
here, I think, as well as in l. 24. The one
corruption would naturally lead to the
other, and the sense is much better.
With Capell's *who* the antecedent is
Saturninus, but there seems no reason
why Saturninus should grant, even for
the sake of argument, that he himself
is asleep. Cf. *R3,* I. iii. 287–8: 'I will not
think but they [i.e. my curses] ascend

Cut off the proud'st conspirator that lives.
Tam. My gracious lord, my lovely Saturnine,
　　　Lord of my life, commander of my thoughts,
　　　Calm thee, and bear the faults of Titus' age,
　　　Th' effects of sorrow for his valiant sons,　　　　30
　　　Whose loss hath pierc'd him deep and scarr'd his heart;
　　　And rather comfort his distressed plight
　　　Than prosecute the meanest or the best
　　　For these contempts. [*Aside.*] Why, thus it shall become
　　　High-witted Tamora to gloze with all:　　　　35
　　　But, Titus, I have touch'd thee to the quick;
　　　Thy life-blood out, if Aaron now be wise,
　　　Then is all safe, the anchor in the port.

Enter Clown.

How now, good fellow! would'st thou speak with us?
Clo. Yea, forsooth, and your mistress-ship be emperial.　　　40
Tam. Empress I am, but yonder sits the emperor.
Clo. 'Tis he. God and Saint Stephen give you godden. I
　　　have brought you a letter and a couple of pigeons
　　　here.　　　　　　　　　　　　　　　[*He reads the letter.*
Sat. Go, take him away, and hang him presently.　　　　45
Clo. How much money must I have?
Tam. Come, sirrah, you must be hanged.
Clo. Hang'd, by' lady! then I have brought up a neck to
　　　a fair end.　　　　　　　　　　　　　　　[*Exit.*

34. [*Aside.*]] F (*end of l. 35*); *not in Qq.*　　36–7. quick;... out,] *Maxwell;* quicke,
... out: *Qq,F.*　　life-blood] life-blood's *Koeppel conj.*　　38. anchor] Anchor's
Q3,F.　　40. mistress-ship] *Johnson;* Mistriship *Q1;* Mistership *Q2–3,F.*　　42.
godden] good den *Q3,F.*　　45–6. presently.... have?] presently? ... haue.
Q1–2.　　48. by' lady] be Lady *Qq;* ber Lady *F.*

the sky, / And there awake God's
gentle-sleeping peace.'
　35. *gloze*] use fair words.
　36. *touch'd*] wounded. The phrase
'touch on the quick' is quoted by
Tilley, Q13, from Skelton's *Magnificence* (*c.* 1516).
　37. *Thy ... out*] I think this means
'once thy life-blood is out', and is subordinate to 'Then all is safe.' Koeppel's
conjecture is in *Englische Studien*, 35
(1906), 126.

　42. *godden*] See on IV. ii. 51.
　48. *by' lady*] The Q spelling is
paralleled in another text probably
printed from Shakespeare's MS., Q2 of
Ham., II. ii. 454: 'by lady' (Q1 : *burlady;*
F: *Byrlady*). 'By (be) lady' is quite a
common form and occurs in the early
editions of *The Batchelars Banquet*
(1603), p. 10, l. 13, of F. P. Wilson's
edition (1929), and in *Eastward Ho!*
(ed. Herford and Simpson), II. ii. 374;
The Trial of Treasure, sig. C3ᵛ; *Jack*

Sat. Despiteful and intolerable wrongs! 50
Shall I endure this monstrous villainy?
I know from whence this same device proceeds.
May this be borne as if his traitorous sons
That died by law for murther of our brother
Have by my means been butchered wrongfully? 55
Go, drag the villain hither by the hair;
Nor age nor honour shall shape privilege.
For this proud mock I'll be thy slaughterman,
Sly frantic wretch, that holp'st to make me great,
In hope thyself should govern Rome and me. 60

Enter Æmilius.

What news with thee, Æmilius?
Æmil. Arm, my lords! Rome never had more cause.
The Goths have gathered head, and with a power
Of high-resolved men, bent to the spoil,
They hither march amain, under conduct 65
Of Lucius, son to old Andronicus;
Who threats, in course of his revenge, to do
As much as ever Coriolanus did.
Sat. Is warlike Lucius general of the Goths?

---

53. borne] borne, *Q2–3;* borne? *F.*   55. butchered] butcher'd *F.*   wrong-
fully?] wrongfully. *Q1–2.*   60. Æmilius] *Theobald; Nutius (Nuntius Q2–3,F)
Emillius Qq,F.*   62. Arm] Arm, arm *Warburton (Ravenscroft).*   lords] lord
Capell (Ravenscroft).   63. gathered] gather'd *F.*   67. his] *Rowe;* this *Qq,F.*

Straw (Malone Soc. Reprints), l. 505;
Locrine, II. iv. 90; *Mucedorus,* II. ii. 42;
R. Johnson, *Tom a Lincoln,* in *Early
English Prose Romances,* ed. W. J.
Thoms, p. 640; Beaumont and Fletcher, *Knight of the Burning Pestle,* I. i
(ed. Waller, VI. 176); *Wild Goose
Chase,* III. i (ed. Waller, IV. 357). I
multiply examples in the hope of en-
suring that the expression never again
gets emended.

53. *this . . . as if*] Virtually 'this accu-
sation that'; cf. on III. ii. 72.

57. *shape privilege*] create immunity.

58. *slaughterman*] executioner: *deaths-
man* also occurs in this sense, *2H6,* III.
ii. 217.

59. *holp'st*] Still commoner in
Shakespeare than the modern (weak)
past.

60. S.D. app. crit. Nutius] In error
for 'Nuntius' (= messenger), contracted 'Nūtius'. The use of this word
is no indication of classical imitation:
it is found already in Miracle Plays, cf.
York Mystery Plays, ed. L. Toulmin
Smith, p. 148.

62. *Arm . . . lords*] The corrections by
Warburton and Capell are both
plausible.

67. *his*] The confusion of *this* and *his*
is so common that I accept Rowe's
correction, which gives a more normal
expression.

These tidings nip me, and I hang the head   70
As flowers with frost, or grass beat down with storms.
Ay, now begins our sorrows to approach:
'Tis he the common people love so much;
Myself hath often heard them say,
When I have walked like a private man,   75
That Lucius' banishment was wrongfully,
And they have wish'd that Lucius were their emperor.

Tam. Why should you fear? is not your city strong?

Sat. Ay, but the citizens favour Lucius,
And will revolt from me to succour him.   80

Tam. King, be thy thoughts imperious, like thy name!
Is the sun dimm'd, that gnats do fly in it?
The eagle suffers little birds to sing,
And is not careful what they mean thereby,
Knowing that with the shadow of his wings   85
He can at pleasure stint their melody;
Even so mayest thou the giddy men of Rome.
Then cheer thy spirit; for know thou, emperor,
I will enchant the old Andronicus
With words more sweet, and yet more dangerous,   90
Than baits to fish, or honey-stalks to sheep,
When as the one is wounded with the bait,
The other rotted with delicious feed.

---

78. your] our *F.*   88. know thou,] *Kittredge;* know thou *Qq,F;* know, thou *F4.*
93. feed] *Q3;* seede *Q1–2;* foode *F.*

---

72. *begins*] See on II. i. 26.

74–5. *Myself . . . man*] A curious isolated reference to the theme of the disguised ruler (in the manner of Harun al Rashid), common on the English stage in Shakespeare's time; e.g. *Measure for Measure,* Chapman's *Blind Beggar of Alexandria,* Middleton's *Phoenix.* See W. Creizenach, *The English Drama in the Age of Shakespeare* (1916), pp. 221–3. The practice is recommended by Sir Thomas Elyot in his *Governour* (1531), III. xxvi.

76. *wrongfully*] See on I. i. 475–6.

82–3. *Is . . . sing*] Wilson compares *Lucr.,* 1014–15: 'Gnats are unnoted whereso'er they fly, / But eagles gaz'd upon with every eye.' The link between eagles and gnats is probably (Tilley, E1) by way of the Erasmian proverb: 'Aquila non captat muscas' (*O.D.E.P.,* p. 163: 'Eagles catch no flies,' first quotation from Pettie, 1581: *O.D.E.P.,* wrongly, 1586).

86. *stint*] stop.

91. *honey-stalks*] stalks of clover. Not found elsewhere, though 'honeysuckle' is found for 'red clover' in Warwickshire (On.). A surfeit of it is sometimes fatal to sheep; Wilson compares Thomas Hardy's *Far from the Madding Crowd.*

92. *When as*] when. The phrase is fairly common in Shakespeare, and as it is now obsolete there seems no point in spelling it *whenas.*

Sat. But he will not entreat his son for us.

Tam. If Tamora entreat him, then he will: 95
    For I can smooth and fill his aged ears
    With golden promises, that, were his heart
    Almost impregnable, his old ears deaf,
    Yet should both ear and heart obey my tongue.
    Go thou before, be our ambassador: 100
    Say that the emperor requests a parley
    Of warlike Lucius, and appoint the meeting
    Even at his father's house, the old Andronicus.

Sat. Æmilius, do this message honourably,
    And if he stand on hostage for his safety,   105
    Bid him demand what pledge will please him best.

Æmil. Your bidding shall I do effectually.   [*Exit.*

Tam. Now will I to that old Andronicus,
    And temper him with all the art I have,
    To pluck proud Lucius from the warlike Goths.   110
    And now sweet emperor, be blithe again,
    And bury all thy fear in my devices.

Sat. Then go incessantly, and plead to him.   [*Exeunt.*

---

96. ears] eare *Q3,F.*   98. ears] yeares *Qq.*   100. before, be] *Capell;* before
to be *Qq;* before to *F.*   103.] *not in Q3,F.*   105. on] *F4;* in *Qq,F.*   safety]
saftie *Q1.*   113. incessantly] *Capell;* sucessantly *Q1;* successantly *Q2–3.F.*
to] for *F.*

96. *smooth*] flatter.

98. *ears*] See on II. iii. 160 for the Q
spelling.

100. *be our ambassador*] F's *to* is perhaps just possible, in the sense 'in the
capacity of', but would be intolerably
ambiguous after *Go*. On the other hand
to would be readily inserted by a compositor if his copy had no comma after
before.

105. *stand on*] insist on. *N.E.D.,*
stand 72e, retains 'stand in' as the only
example of 'insist upon having'. No
editors have followed, and the F4 correction seems more probable, though
perhaps some weight should be given
to the fact that F2–3 did not make it.

safety] For the Q1 spelling cf. *Ham.*
(Q2), I. iii. 21: 'safty' (where, however, the text is suspect).

109. *temper*] work on, cf. *Gent.,* III. ii.

64–5: 'temper her, by your persua-
sion, / To hate young Valentine'.

113. *incessantly*] immediately (a rare
but authenticated sense). There is
better evidence for Capell's conjecture
than he himself knew. The substantive
Q1 text is *sucessantly*, which could arise
from a misreading of *Jn* as *Su* (the
capital *J* is admittedly unexpected).
Q2 then emends to the more plausible,
but non-existent, *successantly*, which has
been variously interpreted as 'following after another' and 'successfully'.
Wilson, pl. lvi, in accordance with his
theory of Shakespeare's burlesque intention, treats it as a deliberate *vox
nihili.* As H. F. Brooks points out to me,
'incessantly' is a word of Lady Wish-
fort's: *The Way of the World,* IV. xiii,
end; V. viii (the latter cited in
N.E.D.).

ACT V

SCENE I

Enter LUCIUS *with an army of Goths, with drums and soldiers.*

Luc. Approved warriors and my faithful friends,
　I have received letters from great Rome
　Which signifies what hate they bear their emperor
　And how desirous of our sight they are.
　Therefore, great lords, be, as your titles witness, 　　5
　Imperious, and impatient of your wrongs;
　And wherein Rome hath done you any scath,
　Let him make treble satisfaction.
First Goth. Brave slip, sprung from the great Andronicus,
　Whose name was once our terror, now our comfort, 　10
　Whose high exploits and honourable deeds

ACT V

Scene 1

Act V Scene 1] *Rowe; Actus Quintus. F; not in Qq.* 　　　Enter] *Flourish. Enter. F.*
drums] *Drum Q3,F.* 　　9.*First Goth*] *Capell (so ll. 121, 162); Goth Qq,F.* 　　sprung]
sprong *Q1.*

soldiers] An 'army with soldiers' is an
odd expression, and Capell substituted
colours for *soldiers.* Wilson suggests that
'Drums and Soldiers' was 'a prompter's
marginal note'—for such notes made
on author's 'foul papers' while, or before, preparing the prompt-copy, see
Greg, *Editorial Problem,* pp. 123–4
(*Merchant of Venice*), 140 (*Comedy of
Errors*). Wilson's reference to p. 96 of
his edition is misleading, since what is
there discussed is the copy for F1, not
Q1.
　1. *Approved . . . friends*] Wilson finds
this construction and rhythm characteristic of Peele, but cf. also *2H6,* I. i.
24: 'Great king of England, and my

gracious lord'; *R3,* v. ii. 1: 'Fellows in
arms, and my most loving friends';
Marlowe, *1 Tamburlaine* (ed. Ellis-
Fermor), III. i. 1: 'Great kings of Bar-
bary, and my portly bassoes'.
　Approved] tried.
　2. *letters*] As often, for a single com-
munication.
　3. *signifies*] See on II. i. 26. The singular meaning of *letters* may make this a
little more natural.
　7. *Rome*] Not, I think (Wilson), equivalent to *Saturnine.* Rather, the Goths
are to revenge on Saturnine all the
wrongs Rome has *ever* done them.
　scath] harm.
　9. *slip*] scion.

Ingrateful Rome requites with foul contempt,
Be bold in us: we'll follow where thou lead'st,
Like stinging bees in hottest summer's day
Led by their master to the flow'red fields,   15
And be adveng'd on cursed Tamora.
Goths. And as he saith, so say we all with him.
Luc. I humbly thank him, and I thank you all.
But who comes here, led by a lusty Goth?

Enter a Goth, leading of AARON *with his Child
in his arms.*

Second Goth. Renowned Lucius, from our troops I stray'd   20
To gaze upon a ruinous monastery;
And as I earnestly did fix mine eye
Upon the wasted building, suddenly
I heard a child cry underneath a wall.
I made unto the noise, when soon I heard   25
The crying babe controll'd with this discourse:
'Peace, tawny slave, half me and half thy dame!
Did not thy hue bewray whose brat thou art,
Had nature lent thee but thy mother's look,
Villain, thou might'st have been an emperor: 30

13. Be bold] Behold *F*.   us:] us; *Theobald;* vs *Q1–2;* vs, *Q3,F*.   16. adveng'd]
auengd *Q3,F*.   17. *Goths*] *F2 (Omn.); not in Qq,F*.   20. *Second Goth] Capell;
Goth Qq,F*.   Renowmed] Renowned *Q3,F*.   23. building, suddenly]
building suddenly, *Q1–2*.   27. dame] dam *Q2–3,F*.

13. *bold*] confident.
15. *master*] i.e. the queen, or, as it
was believed in Shakespeare's time,
the king. In *H5*, I. ii. 190 and 196, he is
their 'king' and 'emperor', and in *2H6*,
III. ii. 126, 'their leader'.
16. *adveng'd*] A Latinate form of
aveng'd.
cursed Tamora] She is evidently
thought of as a renegade to her nation.
If the chap-book (see Introduction,
p. xxvii) represents Shakespeare's immediate source, we cannot explain the
epithet from the German version, in
which she has poisoned the Gothic
king.
22. *earnestly*] attentively.
26. *controll'd*] See on III. i. 259.

27. *tawny*] black; not (Herford) 'a
hue between black and white', cf.
H. T. Price, *Papers of the Michigan
Academy*, 21 (1935), 505–6, who cites
examples to show that *tawny* could
often mean *black* in Elizabethan English, and quotes R. Scot, *Discovery of
Witchcraft*, p. 312, for the belief that the
children of a black father and a white
mother were always black, which,
however, Shakespeare does not share
—cf. IV. ii. 155.
dame] mother, cf. *2H4*, III. ii. 125,
Lucr., 1477. There is no need to read
dam here or at V. ii. 144.
28. *bewray*] make known.
brat] Not necessarily a term of ab-
use.

But where the bull and cow are both milk-white,
They never do beget a coal-black calf.
Peace, villain, peace!' even thus he rates the babe,
'For I must bear thee to a trusty Goth,
Who, when he knows thou art the empress' babe,   35
Will hold thee dearly for thy mother's sake.'
With this, my weapon drawn, I rush'd upon him,
Surpris'd him suddenly, and brought him hither
To use as you think needful of the man.

Luc. O worthy Goth, this is the incarnate devil   40
That robb'd Andronicus of his good hand:
This is the pearl that pleas'd your empress' eye,
And here's the base fruit of her burning lust.
Say, wall-ey'd slave, whither would'st thou convey
This growing image of thy fiend-like face?   45
Why dost not speak? What, deaf? not a word?
A halter, soldiers, hang him on this tree,
And by his side his fruit of bastardy.

Aar. Touch not the boy, he is of royal blood.

Luc. Too like the sire for ever being good.   50
First hang the child, that he may see it sprawl—
A sight to vex the father's soul withal.
Get me a ladder.
            [*A ladder brought, which Aaron is made to ascend.*

Aar.   Lucius, save the child;
And bear it from me to the empress.
If thou do this, I'll show thee wondrous things   55
That highly may advantage thee to hear:
If thou wilt not, befall what may befall,
I'll speak no more but 'Vengeance rot you all!'

---

37. drawn] drawen *Q1.*   43. her] *Q1–2 (Capell);* his *Q3,F.*   53. [*A ladder . . .
ascend.*]] *Capell substantially; not in Qq,F.   Aar.* Lucius] *Theobald; Qq,F give
whole line to Aaron.*   58. more but 'Vengeance . . . all!'] *Globe;* more, but
vengeance . . . all. *Q1–2;* more but vengeance . . . all. *Q3;* more: but vengeance
. . . all. *F;* more: but Vengeance . . . all. *F4.*

39. *use . . . of*] deal with.
42. *pearl . . . eye*] See *O.D.E.P.*, p. 48:
'A black man is a pearl in a fair
woman's eye'. This is the earliest
quotation, and the next is also Shakespearian, *Gent.*, v. ii. 12.

44. *wall-ey'd*] fierce-looking (lit. with
the iris of the eye discoloured).
51. *sprawl*] 'struggle in the death
agony' (On.). Cf. *3H6*, v. v. 39.
58. '*Vengeance . . . all!*'] I think F4
intended to represent this as a quota-

Luc. Say on, and if it please me which thou speak'st,
    Thy child shall live, and I will see it nourish'd.   60
Aar. And if it please thee! why, assure thee, Lucius,
    'Twill vex thy soul to hear what I shall speak;
    For I must talk of murthers, rapes, and massacres,
    Acts of black night, abominable deeds,
    Complots of mischief, treason, villainies,   65
    Ruthful to hear, yet piteously perform'd;
    And this shall all be buried in my death,
    Unless thou swear to me my child shall live.
Luc. Tell on thy mind; I say thy child shall live.
Aar. Swear that he shall, and then I will begin.   70
Luc. Who should I swear by? thou believest no god:
    That granted, how canst thou believe an oath?
Aar. What if I do not? as, indeed, I do not;
    Yet, for I know thou art religious,
    And hast a thing within thee called conscience,   75
    With twenty popish tricks and ceremonies,
    Which I have seen thee careful to observe,

---

65. treason] treasons *Maxwell conj.*   67. in] by *Q3,F.*

tion, by printing *Vengeance* with a capital. This persists in some eighteenth-century editions, but eventually disappears.

59. *and*] A genuine connective, I think, though some editors, influenced by Aaron's repetition in l. 61, write 'an'. What the repetition actually shows is the absence of any sense in sixteenth-century English that two different 'words' are in question.

60. *nourish'd*] Perhaps monosyllabic, cf. l. 84, and *2H6*, iii. i. 348: 'Whiles I in Ireland nourish a mighty band'. This pronunciation is represented by the earlier spelling *nursh*.

65. *treason*] The isolated singular is suspicious, and the plural, for *acts of treason*, is common, cf. *Mer.V.*, v. i. 85: 'fit for treasons, stratagems, and spoils'.

66. *Ruthful*] lamentable.

piteously] so as to excite pity.

71–2. *Who . . . oath?*] There is an

interesting parallel in Machiavelli's *Arte of Warre*, translated by Peter Whithorn (2nd ed., London, 1588), p. 106 (end of Bk vii), on the subject of mercenaries: 'By what God or by what sainctes may I make them to sweare? By those y^t they worship, or by those that they blaspheme? Who they worship I know not any: but I know well they blaspheme all. How should I beleeue that they will keepe their promise to them, whom euery hower they dispise? How can they that dispise God, reuerence men? Then what good fashion should that bee, which might be expressed in this matter?' Wilson compares *R3*, iv. iv. 369 ff. but the point is not quite the same.

74. *for*] because.

76. *popish*] Wilson sees in this the hand of the anti-papal Peele. But considering who the speaker is, it would be at least as appropriate from a writer sympathetic to Catholicism.

Therefore I urge thy oath; for that I know
An idiot holds his bauble for a god,
And keeps the oath which by that god he swears,   80
To that I'll urge him: therefore thou shalt vow
By that same god, what god soe'er it be,
That thou adorest and hast in reverence,
To save my boy, to nourish and bring him up;
Or else I will discover nought to thee.   85

Luc. Even by my god I swear to thee I will.

Aar. First know thou, I begot him on the empress.

Luc. O most insatiate and luxurious woman!

Aar. Tut, Lucius, this was but a deed of charity
To that which thou shalt hear of me anon.   90
'Twas her two sons that murdered Bassianus;
They cut thy sister's tongue and ravish'd her,
And cut her hands and trimm'd her as thou sawest.

Luc. O detestable villain! call'st thou that trimming?

Aar. Why, she was wash'd, and cut, and trimm'd, and
'twas   95
Trim sport for them which had the doing of it.

Luc. O barbarous beastly villains like thyself!

Aar. Indeed, I was their tutor to instruct them.

---

88. and] *not in Q3,F.*   93. hands] hands off *F.*   95–6.] *divided by Capell;
Qq,F divide after* trimm'd.   96. which] that *Q2–3,F.*   97. barbarous]
barberous, *Qq.*

78–81. *for . . . him*] I now (1961)
follow H. F. Brooks in the interpretation of this passage. It is addressed to
Lucius, and contains a parallel to the
oath Aaron is urging upon him: 'because I know an idiot . . . swears, to
that oath I will (when occasion arises)
urge him. Therefore (on the same
principle) thou shalt etc.'.

79. *bauble*] the court fool's stick.

82–3. *what . . . reverence*] Alexander
punctuates with a dash before and
after these words, since Qq,F put no
comma after 'be'. But I think 'what . . .
be' must (as earlier editors have taken
them) be parenthetic.

84. *nourish*] See on l. 60.

88. *luxurious*] lustful; the normal

Shakespearian sense, as with 'luxury',
e.g. *Ham.*, I. v. 83.

90. *To*] compared with.

93. *wash'd . . . trimm'd*] 'As by a
barber' (Wilson). But *trim* also has a
bawdy sense, as in Fletcher, *Loyal
Subject*, II. i. 92 (cited by Delius), *False
One*, II. iii. 88; Dekker, *Match Me
in London*, I. i. 53–5. E. Partridge,
*Dictionary of Slang and Unconventional
English*, cites 'trim the buff' in this
sense.

94. *detestable*] Stress on first syllable.

97. *barbarous*] A pun on 'barber' in
the Q spelling is unlikely. The spelling
occurs also at v. iii. 4, and in *Jack
Straw* (also a Danter play, 1593), sig.
D2v.

That codding spirit had they from their mother,
As sure a card as ever won the set;   100
That bloody mind I think they learn'd of me,
As true a dog as ever fought at head.
Well, let my deeds be witness of my worth.
I train'd thy brethren to that guileful hole
Where the dead corpse of Bassianus lay;   105
I wrote the letter that thy father found,
And hid the gold within that letter mentioned,
Confederate with the queen and her two sons:
And what not done, that thou hast cause to rue,
Wherein I had no stroke of mischief in it?   110
I play'd the cheater for thy father's hand,
And, when I had it, drew myself apart,
And almost broke my heart with extreme laughter.
I pry'd me through the crevice of a wall
When, for his hand, he had his two sons' heads;   115
Beheld his tears, and laugh'd so heartily
That both mine eyes were rainy like to his:
And when I told the empress of this sport,

---

107. that] the Q2–3,F.   mentioned] mention'd F.   110. it?] Rowe; it, Q1–2;
it. Q3,F.

---

99. *codding*] Usually glossed 'lustful'
(from *cod* = testicle), but not recorded
elsewhere. Ridley suggests 'eager to
"cod"' in the dialect sense of 'score
off'. This is attractive (though not
recorded before the nineteenth century) and I think a pun on both senses
is possible.

100. *sure . . . card*] 'expedient certain
to obtain its object' (*N.E.D.*). Both
O.D.E.P., p. 632, and Tilley, C74, cite
Thersytes (c. 1560) which antedates the
earliest *N.E.D.* quotation. A 'Master
Surecard' is mentioned in *2H4*, III. ii.
96.

set] game.

102. *at head*] A reference to bull-
dogs 'whose generosity and courage
are always shown by meeting the bull
in front and seizing him by the nose'
(Johnson). Cf. Jonson (ed. Herford
and Simpson), *Epicoene*, IV. ii. 31–3:
'Trv. You fought high and faire, sir

Iohn. Cle. At the head. Dav. Like an
excellent beare-dog.'

104. *train'd*] enticed.

109–10. *what . . . it?*] A mixture of
constructions, (a) 'what was not done
. . . rue?' (b) 'what was done wherein,
etc.?'

111. *cheater*] 'officer appointed to
look after property forfeited to the
Crown (escheats); hence, because of
his opportunities, fig. in the modern
sense' (Wilson based on On.).

113. *broke my heart*] died. H. T. Price
(*Papers of the Michigan Academy*, 21
(1935), 504) compares Marlowe,
Massacre at Paris (ed. Bennett), x. 15:
'my heart doth break: I faint and die.'

114. *I . . . wall*] Was this shown on
the stage, from behind the traverse, in
III. i? It would be an effective piece of
stage-business.

me] For this idiom see Abbott §220,
Franz §294.

She sounded almost at my pleasing tale,
And for my tidings gave me twenty kisses.   120
First Goth. What, canst thou say all this, and never blush?
Aar. Ay, like a black dog, as the saying is.
Luc. Art thou not sorry for these heinous deeds?
Aar. Ay, that I had not done a thousand more.
Even now I curse the day, and yet, I think,   125
Few come within the compass of my curse,
Wherein I did not some notorious ill:
As kill a man, or else devise his death;
Ravish a maid, or plot the way to do it;
Accuse some innocent, and forswear myself;   130
Set deadly enmity between two friends;
Make poor men's cattle break their necks;
Set fire on barns and haystalks in the night,
And bid the owners quench them with their tears.
Oft have I digg'd up dead men from their graves,   135
And set them upright at their dear friends' door,
Even when their sorrows almost was forgot,
And on their skins, as on the bark of trees,
Have with my knife carved in Roman letters,
'Let not your sorrow die, though I am dead.'   140
But I have done a thousand dreadful things
As willingly as one would kill a fly,
And nothing grieves me heartily indeed

121–4.] *Qq centre prefixes.*   126. the] few *F.*   132. break] stray and break *Z. Jackson conj.;* fall and break *Hudson.*   133. haystalks] haystakes *Q2;* haystackes *Q3,F.*   134. their] the *F.*   141. But] Tut, *Q2–3,F.*

119. *sounded*] swooned. It is pointless to half-modernize to *swounded*, itself obsolete.

122. *like ... dog*] See *O.D.E.P.*, p. 53, where the first quotation is from Gosson (1579).

125–7. *Even ... ill*] See Introduction, p. xxi. 'Within the compass of my curse' recurs in *R3*, I. iii. 284.

132. *break their necks*] Hudson in explaining his conjecture (which is as good as any) suggests that Aaron set pitfalls for the cattle.

133. *haystalks*] The *English Dialect Dictionary* records this form of

'stack' for Hertfordshire (1750).

135–7. *Oft ... forgot*] The fact that a comparable incident actually occurs on the stage in Marlowe's *Jew of Malta*, IV. ii, suggests the priority of Marlowe: cf. L. Kirschbaum, *Modern Language Quarterly*, 7 (1946), 56.

136. *friends*] probably 'relations'': a sense still current in Scotland.

137. *sorrows*] See on II. i. 26.

141. *But*] The sense seems to be 'but why should I go on itemizing?' (H. F. Brooks). Q2's *Tut* has some attractiveness, but the compositor may have recalled l. 89.

But that I cannot do ten thousand more.

Luc. Bring down the devil, for he must not die   145
  So sweet a death as hanging presently.

Aar. If there be devils, would I were a devil,
  To live and burn in everlasting fire,
  So I might have your company in hell,
  But to torment you with my bitter tongue!   150

Luc. Sirs, stop his mouth, and let him speak no more.

Enter ÆMILIUS.

Goth. My lord, there is a messenger from Rome
  Desires to be admitted to your presence.

Luc. Let him come near.
  Welcome, Æmilius: what's the news from Rome?   155

Æmil. Lord Lucius, and you princes of the Goths,
  The Roman emperor greets you all by me;
  And, for he understands you are in arms,
  He craves a parley at your father's house,
  Willing you to demand your hostages,   160
  And they shall be immediately delivered.

First Goth. What says our general?

Luc. Æmilius, let the emperor give his pledges
  Unto my father and my uncle Marcus,
  And we will come. March away.   [*Exeunt.*   165

---

165. March away] Away. [*March. Exeunt.*] *Capell.*   *Exeunt.*] *not in* Q1–2;
Flourish. Exeunt F.

146. *presently*] immediately.

148–50. *To live . . . tongue*] The resemblance (Noble) to Revelations, xx. 10, is not very close.

149. *So*] See on II. i. 102.

151. Enter ÆMILIUS] It has been customary here to give an entry for 'a Goth' and to transfer Æmilius' entry to after l. 154. This is unnecessary. One of the Goths already on the stage announces Æmilius' arrival to Lucius. Wilson satisfactorily expands the Qq,F direction by reading here: *A Goth comes up* and after l. 154 ÆMILIUS *is brought forward*; but it is a little anomalous not to give Æmilius a formal entry.

165. *March away*] The absence of an *Exeunt* in Q1–2 (not known to Capell) tells in favour of his correction.

SCENE II

Enter TAMORA, *and her two sons, disguised.*

Tam. Thus, in this strange and sad habiliment,
    I will encounter with Andronicus,
    And say I am Revenge, sent from below
    To join with him and right his heinous wrongs;
    Knock at his study, where they say he keeps,   5
    To ruminate strange plots of dire revenge;
    Tell him Revenge is come to join with him
    And work confusion on his enemies.
                [*They knock, and Titus opens his study door.*

Tit. Who doth molest my contemplation?
    Is it your trick to make me ope the door,   10
    That so my sad decrees may fly away
    And all my study be to no effect?
    You are deceiv'd; for what I mean to do
    See here in bloody lines I have set down;
    And what is written shall be executed.   15

Tam. Titus, I am come to talk with thee.

Tit. No, not a word; how can I grace my talk,
    Wanting a hand to give it action?

Scene II

Scene II.] *Rowe; not in Qq,F.*   1. habiliment] habilliament *Qq1,3,F;* habilla-
ment *Q2.*   18. it action] *F;* that accord *Qq;* it that accord *Pope.*

1. *sad*] dismal; Wilson compares *R2*,
v. v. 70–1: 'that sad dog / That brings
me food'.

2. *encounter with*] meet.

5. *keeps*] dwells; cf. *Ham.*, II. i. 7–8:
'what Danskers are in Paris . . . where
they keep'.

9. *Who . . . contemplation*] This line is
quoted from memory ('Whoe does
molest oᵣ Contemplations'), and in
jest, by a clown in *The Welsh Embassador* (Malone Society Reprint), l. 1963.
See on IV. i. 102.

11. *That . . . away*] Possibly an allusion to the Sibyl's leaves: see on IV. i.
105.

    sad decrees] 'solemn resolutions'
(Ridley).

18. *Wanting . . . action*] I accept the F
reading with some confidence. Q cannot be accepted as it stands, but would
need to be emended as by Pope. The
MS. may have read *giue yt acc(i)on(e).*
The *cc* spelling is common and so is
-con for *-cion*, and a final *e*, which could
be corrupted to *d*, is not inconceivable
(for 'superfluous *e* mute" see J. D.
Wilson, *The Manuscript of Shakespeare's
Hamlet*, p. 116). For the meaning, see
B. L. Joseph, *Elizabethan Acting* (London, 1951), especially p. 39, quoting
John Bulwer, *Chironomia* (London,
1644), p. 16: 'The moving and significant extension of the *Hand* is knowne
to be so absolutely pertinent to speech,
that we together with a speech expect

Thou hast the odds of me; therefore no more.

Tam. If thou didst know me, thou would'st talk with me.   20

Tit. I am not mad; I know thee well enough:

 Witness this wretched stump, witness these crimson
  lines;

 Witness these trenches made by grief and care;

 Witness the tiring day and heavy night;

 Witness all sorrow that I know thee well   25

 For our proud empress, mighty Tamora.

 Is not thy coming for my other hand?

Tam. Know thou, sad man, I am not Tamora;

 She is thy enemy, and I thy friend:

 I am Revenge, sent from th' infernal kingdom   30

 To ease the gnawing vulture of thy mind

 By working wreakful vengeance on thy foes.

 Come down and welcome me to this world's light;

 Confer with me of murder and of death.

 There's not a hollow cave or lurking-place,   35

 No vast obscurity or misty vale,

 Where bloody murther or detested rape

 Can couch for fear, but I will find them out,

 And in their ears tell them my dreadful name,

 Revenge, which makes the foul offender quake.   40

Tit. Art thou Revenge? and art thou sent to me

 To be a torment to mine enemies?

Tam. I am; therefore come down and welcome me.

---

28. Know thou,] *F4*; Know thou *Qq,F*; Know, thou *Capell.*   31. thy] the *F.*
32. thy] my *F.*   40. offender] offenders *Q3,F.*   42. mine] thine *Q2 (Edin.*
copy).

---

the due motion of the *Hand* to explaine,
direct, enforce, apply, apparrell, & to
beautifie the words men utter, which
would prove naked, unless the cloath-
ing *Hands* doe neatly move to adorne
and hide their nakednesse, with their
comely and ministeriall parts of
speech.' Dr Joseph discusses both the
Quarto and Folio readings (pp. 53,
59): cf. also *2H6*, v. i. 8–9: 'I cannot
give due action to my words / Except
a sword or sceptre balance it.' W. F.
Schirmer (*Sh. Jb.*, 81 (1935), 21, n. 4)
cites Quintilian, xi. 3 [65 ff. and 85],

and Wilson, *Arte of Rhetorique* (ed.
G. H. Mair, Oxford, 1909), pp. 220–1.
There is an allusion to this scene in
Middleton's *Father Hubburd's Tales*
(Works, ed. Bullen, viii. 94): 'my
lamentable action of one arm, like old
Titus Andronicus'.

 19. *odds of*] advantage over.

 31. *gnawing vulture*] An allusion to
the Prometheus story (see on ii. i.
17).

 32. *wreakful vengeance*] This sort of
pleonasm is normal in the minor
drama of the time.

Tit. Do me some service ere I come to thee.
   Lo, by thy side where Rape and Murder stands;
   Now give some surance that thou art Revenge:
   Stab them, or tear them on thy chariot-wheels,
   And then I'll come and be thy waggoner,
   And whirl along with thee about the globe.
   Provide two proper palfreys, black as jet,   50
   To hale thy vengeful waggon swift away,
   And find out murderers in their guilty caves:
   And when thy car is loaden with their heads,
   I will dismount, and by thy waggon-wheel
   Trot like a servile footman all day long,   55
   Even from Hyperion's rising in the east
   Until his very downfall in the sea:
   And day by day I'll do this heavy task,
   So thou destroy Rapine and Murder there.
Tam. These are my ministers, and come with me.   60
Tit. Are these thy ministers? what are they call'd?

---

49. globe.] *Capell conj.; globes. Qq,F;* globe, *W. S. Walker conj.*   50. two] *Rowe;* thee two *Qq,F.*   black] as blacke *Q3,F.*   52. murderers] *Capell;* murder *Qq,F.*   caves] *F2;* cares *Qq,F.*   54. thy] *Q1 (Rowe);* the *Q2–3,F.*   56. Hyperion's] *F2 (Hiperions); Epeons Qq; Eptons F.*   57. very] weary *Wilson conj.*   61. these] *Dyce;* them *Qq,F;* they *F2.*

46. *surance*] assurance.

49. *globe*] I think this correction is certain: only the terrestrial globe can be in question. Capell wrote: ' "*globes*", (if not a mistake), implies a plurality of worlds constituted as earth is': for this reason I credit him with the conjecture. Walker may well have been right in further proposing to replace the full-stop at the end of this line by a less heavy stop, and to treat *Provide* as infinitive, parallel to *come* and *whirl*.

50. *proper*] handsome; frequent in Shakespeare.

black as jet] See Tilley, J49.

56. *Hyperion's*] The MS. probably read 'Epions', using the customary abbreviation for 'per' (J. G. McManaway in *Shakespeare Survey*, 3 (1950), p. 144). Hyperion is the sun-god.

57. *very*] Wilson's conjecture is attractive but not essential; cf. *Err.*, I.

ii. 7: 'Dies ere the weary sun set in the west'.

59. *So*] See on II. i. 102.

Rapine] rape: so also ll. 83, 103. H. Nørgaard, *Eng. Studies*, 45 (1964), 138, quotes instances of this sense from Whetstone (1582) and R. Robinson (1574). Gower's version of the Tereus story (*Confessio Amantis*, v) has *Ravine* in the sense 'robbery by violence'; cf. especially ll. 5524–8 on 'Lovers . . . That whan noght elles mai availe, / Anon with strengthe thei assaile / And gete of love the sesine [possession], / Whan thei se time, be Ravine', also ll. 5530, 5627, 5919 (*raviner*), and 5650, 6050 (noted by Steevens), 6064 (*ravine*).

61. *Are these*] I cannot quite believe in Qq,F's *them*, though F has *them* as nominative in *John*, IV. ii. 50–1: 'for the which myself and them / Bend their

Tam. Rape and Murder; therefore called so
    'Cause they take vengeance of such kind of men.
Tit. Good Lord, how like the empress' sons they are,
    And you the empress, but we worldly men   65
    Have miserable, mad, mistaking eyes.
    O sweet Revenge, now do I come to thee;
    And, if one arm's embracement will content thee,
    I will embrace thee in it by and by.   [*Exit.*
Tam. This closing with him fits his lunacy.   70
    Whate'er I forge to feed his brain-sick humours,
    Do you uphold and maintain in your speeches,
    For now he firmly takes me for Revenge;
    And, being credulous in this mad thought,
    I'll make him send for Lucius his son,   75
    And whilst I at a banket hold him sure,
    I'll find some cunning practice out of hand

---

62. Rape] Rapine *F2*.   65. worldly] wordlie *Q1*.   66. mad, mistaking] mad mistaking *Qq,F*; mad-mistaking *W. S. Walker*.   69. *Exit*] *Exit above Rowe.* 71. humours] fits *Q2–3,F*.   76. banket] banquet *Q2–3,F*.

best studies', where some editors think it to have been erroneously repeated from the previous line.

what . . . call'd?] Wilson calls this question 'an inconsistency surely too glaring to be explained as Titus's lunacy'. In my 1953 edition, I wrote, 'It is not at all clear, though the editors do not comment on it, how Titus knows at l. 45 who Tamora's attendants are'. In this edition, I am privileged to publish in an Appendix an admirable solution by Dr H. F. Brooks.

62. *Rape . . . so*] An effectively solemn headless line.

65. *worldly*] of this world; without the modern connotations. In 1953 I retained the Q1 form as an archaism (see *N.E.D.*), but at this date it is almost certainly a misprint.

69.] The whole question of the gallery has been re-opened by R. Hosley in *Shakespeare Quarterly*, 8 (1957), and *Shakespeare Survey*, 10 (1957). In the latter article (p. 86, n. 4) Hosley rejects the use of the

gallery in this scene. Certainly it is unproved, and Titus can perfectly well withdraw into a 'study' behind the main stage. I am glad that Hosley also agrees that the gallery is not called for in v. iii (see my note on l. 66).

70. *closing*] agreeing, cf. *Meas.*, v. i. 341: 'Hark how the villain would close ("climb down", On.) now'.

71. *forge*] invent; cf. Falstaff's 'apprehensive, quick, forgetive' (*2H4*, IV. iii. 107).

humours] Q2's *fits* is not just (Wilson) 'repeated by the compositor from l. 70', though that line no doubt influenced his choice of a word. But the corruption of the corresponding word on the verso (l. 106: *shalt* Q1; *maist* Q2) shows that the word was illegible (it is very badly printed in the surviving copy). The line begins a new page.

76. *banket*] See on III. ii. S.D. before 1, and cf. ll. 194, 203.

77. *practice*] scheme.

out of hand] on the spur of the moment.

To scatter and disperse the giddy Goths,
Or, at the least, make them his enemies.
See, here he comes, and I must ply my theme.   80

Enter TITUS.

Tit. Long have I been forlorn, and all for thee:
Welcome, dread Fury, to my woeful house:
Rapine and Murther, you are welcome too.
How like the empress and her sons you are.
Well are you fitted, had you but a Moor: 85
Could not all hell afford you such a devil?
For well I wot the empress never wags
But in her company there is a Moor;
And would you represent our queen aright,
It were convenient you had such a devil: 90
But welcome as you are: what shall we do?
Tam. What would'st thou have us do, Andronicus?
Dem. Show me a murtherer, I'll deal with him.
Chi. Show me a villain that hath done a rape,
And I am sent to be reveng'd on him.   95
Tam. Show me a thousand that hath done thee wrong,
And I will be revenged on them all.
Tit. Look round about the wicked streets of Rome,
And when thou find'st a man that's like thyself,
Good Murther, stab him; he's a murtherer.   100
Go thou with him; and when it is thy hap
To find another that is like to thee,
Good Rapine, stab him; he is a ravisher.
Go thou with them; and in the emperor's court
There is a queen attended by a Moor;   105
Well shalt thou know her by thine own proportion,
For up and down she doth resemble thee:
I pray thee, do on them some violent death;
They have been violent to me and mine.
Tam. Well hast thou lesson'd us; this shall we do.   110

80. ply] play *F.*   *Enter* TITUS.] *Rowe; not in Qq,F.*   91. are: what] *Pope;* are,
what *Qq,F.*   96. hath] haue *Q2–3,F.*   97. I will] Ile *F.*   106. shalt] maist
Q2–3,F.   thine] thy *Q3,F.*

87. *wags*] goes about.   106. *shalt*] See on l. 71.
96. *hath*] See on II. iv. 17.   107. *up and down*] exactly.

But would it please thee, good Andronicus,
To send for Lucius, thy thrice-valiant son,
Who leads towards Rome a band of warlike Goths,
And bid him come and banquet at thy house,
When he is here, even at thy solemn feast,   115
I will bring in the empress and her sons,
The emperor himself, and all thy foes,
And at thy mercy shall they stoop and kneel,
And on them shalt thou ease thy angry heart.
What says Andronicus to this device?   120
Tit. Marcus, my brother, 'tis sad Titus calls.

Enter MARCUS.

Go, gentle Marcus, to thy nephew Lucius;
Thou shalt inquire him out among the Goths:
Bid him repair to me and bring with him
Some of the chiefest princes of the Goths;   125
Bid him encamp his soldiers where they are.
Tell him, the emperor and the empress too
Feast at my house, and he shall feast with them:
This do thou for my love; and so let him,
As he regards his aged father's life.   130
Marc. This will I do, and soon return again.   [*Exit.*
Tam. Now will I hence about thy business,
And take my ministers along with me.
Tit. Nay, nay, let Rape and Murder stay with me,
Or else I'll call my brother back again   135
And cleave to no revenge but Lucius.
Tam. [*Aside to her sons.*] What say you, boys? will you abide
          with him,
Whiles I go tell my lord the emperor
How I have govern'd our determin'd jest?
Yield to his humour, smooth and speak him fair,   140
And tarry with him till I turn again.

121. *Enter* MARCUS.] *so Theobold; after l. 120 Qq,F.*   128. Feast] Feasts *F.*
131. *Exit.*] *not in Qq,F.*   136. Lucius] Lucius' *W. S. Walker.*   137. [*Aside . . .
sons.*]] *Hanmer; not in Qq,F.*   abide] *Q1 (Rowe)*; bide *Q2–3,F.*   140. Yield]
Yeede *Q2 (Yeeld with imperfect l resembling an apostrophe Q1).*

139. *govern'd our determin'd jest*] put in-   140. *smooth*] See on IV. iv. 96.
to practice the jest we determined on.   *speak him fair*] humour him.

Tit. [*Aside.*] I knew them all, though they suppos'd me mad,
     And will o'erreach them in their own devices,
     A pair of cursed hell-hounds and their dame.
Dem. Madam, depart at pleasure; leave us here.   145
Tam. Farewell, Andronicus: Revenge now goes
     To lay a complot to betray thy foes.
Tit. I know thou dost; and, sweet Revenge, farewell.

                                  [*Exit Tamora.*

Chi. Tell us, old man, how shall we be employ'd?
Tit. Tut, I have work enough for you to do.   150
     Publius, come hither, Caius, and Valentine.

           Enter PUBLIUS *and others.*

Pub. What is your will?
Tit. Know you these two?
Pub. The empress' sons, I take them, Chiron and Demetrius.
Tit. Fie, Publius, fie, thou art too much deceiv'd;   155
     The one is Murder, and Rape is the other's name;
     And therefore bind them, gentle Publius;
     Caius and Valentine, lay hands on them.
     Oft have you heard me wish for such an hour,
     And now I find it: therefore bind them sure,   160
     And stop their mouths if they begin to cry.   [*Exit.*
Chi. Villains, forbear, we are the empress' sons.
Pub. And therefore do we what we are commanded;
     Stop close their mouths, let them not speak a word;
     Is he sure bound? look that you bind them fast.   165

    Enter TITUS ANDRONICUS *with a knife, and* LAVINIA *with
                  a basin.*

Tit. Come, come, Lavinia; look, thy foes are bound.
     Sirs, stop their mouths, let them not speak to me,

---

142. [*Aside.*]] *Rowe, not in* Qq,F.   knew . . . suppos'd] know . . . suppose *Q2–3,F.*
144. dame] Dam *Q3,F.*   148. *Exit Tamora.*] *Capell (after l. 147 Rowe); not in*
Qq,F.   150. Tut] But *Q3.*   152. *Enter . . . others.*] *Rowe substantially; not in* Qq,F.
154. and] *Theobald; not in* Qq,F.   156. and] *not in Q2–3,F.*   161.] *not in F (but
with comma at end of l. 160*).   *Exit.*] *Rowe; not in* Qq,F.   165. fast.] fast.
Exeunt. F.

144. *dame*] See on v. i. 27.   163. *therefore*] for that very reason.

But let them hear what fearful words I utter.
O villains, Chiron and Demetrius,
Here stands the spring whom you have stain'd with
    mud,   170
This goodly summer with your winter mix'd:
You kill'd her husband, and for that vild fault
Two of her brothers were condemn'd to death,
My hand cut off and made a merry jest:
Both her sweet hands, her tongue, and that more dear
Than hands or tongue, her spotless chastity,   176
Inhuman traitors, you constrain'd and forc'd.
What would you say if I should let you speak?
Villains, for shame you could not beg for grace.
Hark, wretches, how I mean to martyr you.   180
This one hand yet is left to cut your throats,
Whiles that Lavinia 'tween her stumps doth hold
The basin that receives your guilty blood.
You know your mother means to feast with me,
And calls herself Revenge, and thinks me mad.   185
Hark, villains, I will grind your bones to dust,
And with your blood and it I'll make a paste,
And of the paste a coffin I will rear,
And make two pasties of your shameful heads,
And bid that strumpet, your unhallowed dam,   190
Like to the earth swallow her own increase.

182. Whiles] Whilst *Q2–3,F*.   191. own] *not in F*.

170. *spring . . . mud*] Parrott, p. 35, cites *Lucr.*, 577: 'Mud not the fountain that gave drink to thee,' noting that in both passages the words are addressed to a ravisher (or would-be ravisher) and refer to his victim. The *Lucr.* lines refer more specifically to ingratitude, and I believe they combine a recollection of the *Titus* line with a recollection of Southwell's *St Peter's Complaint*, st. 18, which ends: 'But I, that drunk the drops of heavenly flud, / Bemyr'd the Giver with returning mud.' On the relationship between Southwell and *Lucr.*, see Fr. Christopher Devlin in

The Month, September 1950. Tilley, D345, quotes 'Cast no dirt into the well that has given you water' as a proverb first recorded by Ray in 1678.

188. *coffin*] The normal word for a pie-crust, not a sinister metaphor, though perhaps with double sense. In Dekker (ed. Bowers), *Patient Grissil*, IV. iii. 124–5, there is a pun on this sense of coffin: 'the coffins of pyes, wherein the dead bodies of birdes should have been buried'. See also Oppel, p. 50.

191. *Like . . . increase*] See on II. iii. 239.

This is the feast that I have bid her to,
And this the banket she shall surfeit on;
For worse than Philomel you us'd my daughter,
And worse than Progne I will be reveng'd.   195
And now prepare your throats—Lavinia, come,
Receive the blood: and when that they are dead,
Let me go grind their bones to powder small,
And with this hateful liquor temper it,
And in that paste let their vile heads be bak'd.   200
Come, come, be every one officious
To make this banket, which I wish may prove
More stern and bloody than the Centaurs' feast.

                [He cuts their throats.

So, now bring them in, for I'll play the cook,
And see them ready against their mother comes.   205

                    [Exeunt.

SCENE III

Enter LUCIUS, MARCUS, *and the Goths, with* AARON,
prisoner.

Luc. Uncle Marcus, since 'tis my father's mind
    That I repair to Rome, I am content.
Goth. And ours with thine, befall what fortune will.
Luc. Good uncle, take you in this barbarous Moor,

---

193. banket] banquet *Q2–3,F.*   200. vile] vilde *Q3;* vil'd *F.*   202. may]
might *F.*   204. I'll] I will *W. S. Walker.*   205. against] gainst *F.*

Scene III

Scene III.] *Capell; not in Qq,F.*   with AARON, *prisoner*] *Rowe; not in Qq,F.*

194–5. *Philomel . . . Progne*] See on
II. iv. 26.

199. *temper*] moisten.

201. *officious*] busy, without the
hostile modern implication.

203. *Centaurs' feast*] A battle between the Centaurs and the Lapithae
followed the marriage of Pirithous and
Hippodamia: see, amongst other
sources, Ovid, *Met.*, XII. 210 ff.

204. *So . . . cook*] With normal scansion, we get an inappropriate stress on

them. Walker, followed by H. T. Price
(*English Institute Essays, 1947*, p. 152),
and by Alexander, may be right in
treating *So* as extrametrical and
reading *I will.*

205. *against*] by the time that.

Scene III

3. *ours*] Prob. 'our mind' from l. 1
(Delius) rather than (Malone) 'our
content', supplied out of adj. 'content'
in l. 2.

This ravenous tiger, this accursed devil;   5
Let him receive no sust'nance, fetter him,
Till he be brought unto the empress' face,
For testimony of her foul proceedings:
And see the ambush of our friends be strong;
I fear the emperor means no good to us.   10

Aar. Some devil whisper curses in my ear,
And prompt me that my tongue may utter forth
The venomous malice of my swelling heart!

Luc. Away, inhuman dog, unhallowed slave!
Sirs, help our uncle to convey him in.   15

            [*Exeunt Goths with Aaron.*
The trumpets show the emperor is at hand.

Sound trumpets. Enter Emperor and Empress, with ÆMILIUS,
Tribunes and others.

Sat. What, hath the firmament mo suns than one?
Luc. What boots it thee to call thyself a sun?
Marc. Rome's emperor, and nephew, break the parle;
These quarrels must be quietly debated: 20
The feast is ready which the careful Titus
Hath ordain'd to an honourable end,

---

7. empress'] *Q1–2* (Empresse), *Malone;* Emperours *Q3;* Emperous *F.*   11.
Aar.] Moore. Qq.   my] *Q1,F;* mine *Q2–3.*   15. *Exeunt . . . Aaron.] Rowe (after*
l. 14) ; not in Qq,F; F adds Flourish at end of this line.   16. ÆMILIUS,] *Dyce; not in*
Qq,F.   17. *Sat.] King. Qq.*   mo] more *F.*   22. ordain'd] ordained *Q3,F.*

---

13. *The . . . heart*] Verity quotes *1H6,*
III. i. 26: 'From envious malice of thy
swelling heart', and Wilson [Peele],
Alcazar, II. iii. 3. Add (Robertson)
Arden of Feversham, I. 327: 'the ran-
corous venome of thy mis-swolne hart'.

17. *mo*] more, usually of number.
From O.E. *ma,* originally an adverb
constructed with genitive, like Latin
plus. Tilley, S992, compares *1H4,* v.
iv. 65: 'Two stars keep not their
motion in one sphere,' and quotes
Erasmus, *Similia* 608B: 'Ut plures
apparere Soles prodigium est: Ita
plures esse Monarchas aut Impera-
tores', and Young, *Civile Conversation*
(1586): 'Two kinges in one kingdome

doe not agree well together.' Sidney
plays on the notion in some verses in
the *Arcadia* (*Works,* ed. Feuillerat, II.
38).

19. *break*] interrupt, the 'parle' being
the slanging-match that ll. 17–18 have
initiated. Johnson interpreted 'begin
the parley', and On. 4 gives 'open (ne-
gotiations)' as his first gloss, though
adding '(or? = "break off")'.

21. *careful*] Probably 'afflicted with
cares' rather than 'taking trouble'.
There might be an ironic pun, though
it could only be Shakespeare's irony,
not Marcus', as he does not know the
special kind of care that Titus has
taken.

For peace, for love, for league, and good to Rome:
Please you, therefore, draw nigh, and take your places.
Sat. Marcus, we will.   25

> *Trumpets sounding, enter* TITUS, *like a cook, placing the*
> *dishes, and* LAVINIA, *with a veil over her face.*

Tit. Welcome, my lord; welcome, dread queen;
Welcome, ye warlike Goths; welcome Lucius;
And welcome, all: although the cheer be poor,
'Twill fill your stomachs; please you eat of it.
Sat. Why art thou thus attir'd, Andronicus?   30
Tit. Because I would be sure to have all well
To entertain your highness and your empress.
Tam. We are beholding to you, good Andronicus.
Tit. And if your highness knew my heart, you were.
My lord the emperor, resolve me this: 35
Was it well done of rash Virginius
To slay his daughter with his own right hand,
Because she was enforc'd, stain'd, and deflow'r'd?
Sat. It was, Andronicus.

25. *Sat.*] *King. Q1; Empe. Q2.*   will.] will. *Hoboyes. A Table brought in. F.*
Trumpets sounding, enter] *Sound trumpets, enter (euter Q2) Q2–3; Enter F.*   dishes]
meate on the table Q2–3,F.   26. lord] *gracious Lord Q2–3,F.*   28. all:] all
Q1–2; all, Q3.   30. *Sat.*] *King. Q1–2 (so ll. 39, 41, 48, 53 (Q3), 59).*   attir'd]
attired Qq.

33. *beholding*] See on I. i. 396.
36–8. *Was . . . deflow'r'd*] In earlier editions, I canvassed various ideas based on the assumption that Virginius' daughter was not ravished in any current versions of the story. It has now been pointed out by H. Nørgaard, *Eng. Studies,* 45 (1964), 139–41, that this is not so. The existence of the same version in *Alphonsus, Emperor of Germany* (in *Tragedies of George Chapman,* ed. Parrott), IV. iii. 64, had been noticed, and unconvincingly explained, by J. M. Robertson. But it is a well-established version, going back to Florus, *Epitome.* Nørgaard suggests as immediate source Ludowicke Lloyd, who twice told the story in this form, in *The Pilgrimage of Princes* (1573) and in

The Consent of Tune (1590). Earlier solutions to the problem, which can now be seen to be at best very improbable, are: 1. Shakespeare revised, and got wrong, a Peele original (Wilson). 2. *Because* is an error for *Before* (Delius). The corruption could have resulted from anticipation of l. 41, or been deliberately introduced on the assumption that consistency with ll. 41–2 required it. 3. The coincidence with *Alphonsus, Emperor of Germany* is explained by Peele's authorship of both passages (Robertson, *Introduction to the Study of the Shakespeare Canon,* pp. 154–5). But this coincidence only seemed odd in the absence of other evidence of the currency of this version of the story.

Tit. Your reason, mighty lord?   40
Sat. Because the girl should not survive her shame,
    And by her presence still renew his sorrows.
Tit. A reason mighty, strong, and effectual;
    A pattern, president, and lively warrant
    For me, most wretched, to perform the like.   45
    Die, die, Lavinia, and thy shame with thee;
    And with thy shame thy father's sorrow die! [*He kills her.*
Sat. What hast thou done, unnatural and unkind?
Tit. Kill'd her for whom my tears have made me blind.
    I am as woeful as Virginius was,   50
    And have a thousand times more cause than he
    To do this outrage: and it now is done.
Sat. What, was she ravish'd? tell who did the deed.
Tit. Will't please you eat? will't please your highness feed?

43. and] *om. Hanmer.*   47. *He kills her.*] *not in Q1–2.*   48. thou] *not in F.*
52.] *not in F.*   now is] is now *Q3.*

41. *Because . . . shame*] Perhaps, simply, 'because it was not right that she should survive', but I suspect, rather, an elliptical construction. Titus has asked 'Why do you say he was right?' and Saturninus answers: [He was right because he acted] in order that, etc. Such a telescoping is facilitated by the double sense of 'because' in Elizabethan English. A writer can pass from one to the other in the same sentence: cf. Sidney's Dedication of *Arcadia* (ed. Feuillerat, p. 4): 'this say I, because it may be ever so; or to say better, because it will be ever so.' A passage in Shakespeare very similar to the present is *1H6*, III. i. 36–7: 'It is not that that hath incens'd the duke: / It is because no man should sway but he,' where we move from cause in the first line to purpose in the second. *N.E.D.*, Schmidt, Onions, and Franz fail to quote Shakespearian instances of 'because ' = in order that. Abbott (§117) quotes *2H6*, III. ii. 99–100, to which add *Troil.*, III. ii. 216–18. The easy transition from one sense of *because* to the other is also illustrated in in Jonson, *Neptune's Triumph*, 228–9, and in Dekker, *Foure Birds of Noah's*

Arke (1609), sig. A5 (ed. F. P. Wilson, pp. 9–10): 'Nothing that is set downe is tedious, because I had a care of thy memorie. Nothing is done twice, because thou mayst take delight in them.' See also Donne, *Sermons* (ed. Simpson and Potter), VIII. 8. 696–8, 'Neither does it become us in any case, to say God layes this upon him, because he is so ill, but because he may be better.' So in Latin, *causa* can be followed by *quod* and *ne* in the same sentence: Caesar, *B.G.*, VI. ix. 1–2.

43. *and*] Hanmer's deletion of this may well be right.

44. *president*] precedent; the most usual Shakespearian spelling with this meaning.

lively] striking (Wilson); Greg, *R.E.S.*, I (1925), 477, notes that this is *N.E.D.*'s sense 4c, the first quotation for which postdates *Titus* but illustrates it well: 'they shew the Indians their blind errors, by lively and plain reasons' (E. Grimstone, *D'Acosta's Hist. Indies*, 1604). There is perhaps play on the literal sense 'living' (cf. III. i. 105), to which On. refers this passage.

Tam. Why hast thou slain thine only daughter thus?   55
Tit. Not I; 'twas Chiron and Demetrius:
    They ravish'd her, and cut away her tongue;
    And they, 'twas they, that did her all this wrong.
Sat. Go fetch them hither to us presently.
Tit. Why, there they are, both baked in this pie;   60
    Whereof their mother daintily hath fed,
    Eating the flesh that she herself hath bred.
    'Tis true, 'tis true; witness my knife's sharp point.
                                   [*He stabs the Empress.*
Sat. Die, frantic wretch, for this accursed deed.   [*Kills Titus.*
Luc. Can the son's eye behold his father bleed?   65
    There's meed for meed, death for a deadly deed.
                                   [*Kills Saturninus.*
Marc. You sad-fac'd men, people and sons of Rome,
    By uproars sever'd, as a flight of fowl
    Scatter'd by winds and high tempestuous gusts,
    O, let me teach you how to knit again   70
    This scattered corn into one mutual sheaf,

---

55. thus] *not in Q3* (*with no stop after* daughter), *F.*   60. are, both] *Grey;* are both *Q1;* are both, *Q2–3,F.*   this] that *Q2–3,F.*   64. *Sat.*] *Emperour. Q1; Empe. Q2–3.   Kills Titus.*] *Rowe substcntially; not in Qq,F.*   66. *Kills Saturninus.*] *Rowe substantially; not in Qq,F.*   68. as] like *Q3,F.*   69. Scatter'd] Scattered *Q3,F.*   tempestuous] tempestious *Q2–3.*   71. scattered] scattred *Q2–3,F.*

---

59. *presently*] immediately.

60. *are, both*] I credit this punctuation to Zachary Grey since it appears (but without comment) in his *Notes on Shakespeare* (1754), II. 136. Professor Alexander adopts it and it seems to me rhythmically superior to the Q2 punctuation.

this] See Introduction, p. xii.

66. *meed for meed*] Cited by Tilley, M800, 'Measure for measure'.

Kills Saturninus] It has been customary since Capell to send 'Lucius, Marcus, and others' to the upper stage at this point, and bring them down again at l. 145. This is no doubt based on ll. 130 ff. I am not convinced that those lines require the speaker and his friends to be visibly higher than their audience: on the dangers of inference to staging from dialogue interpreted too naturalistically, see G. F. Reynolds, *J.E.G.P.*, 42 (1943), 124. Neither ascent nor descent is here covered by dialogue, as is usual: cf. G. F. Reynolds, *The Staging of Elizabethan Plays* (New York, 1940), pp. 99–100; as at v. ii. 70 (*possibly* a descent) Titus has eleven lines for coming down. If it is felt that ll. 130 ff. demand some sort of raised position, one might suggest a movable scaffolding. There is evidence for the existence of this, though its nature is obscure: cf. W. Smith, *R.E.S.*, n.s. 2 (1951), 22–6, especially the reference to *Troil.*, I. ii. 191–5: 'Shall we stand up here? . . . there's an excellent place; here we may see most bravely.'

71. *mutual sheaf*] a sheaf whose parts belong together (Delius, quoting *Ant.*, I. i. 37: 'such a mutual pair');

These broken limbs again into one body;
Lest Rome herself be bane unto herself,
And she whom mighty kingdoms cur'sy to,
Like a forlorn and desperate castaway,   75
Do shameful execution on herself.
But if my frosty signs and chaps of age,
Grave witnesses of true experience,
Cannot induce you to attend my words,
Speak, Rome's dear friend, as erst our ancestor,   80
When with his solemn tongue he did discourse
To love-sick Dido's sad-attending ear
The story of that baleful burning night
When subtle Greeks surpris'd King Priam's Troy.
Tell us what Sinon hath bewitch'd our ears,   85
Or who hath brought the fatal engine in
That gives our Troy, our Rome, the civil wound.
My heart is not compact of flint nor steel,
Nor can I utter all our bitter grief,

72–3. body; Lest] *Capell;* bodie. *Romane Lord.* Let *Qq;* body. *Goth.* Let *F.*
74. cur'sy] *Qq,F* (cursie) *;* curtsie *F3.*   75. castaway] cast away *Qq.*   82. sad-
attending] *W. S. Walker;* sad attending *Qq,F.*   83. baleful burning] baleful-
burning *W. S. Walker.*

---

not quite the same sense as in l. 134.

72. *broken limbs*] Cf. Seneca, *Thyestes*, 432–3: 'lacerae domus / componit artus'.

73. *Lest*] Capell's emendation is in itself satisfactory, but does not explain everything. Wilson suggests that ' "Romane Lord" was Shakespeare's heading to a marginal addition, or slip, which he intended to be tacked on to Marcus's lines 67–72'. But he would surely never have referred to Marcus in such an impersonal fashion. If the lines were on a loose sheet, they most likely had no heading at all. Sisson (*New Readings*, II. 144–5) has a defence of Q which I find quite unconvincing. H. F. Brooks suggests that some tangle of corrections at the beginning of the line might have seemed to give 'L. Rom.' or the like, expanded to 'Romane Lord' as a speech-prefix.

bane] destroyer.

74. *cur'sy*] this phonetic spelling (cf. Wyld, p. 302) seems worth preserving.

77. *frosty . . . chaps*] white hair and cracks in the skin.

80. *ancestor*] Aeneas.

82. *sad-attending*] seriously attending.

85. *Sinon*] whose false story induced the Trojans to admit the wooden horse.

86. *fatal engine*] Virgil's *fatalis machina* (*Aen.*, II. 237), as J. A. K. Thomson points out, *Shakespeare and the Classics* (1952), p. 56. J. M. Robertson, *Introduction to the Study of the Shakespeare Canon* (1924), p. 183, cites some rather striking parallels to this passage in Peele's *Tale of Troy* (1589), 400 ff.

87. *civil*] inflicted in civil war; cf. *Rom.*, Prol. 4: 'Where civil blood makes civil hands unclean'.

88. *compact*] composed. See on I. i. 462, and cf. *MND.*, v. i. 8: 'of imagination all compact'.

But floods of tears will drown my oratory,   90
And break my utt'rance, even in the time
When it should move ye to attend me most,
And force you to commiseration.
Here's Rome's young captain, let him tell the tale,
While I stand by and weep to hear him speak.   95

Luc. Then, gracious auditory, be it known to you,
That Chiron and the damn'd Demetrius
Were they that murdered our emperor's brother;
And they it were that ravished our sister.
For their fell faults our brothers were beheaded,   100
Our father's tears despis'd, and basely cozen'd
Of that true hand that fought Rome's quarrel out
And sent her enemies unto the grave.
Lastly, myself unkindly banished,
The gates shut on me, and turn'd weeping out,   105
To beg relief among Rome's enemies;
Who drown'd their enmity in my true tears,
And op'd their arms to embrace me as a friend:
I am the turn'd forth, be it known to you,
That hath preserv'd her welfare in my blood   110
And from her bosom took the enemy's point,
Sheathing the steel in my advent'rous body.
Alas, you know I am no vaunter, I;

91. my] my very *Q3,*F.   92. ye] you *Q2–3,*F.   93. And force you to] Lending your kind (*F adds* hand) *Q2–3,*F. 94. Here's Rome's young] Here is a (our *W. S. Walker*) *Q2–3,*F.   95. While I stand by] Your harts will throb *Q2–3,*F. 96. Then] This *F.* gracious] noble *Q2–3,*F.   97. Chiron and the damn'd] cursed Chiron and *Q2–3,*F.   98. murdered] *Rowe;* murdred *Qq,*F.   100. faults] fault *Hudson.*   109. I] And (and *Q3*) I *Q3,*F.   the] *not in* F.   turn'd] *F4;* turned *Qq,*F.

93–7. *And . . . Demetrius*] See Introduction, p. xii. In l. 94 Walker (and Dyce who followed him) deserves credit for not acquiescing in the traditional text.

98. *murdered*] Qq,F's *murdred* cannot represent an alternative pronunciation, so I have normalized.

99. *they it were*] For this agreement of the verb with the complement instead of the subject, already archaic at this time, see *N.E.D. it,* 2.

100. *faults*] *Fault* would be more natural in modern English, but apparently the share of the guilt belonging to each is thought of separately (cf. on III. i. 238). But the emendation may be correct: cf. II. iii. 291.

101. *cozen'd*] cheated. According to sense this goes with *father.* In l. 105, *turn'd* is in a similar loose construction.

104. *unkindly*] unnaturally (this is at least part of the sense: cf. II. i. 116 for the noun *kind*).

112. *advent'rous*] See on II. iii. 285.

My scars can witness, dumb although they are,
That my report is just and full of truth.   115
But soft, methinks I do digress too much,
Citing my worthless praise: O, pardon me;
For when no friends are by, men praise themselves.
Marc. Now is my turn to speak. Behold the child;
Of this was Tamora delivered,   120
The issue of an irreligious Moor,
Chief architect and plotter of these woes.
The villain is alive in Titus' house,
And as he is to witness, this is true.
Now judge what cause had Titus to revenge   125
These wrongs unspeakable, past patience,
Or more than any living man could bear.
Now have you heard the truth: what say you, Romans?
Have we done aught amiss, show us wherein,
And, from the place where you behold us pleading,   130
The poor remainder of Andronici
Will hand in hand all headlong hurl ourselves,
And on the ragged stones beat forth our souls,

---

119. the] this *Q3,F.*   124. And . . . is to witness,] *Maxwell;* And . . . is to witnes *Qq;* And . . . is, to witnesse *F;* Damn'd . . . is, to witness *Theobald.*   true.] true, *Qq.*   125. cause] *F4;* course *Qq,F.*   revenge] reuenge. *Q1–2.*   127. bear.] beare, *Q1.*   128. have you] you haue *Q2–3,F.*   truth:] truth. *Wilson;* truth, *Qq,F.*   129. amiss,] amisse? *Q3,F.*   130. pleading] now *Q2–3,F.*   131. Andronici] *Andronicie Qq.*   132. hurl ourselves] cast vs downe *Q2–3,F.*   133. souls] braines *Q2–3,F.*

---

118. *when . . . themselves*] O.D.E.P., p. 447, and Tilley, N117, cite from Barclay's *Ship of Fools* (1509): 'Men . . . / In theyr olde prouerbes often comprehende / That he that is among shrewyd neyghbours / May his owne dedes laufully commende.'

124. *And . . . true*] I think these are the only changes required in the Q text. It could, as Delius saw, be construed without any changes, making 'As he is to witness [that] this is true' subordinate to 'Now judge, etc.' But 'Now judge' seems to begin a new sentence—he has given all the facts and now he asks for a verdict—and the Q punctuation is certainly faulty at the end of ll. 125 and 127. With the text printed, the meaning is *either* 'as he is to witness' exactly as in modern English, *or*, if this seems a little tame, the *as* may be the *as* of asseveration, = 'as surely as'. A comparable (though not closely similar) line is *R2*, III. iii. 119: 'This swears he, as he is a prince, is just.' Theobald's forcible-feeble *Damn'd* has been surprisingly popular, but is not adequately supported by comparing *Oth.*, I. ii. 63: 'Damn'd as thou art', though both are applied to Moors. For misplaced ingenuity, Kellner's *Audashious* (for *And as he is*) is worth mentioning.

130–3. *And . . . souls*] See Introduction, p. xii.

133. *ragged*] See on II. iii. 230.

And make a mitual closure of our house.
Speak, Romans, speak, and if you say we shall,   135
Lo, hand in hand, Lucius and I will fall.

Æmil. Come, come, thou reverent man of Rome,
And bring our emperor gently in thy hand,
Lucius our emperor; for well I know
The common voice do cry it shall be so.   140

All. Lucius, all hail, Rome's royal emperor!

Marc. [*To Attendants.*] Go, go into old Titus' sorrowful
house,
And hither hale that misbelieving Moor,
To be adjudg'd some direful slaught'ring death,
As punishment for his most wicked life.   145
                                   [*Exeunt Attendants.*

All. Lucius, all hail, Rome's gracious governor!

Luc. Thanks, gentle Romans: may I govern so,
To heal Rome's harms, and wipe away her woe.
But, gentle people, give me aim awhile,

---

137. Come, come,] Come, Marcus, come, *Maxwell conj.*   141. *All.*] *Rom.*
Capell (*Omnes Ravenscroft*); *Marcus. Qq*; *Mar. F.*   142. *Marc.* [*To Attendants*]]
Capell; not in *Qq,F.*   144. adjudg'd] adiudge *Q1–2.*   direful slaught'ring]
direful-slaught'ring *W. S. Walker.*   slaught'ring] slaughtering *F.*   145.
Exeunt Attendants.] *Camb.*; not in *Qq,F.*   146. *All.*] *Rom. Capell*; not in *Qq,F.*
Rome's] *Q1* (*Rowe*); to Romes *Q2–3,F.*

---

134. *mutual closure*] common end.
This meaning of *mutual*, 'now regarded
as incorrect', is 'the commonest
Shakespearian sense' (On.).

137. *Come, come*] An odd repetition,
though cf. l. 160. For my conjecture,
cf. IV. iii. 1, and III. i. 143: 'Mark,
Marcus, mark.' It is conceivable that
Marcus was abbreviated to *M.* in the
MS. and that the compositor did not
know what to make of it.

reverent] See on II. iii. 296.

141. *All*] Knight's argument that
here and at l. 146 'Marcus is the tribune of the people, and speaks authori-
tatively what "the common voice" has
required' is unconvincing, with its
sharp transition from l. 141 to l. 142.
Capell had already written: 'the pretence that Marcus speaks for them is
indeed foolish, and will never be set up

by persons of understanding'. More
likely the change of speaker at both
points was inadequately indicated
in the MS., perhaps only by a dash,
and the compositor had to do his
best.

149. *give me aim*] The literal meaning
of this idiom is (On.) 'to guide someone in his aim by informing him of the
result of a preceding shot', but something less specific is required here, and
a number of passages in Dekker give a
clue. 'The English, the Dutch, and the
Spanish, stoode aloofe and gaue ayme,
whilst thou shotst arrowes vpright,
that fell vpon thine owne head' (*The
Seven Deadly Sins of London*, ed. H.
Brett-Smith, p. 9); 'France, Spaine,
and Belgia, lift vp their heads, preparing to do asmuch for *England* by
giuing ayme, whilst she shot arrowes

For nature puts me to a heavy task.   150
Stand all aloof; but, uncle, draw you near
To shed obsequious tears upon this trunk.
O, take this warm kiss on thy pale cold lips,
These sorrowful drops upon thy blood-stain'd face,
The last true duties of thy noble son.   155
Marc. Tear for tear and loving kiss for kiss
   Thy brother Marcus tenders on thy lips:
   O, were the sum of these that I should pay
   Countless and infinite, yet would I pay them.
Luc. Come hither, boy; come, come and learn of us   160
   To melt in showers: thy grandsire lov'd thee well:
   Many a time he danc'd thee on his knee,
   Sung thee asleep, his loving breast thy pillow;
   Many a story hath he told to thee,
   And bid thee bear his pretty tales in mind,   165
   And talk of them when he was dead and gone.
Marc. How many thousand times hath these poor lips,
   When they were living, warm'd themselves on thine!
   O now, sweet boy, give them their latest kiss.
   Bid him farewell; commit him to the grave;   170
   Do them that kindness, and take leave of them.

---

153. pale cold] pale-cold *W. S. Walker.*   154. blood-stain'd] *F3;* blood slaine
Q1–2; bloud-slaine *Q3,F.*   163. Sung] Song *Q1.*   164. story] matter *Q2–3,F.*
165–9.] Meete and agreeing with thine infancie, / In that respect then, like a
louing child, (child. *Q2*) / Shed yet some small drops from thy tender spring, /
Because kind nature doth require it so, / Friends should associate friends in grief
and woe. *Q2–3,F.*   171. them . . . them] *Qq;* him . . . him *F.*

at her owne brest' (*Plague Pamphlets*, ed. F. P. Wilson, p. 20); '*England* hath stood and giuen aime, when Arrowes were shot into all our [? their *or* other] bosomes' (*ibid.,* p. 142); 'they that are ful of coyne, *draw*: they that haue little, stand by & giue *ayme*' (*Lanthorn and Candlelight,* 1608, sig. D2). In all these passages (I owe the second and fourth to Professor F. P. Wilson) the sense seems weakened to little more than 'encourage', which would suit the *Titus* passage well. If this is so, emendations, none of them satisfactory, may be ignored, as may Schmidt's vague paraphrase: 'give room and scope to his thoughts'.

150. *puts me to*] imposes on me.

152. *obsequious*] dutiful towards the dead, with no unfavourable implication.

164–9. *Many . . . kiss*] See Introduction, p. xii.

167. *hath*] See on II. iv. 17.

171. *them . . . them*] With Alexander and Sisson, I now revert to Q, treating as parenthetic l. 170 (which I still think may have been an after-thought, to take the place of l. 171, or to follow it).

Boy. O grandsire, grandsire, ev'n with all my heart
　　Would I were dead, so you did live again!
　　O lord, I cannot speak to him for weeping;
　　My tears will choke me if I ope my mouth.　　　175

Re-enter Attendants, with AARON.

Æmil. You sad Andronici, have done with woes:
　　Give sentence on this execrable wretch
　　That hath been breeder of these dire events.
Luc. Set him breast-deep in earth and famish him;
　　There let him stand and rave and cry for food.　　180
　　If any one relieves or pities him,
　　For the offence he dies. This is our doom.
　　Some stay to see him fast'ned in the earth.
Aar. Ah, why should wrath be mute, and fury dumb?
　　I am no baby, I, that with base prayers　　　185
　　I should repent the evils I have done;
　　Ten thousand worse than ever yet I did
　　Would I perform, if I might have my will.
　　If one good deed in all my life I did,
　　I do repent it from my very soul.　　　190
Luc. Some loving friends convey the emperor hence,
　　And give him burial in his fathers' grave.
　　My father and Lavinia shall forthwith
　　Be closed in our household's monument.
　　As for that ravenous tiger, Tamora,　　　195

---

172. *Boy.*] *Puer. Qq.*　　175. *Re-enter . . .* AARON.] *Rowe (substantially)* ; not in *Qq,F.*
176. *Æmil.*] *Dyce (Ravenscroft)* ; *Romane. Q1* ; *Romaine. Q2–3* ; *Romans. F.*　　184.
Ah] O *F.*　　192. *fathers'*] *Anon. (in Camb.)* ; fathers *Qq,F* ; father's *Rowe.*　　195.
ravenous] *Q1 (Collier MS.)* ; hainous *Q2–3,F.*

173. *so*] See on II. i. 102.
176. *Æmil.*] It seems most unlikely
that an otherwise mute character
should make this speech. On the other
hand, if it is meant for Æmilius, the
vague reference is exactly what we
expect in this sort of text (see on I. i.
299). Hence I follow Dyce with some
confidence.
179.] H. F. Brooks notes that in

Lodge's *Wounds of Civil War* the traitor
page is to be famished to death.
184–90. *Ah . . . soul*] Recalls v. i.
124–44 (Wilson).
192. *fathers'*] More probable than
father's. What is important is that it is
the ancestral tomb.
195. *ravenous*] One of the few correct
guesses attributed by Collier to his
mythical MS.; no doubt from l. 5.

No funeral rite, nor man in mourning weed,
No mournfull bell shall ring her burial;
But throw her forth to beasts and birds to prey.
Her life was beastly and devoid of pity;
And being dead, let birds on her take pity. [*Exeunt.*   200

Finis the Tragedy of Titus Andronicus.

196. rite] right *Q1–2.*   mourning] mournefull *Q3,F.*   weed] weeds *Q2–3,F.*
198. to prey] of prey *F.*   199. beastly] Beast-like *F.*   200. dead . . . pity] so,
shall haue like want of pitty *Q2–3,F. After this line Q2–3,F add:* See iustice
done on Aron that damn'd Moore, / By (From *F*) whom our heauie haps had
their beginning: / Then (Than *Q2*) afterwards to order well the state, / That like
euents may nere it ruinate.   *Exeunt.] not in Q2–3.*   the Tragedy of Titus
Andronicus.] *not in Q2–3,F.*

196. *No . . . rite*] Not, strictly, an
appropriate subject to *shall ring,* but
the transition through *man . . . weed*
makes the expression natural. For the
Q1–2 spelling *right* see on 1. i. 78.

198. *to prey*] With Neilson and Hill,
I see no objection to this in the sense
'for them to prey on'. For what may be
an echo in *Troublesome Reign of King
John,* see Introduction, p. xxi.

APPENDIX

(Contributed by Harold F. Brooks)

(*a*) Ravenscroft on *Titus*,[1] and Cowley on the posthumous Folio editions of Beaumont and Fletcher, Jonson, and Shakespeare.

When Ravenscroft calls *Titus* 'rather a heap of Rubbish than a Structure', it is pretty clear that he is remembering the passage where Cowley, in 1656, censured what he regarded as the uncritical inclusiveness of posthumous collected editions like the First Folio Shakespeare.[2] Posthumous editions of poets, above all, Cowley complains are

> stuffed out, either with counterfeit pieces, . . . or with such, which though of their own *Coyn*, they would have called in themselves for the baseness of the Alloy; whether this proceed from the indiscretion of their *Friends*, who think a vast heap of Stones or Rubbish a better Monument than a little *Tomb* of *Marble*, or by the unworthy avarice of some *Stationers*, who are content to diminish the value of the Author, so they may encrease the price of the Book. . . This has been the case with *Shakespeare, Fletcher, Jonson*, and many others, part of whose Poems I should take the boldness to prune and lop away, if the care of replanting them in print did belong to me; neither would I make any scruple to cut off from some the unnecessary yong *Suckers*, and from others the old withered Branches.[3]

The passage was most likely brought to Ravenscroft's mind by a citation of part of it in Joseph Hindmarsh's 'Advertisement' to the *Remains* of John Oldham, 1684; Hindmarsh published Ravenscroft's *Titus*;[4] and a second edition of the *Remains*, both in 1687. Ravenscroft's actual echo is not from the *Remains*, but apparently from Cowley at first hand.[5]

1. See above, p. xix, and R. F. Hill in *Shakespeare Survey*, 10 (1957), 70, n. 7.
2. See p. 130, n. 1 below.
3. Abraham Cowley, *Poems*, 1656, preface; repr. *Critical Essays of the 17th Century*, ed. J. E. Spingarn, II. 78 f.
4. Also his *London Cuckolds*, 1682, 1688; *Dame Dobson*, 1684; and the Prologue and Epilogue to *Dame Dobson*, s. sh. fol., 1683.
5. In the *Remains* 'heap of Rubbish' is not quoted: Hindmarsh dissociates him-

No doubt he saw, or chose to see, in *Titus*, an instance not only of the inferior but also of the unauthentic work which Cowley had stigmatized in his preface; and he may have been reading Cowley correctly. Yet it is not certain that Cowley meant to say that anything spurious had been included in the Shakespeare First or Second Folio.[1] A collected edition, he contends, should admit neither the unauthentic nor the inferior (for example, the juvenile or the senile). The reference to senile work must be specifically to Jonson; to what Dryden called 'his dotages':[2] and there is nothing unauthentic in the 1640 Folio, nor yet juvenile; it follows Jonson's own well-considered edition of 1616 in excluding his immature comedy, *The Case is Altered*.[3] If only one of Cowley's objections is aimed at the posthumous Jonson Folio, the same may hold good for Shakespeare. The Beaumont and Fletcher Folio of 1647 notoriously contained, without identifying them, Fletcher's collaborations with others besides Beaumont—Sir Aston Cockayne protested at the wrong done to both authors, and to Massinger also, by the want of proper attributions.[4] This uncertainty in which the Fletcher canon was left may perhaps be the sole point concerning the dramatists named by Cowley to which his general stricture about 'counterfeit pieces' has relevance. When he comes to these dramatists in particular, he thinks chiefly of lopping away their senilia and juvenilia. Subsequently, some of Fletcher's plays were classed by Dryden as immature;[5] and Dryden may have been per-

---

self from those publishers who '(as the incomparable Mr. *Cowley* has exprest it) think a rude heap of ill-placed Stones a better Monument than a neat Tomb of Marble'. Dryden had previously adopted the phrase in justifying (like Ravenscroft) an adaptation from Shakespeare: cf. *Troilus and Cressida*, preface (*Essays*, ed. W. P. Ker, I. 204): 'I undertook to remove that heap of rubbish under which many excellent thoughts lay wholly buried.' Ravenscroft probably knew this passage too: but his 'structure' corresponds to Cowley's 'Monument', and, as antithesis to 'heap', with Cowley's 'Tomb of Marble'.

1. It was not till the second issue of the Third, 1664, that *Pericles* and six apocryphal plays were added.

2. *Essays, ed. cit.*, I. 81.

3. *Ben Jonson*, ed. Herford and Simpson, IX. 14, 89–91, 104–6. Two spurious pieces appeared in the 1640 collections of his poems (*ibid.*, 126, 128), but I doubt whether Cowley was thinking of those.

4. His authorities were Massinger himself, and Cotton: cf. 'To my Cousin Mr. Charles Cotton', and 'To Mr. Humphry Mosley and Mr. Humphrey Robinson' (the publishers of the Folio): *Poems*, 1662, pp. 91, 217; cf. p. 186. Cockayne's occasional poems witness to epistolary and conversational discussion.

5.   Your *Ben* and *Fletcher*, in their first young flight
                    Did no *Volpone*, no *Arbaces* write.

(Prologue to *Circe*, 1677, ll. 11 f.), cf. *Essays, ed. cit.*, I. 81: 'The first play that brought Fletcher and [Beaumont] in esteem was their *Philaster*, for before that, they had written two or three very unsuccessfully.'

sonally acquainted with Cowley's views.[1] It is to immaturity, again, that Dryden attributes what he considers inferior plays by Shakespeare: *Pericles*, History plays, *Troilus and Cressida*.[2] In censuring the Shakespeare Folio, it may have been the inclusion of immature, not of spurious, pieces that Cowley had in mind. But one cannot be sure.

One cannot be sure, either, of the bearing of Ravenscroft's Cowleian reminiscence upon his denial of *Titus* to Shakespeare. It allows us to argue that part of the shaky support he relied on was the statement he read into Cowley that the Folio included 'counterfeit pieces'. Alternatively, however, it allows us to argue that far from misreading Cowley he had indeed the support of a complaint against the canon of the Folio, made thirty years before the date of his own Address: thirty years nearer to Shakespeare's lifetime.[3] Yet although, so far as I can see, no conclusion favourable or unfavourable to Ravenscroft's assertions can safely be drawn from it, his debt to Cowley, if we are to discuss what the assertions rest upon, cannot be left out of account.

(b) Act v, Scene ii. Chiron and Demetrius as Rape and Murder.

The editor and I no longer believe that Titus' identification of Tamora's sons with Rape and Murder constitutes a puzzle, nor his subsequent question, 'What are they calld?' an inconsistency pointing perhaps to corruption in the text. Commentators set themselves an insoluble problem if they take Tamora's plan of presenting herself to Titus as Revenge[4] to include presenting her sons as Rape and Murder. If it is assumed that the disguises into which she has put them are emblematic of those crimes, Titus' identifica-

1. They both took part in the meetings to consider the founding of an English Academy (Spingarn, *op. cit.*, II. 328 f., 337).

2.   Shakespeare's own Muse her *Pericles* first bore:
                         The Prince of *Tyre* was elder than the Moore.
                         'Tis miracle to see a first good Play.

(Prologue to *Circe*, ll. 16–18). He criticizes the plots of Elizabethan dramatists, 'especially those which they writ first . . . I suppose I need not name *Pericles Prince of Tyre* nor the historical plays of Shakespeare.' And again: 'in his latter plays he had worn off somewhat of the rust; but the tragedy which I have undertaken to correct was in all probability one of his first endeavours on the stage . . . Shakespeare . . . in the apprenticeship of his writing, modelled [the story] into that play, . . . now called *Troilus and Cressida*' (*Essays, ed. cit.*, I. 165, 203). Dryden's ignorance of Shakespearian chronology only emphasizes his correlation of the inferior with the immature as he conceives them. He is generalizing from his own long apprenticeship, but may be following Cowley too.

3. The ground of the complaint, if Cowley intended it, is another question.

4. See above, v. ii. 61, n. *'what . . . call'd?'*

tion of them is explained, it is true, but at the cost of making it impossible to understand the discussion of their names later on; whereas once it is realized that the disguises and her intentions cast them only for the role of Revenge's ministers, the development of the scene becomes perfectly intelligible.

In announcing herself as Revenge, Tamora speaks of rape and murder, not of course as her companions, but as villainies (half-personified) which she will persecute.[1] Titus responds:

> Lo, by thy side where Rape and Murder stands.

He has recognized, not impersonations designed by Tamora, but the men themselves, and, under cover of his supposed madness,[2] christens them after his knowledge of what they have done. For her, this is at most a madman's intuition: she cannot know he knows. She is faced, however, with his awkward demand that she should prove herself Revenge, and fulfil her promise, by falling upon Rape and Murder in the persons of her companions. She begins to deny the identifications:

> These are my ministers, and come with me;

that is, she assigns them the role she has envisaged them in all along. And Titus replies as though shaken in his madman's rash assurance:

> Are these thy ministers? what are they call'd?

'They are your ministers, then, are they? Well, if I was wrong about them, what do you say their names really are?' But now Tamora decides she can accept the names he has bestowed, while maintaining her explanation: 'Rape and Murder,' she answers,

> therefore called so
> 'Cause they take vengeance of such kind of men.

Thus she accommodates her original conception to what she regards as Titus' 'brainsick humours'.

That this is the right interpretation is clear from Tamora's own comment, aside to her sons:

> This closing with him fits his lunacy.

'This closing with him' is her pretence that he was right after all about the names. They do not originate with her: to humour Titus she accepts them, as the phrase implies, from him.

---

1. Ll. 35, 40.

2. If something of real madness clings about Titus in the scene, one need not, for the present purpose, try to say how much. He is sane enough to see through Tamora, to play up to her belief that he is lunatic, and to organize his (surely not altogether sane) revenge.